NEW AND EXPANDED EDITION

WHAT YOUR CHILD NEEDS TO KNOW WHEN

Includes Evaluation Check Lists for Grades K-8

ROBIN SCARLATA

What Your Child Needs to Know When–*New and Expanded Edition*
Includes Evaluation Check Lists for Grades K-8

First Edition:

ISBN 0-89826-044-2

New and Expanded Edition:

ISBN 0-89826-044-2

1999 Published by: Heart of Wisdom Publishers
(615) 382-5500
http://heartofwisdom.com

ACKNOWLEDGEMENTS

Dedication

And I thank Christ Jesus our Lord, who hath enabled me, for that he counted me faithful, putting me into the ministry;.... This is a faithful saying, and worthy of all acceptation, that Christ Jesus came into the world to save sinners; of whom I am chief. Howbeit for this cause I obtained mercy, that in me first Jesus Christ might shew forth all longsuffering, for a pattern to them which should hereafter believe on him to life everlasting.

—1 TIMOTHY 1:12-:15-16

To my children, and grandchildren,
born and unborn,
may they all meditate on the book of the law day and night, and observe to do according to all that is written therein.

CONTENTS

This you shall find some day. Dear John, when I shall have past away forever, and the cold white stone will be keeping its lonely watch over the lips you have so often pressed, and the sod will be growing green that shall hid forever from your sight the form of one who has so often nestled close to your bossom.

For many long and sleepless nights when all beside my thoughts was at rest. I have wrestled with the consciousness of approching death, until at last it has forced itself upon my mind, and although to you and to my dear children it might seem but nervous imagination, yet Dear John it is so.

Many weary hours have I passed in trying to reconcile myself to leaving you whom I love so well, and the darling children. God has given us, that need a mothers care and prayers.

Oh, how hard to struggle on silently and alone with the sure conviction that I am about to leave all forever and go alone unto the dark valley of death.

But, I know in whom I have trusted and leaning upon his arm, I fear no evil.

I could wish to live if only to watch over you when in pain, sickness and death, but it is not to be so and I submit, you shall share my last thought and prayer on earth.

When I am gone, try and find comfort in Jesus. Never close your eyes to sleep without each reading a verse in the Bible and as my little ones grow up teach them to love the Bible and the church of God.

But, amidst all let memory carry them back to a home where the law of kindness reighed, where the mothers reproving eyes was moistened with tears, and the father frouned more in sorrow than in anger.

I know the spot where you will lay me, often have we stood there together. I loved to visit the place and I know you will love it not the less when I lay there.

This is a letter to my Great, Great Grandfather from my Great, Great Grandmother in 1887 (original spelling). She wrote this letter as she lay at death's door. She died before it was completed. What a joy it was to find the thing she desired most for her children was the needful thing Jesus spoke about to Martha. I hope it touches you in as emotionally powerful a way as it has me.

INTRODUCTION

WHY I WROTE THIS BOOK

In 1990, our family began Family Christian Academy, an umbrella school in Tennessee, as a service to help home schoolers educate their children in the Lord. Since then, FCA has grown to over 5,000 home schoolers from all over the nation.

Each year approaching testing time, we receive hundreds of frantic phone calls from parents saying things such as: "How do I know if we are prepared for the achievement tests?" "When do I teach double digit multiplication?" "What kind of words are on the spelling test?" "When do I teach homophones?" "What are homophones?" etc.

I prepared a workshop to calm frantic home educators. It was from this workshop that this book was developed. The motives behind this book are the same as those of the workshop—to answer questions, apprehensions, and fear. The ultimate goal is to help all home educators and prayerfully to put the dreaded achievement test and the National standards in the proper perspective.

Home schooling causes apprehension enough, in and of itself. Add the stress of tests which measure a parent's effectiveness and ability, and the parent can be pushed right over the edge.

Many feel if their child scores well, it must be luck. If they score poorly, even if it is only in one subtest, mother and father may feel like failures at parenting. Studies have shown, in most cases, the child would have scored much lower if he was left in the school system. It's a shame to see mothers and fathers in such a stressful, judgmental situation over state requirements.

It is very normal to struggle with doubts and to wonder if you are doing enough. I hope this book will give you a glimpse of the true and righteous standards our Lord has for your children. His yoke is easy, His burden is light.

There are many other excellent books written by home schoolers for home schoolers to give you confidence and assurance as you plod through this strange home school land.

What This Book is Not

This book was not written to make achievement tests the focus of home education. Americans are already too concerned with academic success and too little with the whole child. Many elements of learning and development are not captured by standardized tests.

The National Education Associations agenda is an aggressive, socialist, anti-life, anti-family policy. Consider the philosophies studied: Plato and Greek thought, Islam, Marxism, Rationalism/Humanism, Buddhism and Eastern mysticism, and Evolution.

Home school parents can tell their children's strengths and weaknesses from working with them daily. They do not really need achievement tests. First of all, the achievement tests do not test a child's relationship with God. God's spiritual requirements are so much more significant than any academic requirements defined by man. Secondly, home schooling parents generally have higher standards than the school. Children are all unique with individual God-given talents that cannot be measured by a test. Man's teachings, programs, and standards only evaluate a small portion of a large picture. They do not evaluate wisdom for living a prudent and righteous life. Your most important accomplishment will be to teach your child God's holy Word, true wisdom, to prepare him or her for a life of service.

HOW TO USE THIS BOOK

This book is divided into four major sections:

SECTION I: PHILOSOPHY OF EDUCATION

Section I explains how we have been conditioned to believe the state is competent to assess our children's intelligence. This section looks at America's two main world views—Christian and secular. The next chapters in this section clarify the difference between state education and Biblical education, taking a brief look at each major time period to see how public education came to where it is today and how important it is to return to a Bible-centered education.

SECTION II: STATE ACHIEVEMENT TESTS

This section explains what achievements are, explains test terms, test scores, testing limitations, avoiding test anxiety, and answers the most frequently asked test questions. It also critiques testing evaluations and explains better methods of evaluation you can implement with the information and Check Lists in this book.

SECTION III: TEACHING WISDOM

Section III is an introduction to a unique teaching approach based on the philosophy in this book. It describes how to use the Bible as core of the curriculum with a secondary emphasis on writing skills.

SECTION IV: EVALUATION CHECK LISTS

The first two chapters in Section II include two very important Check Lists—a Bible Reading Check List and a Character Quality Check List. The rest of the check lists in Section II include basic skills from the main achievement tests. Fill out the check list of skills at your child's grade level or a level below his level. The results will help you in several areas.

Diagnostic Tool

The Check List is divided by school subjects and then by grade. Each subject division includes teaching advice on that subject and a check list to keep track of your children's skills. The Check Lists are an effective diagnostic tool. Achievement tests measure knowledge of subjects taught and basically how well a child can take a test.

The Check List measures a broad range of abilities or skills that are considered important to success in school. Check Lists show you what to look for in checking the basic skills your child should know in each grade. Check Lists enhance the process of observation, make it more reliable, and help ensure consistency by providing an explanation and illustrations for each performance indicator.

Planning Tool to Develop or Choose Curriculum

If you are using this book to plan your curriculum, simply use the Check List to make a list of things your child has not mastered, make your own modifications to include or emphasize what you consider high priority, and add special items central to your own philosophy. Once you have determined the goals you want to accomplish, schedule and plan your time. Be sure you master the basics in this book.

Studies show combining the check list with a cumulation of the child's work, such as in a portfolio, will give a great deal of information and evidence about children's activities and development that can be used to enhance instruction and to plan future goals. (Meisels, Liaw, Dorfman, and Fails).

Teach to the Test

If you invested in this book to "teach to the test," I recommend you read this book and reexamine your motives. If you teach to the test—the test results will be worthless. You won't know what your child really knows. The results will only reveal whether or not your child has the ability to remember specific information for a short period. Teaching to the test alters what you can interpret from test scores because it involves teaching specific content. It also weakens the direct judgment that can be reasonably drawn about students' knowledge. Rarely would you want to limit your inference about knowledge to the specific questions asked in a specific format. Making inferences about a broader area of skills gives you a better idea of your child's strong and weak areas.

SECTION I
PHILOSOPHY OF EDUCATION

CHAPTER 1

RENEWING YOUR MIND

Prepare to Build

As you were growing up and receiving an education, you were taught in certain ways, with systems and procedures that you eventually assumed to be the "correct way" to teach and evaluate students. Public schools teach using the curriculum of the state, subjects that can be evaluated through national achievement testing. As a child, you might have been allowed to pray in school, but Bible or spiritual training was not a part of the state's curriculum. This "measurable academics only" approach is based on Greek philosophy. Today's parents generally believe achievement testing is the only or the best way to assess a child's development and educational advancement. The purpose of this book is to show you what your child needs to know to be prepared for life and is different from basic academic skills.

An old story explains how easy it is to be conditioned into a wrong thinking pattern. A husband asked his wife why she always cut off the end of the rump roast before roasting it. She replied, "I'm not sure why. I've never thought about it. My mother always cut off the end of the rump roast, so there must be a reason." A few weeks later Mother visited the family. The man asked his wife's mother, "We were wondering, why do you always cut off the end of the rump roast before you roast it?" She replied, "I don't know. I have never thought about it. My mother always cut off the end of the rump roast, so there must be a reason." This made them all curious. They decided to call the wife's mother's mother—the grandmother—to ask her. Grandmother answered the phone. The husband asked her, "Your daughter, granddaughter and I were wondering, why do you always cut off the end of the rump roast before you roast it?" Grandmother replied, "Oh, my roasting pan was too small. I had to cut it off it for it to fit in the pan!"

Many of us have been conditioned to believe "the state" has all the answers and that the state standards are made by a staff of very educated people. These educated people, chosen by the state, surely know more than parents know concerning what children need to prepare for life.

There are many good home school books, support groups and workshops available to help re-condition (un-brainwash) parents who realize the state system does not work. It does not do a good job of educating our children or evaluating our children—there are better ways. It is possible to train and educate our children and maintain God-honoring perspectives.

Students in this country are being intellectually maimed by relativism in our classrooms. Because we have rejected moral absolutes, the curriculum has no central reference point to revolve around, and no foundation on which to rest. College-level courses have become a confusing blur because no one really knows what's right and what's wrong, what's good and what's bad.

-Alan Bloom

Why do I think there are so many misled parents? For many years, I have presented a monthly workshop for parents interested in home education. Each session included a question and answer period. Even though the majority of the parents were considering home education for religious reasons, it was easy to determine most parents have been indoctrinated with a "public school mentality" due to the questions asked. The questions will be answered in Section II. For now, let's look at the motives behind these questions. The most frequently asked questions pertaining to teaching and evaluating home-schooled students:

1. How do I find out if my child is required to take the achievement test?
2. How do I know if I am meeting state standards?
3. How do I know if the curriculum I am using includes everything on the Achievement Tests?
4. Shouldn't I use textbooks, such as the schools use?
5. What about college?
6. What about algebra, higher math, and lab sciences?
7. How will Goals 2000, Outcome-Based Education (OBE), or the new national standards affect the achievement tests?
8. How do I know the material I am using will prepare my child for life?
9. How do I motivate my child to learn?
10. What about grades?
11. How do I really know if I am doing enough?

During my eighty-seven years I have witnessed a whole succession of technological revolutions. But none of them has done away with the need for character in the individual or the ability to think.

-Bernard M. Baruch, *Baruch: My Own Story*, 1957

Decency--generosity--cooperation-assistance in trouble--devotion to duty; these are the things that are of greater value than surface appearances and customs.

-Dwight D. Eisenhower, *letter to Mamie Doud Eisenhower, June 11, 1943.*

It seems the state has conditioned many parents to fear teaching their own children. Even the parents looking into teaching kindergarten or first grade at home fear they are not qualified to teach simple facts such as the alphabet and basic addition. Of course, we all want our children to do the best they can do in all areas. But, what is the most important thing you can do to prepare your children for life? Teach him algebra, computer skills, writing skills? In all the workshops I have given I have heard the previous questions over and over. But never once has anyone ever asked:

1. How can I find out what God's will is for my child?
2. How do I determine my child's God-given gifts?
3. How will I know if my child is saved?
4. What does the Bible say to teach to our children?
5. How did godly men and women teach their children in Bible times?

Let us look forward to the time when we can take the flag of our country and nail it below the Cross, and there let it wave as it waved in the olden times, and let us gather around it an inscribed for our motto: "Liberty and Union, one and inseparable, now and forever," and exclaim, Christ first, our country next!

-Andrew Johnson

Many people tend to view life as quartered: partly religious, partly educational, partly professional, and partly leisure-oriented. Yet, everything we do, regardless of occupation—homemaker, businessman, ditch digger, dentist—we should do unto our King. We should be praising and acknowledging Him in learning, work, recreation, and worship—in all things. In the same way, our children need to see all their lives revolving around our King—their writing, reading, daily routine, studies, experiments, and friendships. We need to renew our minds—consider God's ways first!

Before planning the school year, sit down and plan. The Bible says no one builds a tower unless they first consider what is necessary (Luke 14:28). The story on the following few pages is an example of how tragic planning with the wrong focus can be.

With the National public school system under humanist control, and our nation's public school under similar control, it is obvious to anyone who can see that, under the guise of secularization, the humanists have created the most powerful and pervasive government-funded establishment of religion that has ever existed in the United States.

-A Brief History of Christian Influence in U.S. Colleges
Jay Rogers Director,
Media House International.

Building a Home

A man decided he wanted to build a house. It would not be just any house. He dreamed of a big, beautiful, luxury home. He wanted to build the most beautiful house in town.

He carefully thought about the basic building materials, the lumber, the plumbing, roofing, the bricks and even the nails. He made a list of building materials he would need.

The man found out about a free government program that would help him build his house. He went to the state home builder's office and filled out the proper forms. He was assigned a free set of blueprints, a state government builder, and a lot. The man was thrilled, for by going to the government he was able to save a

"...We must ask how we can kill the god of Christianity. We need only to insure that our schools teach only secular knowledge. If we can achieve this, god would be shortly due for a funeral service."

-G. Bozarth
promoting the religion of humanism

"Education is thus a most powerful ally of Humanism, and every American school is a school of humanism. What can a theistic Sunday School's meeting for an hour once a week and teaching only a fraction of the children, do to stem the tide of a five day program of humanistic teaching."

-Charles Potter
a signer of the Humanist Manifesto.

"I am convinced that the battle for humankind's future must be waged and won in the public school classroom by teachers who correctly perceive their role as proselytizers of a new faith: a religion of humanity... These teachers must embody the same selfless dedication as the most rabid fundamentalist preachers, for they will be ministers of another sort, utilizing a classroom instead of a pulpit to convey humanist values in whatever subject they teach, regardless of the educational level - preschool day care or a large state university. the classroom must and will become an arena of conflict between the old and new - the rotting corpse of Christianity, together with all its adjacent evils and misery, and the new faith of humanism, resplendent in its promise of a world in which the never-realized Christian ideal of 'love thy neighbor' will finally be achieved."

-From an article in *The Humanist* titled "A New Religion for a New Age"

fortune. He didn't have to pay for the blueprints, the builder, or even the lot!

He met with the state builder and showed him his list of building materials. The builder exclaimed, "What a list! You've listed absolutely everything needed to build a spectacular home! I've never seen someone so well prepared. You have everything from chandeliers to the sewage pump." The builder added, "I have just the right tools to build your home. This will be a fine house."

Finally, the house was built, and it was truly a magnificent home made with the very best of tools and building materials.

The state building inspector came to check the home. The building inspector was in awe. He said, "You have a fine home. It is beautiful. You have the very best of all the building materials. Your home is in the top ninety-ninth percentile compared to other homes in this area. Your house has passed the state's standards." The man moved into his new beautiful home.

One day the man and his wife were eating dinner. His wife complained that the doors and windows would not shut. Even the beautiful hand-made kitchen cabinet doors would not shut. As they were talking, it started to rain. It wasn't a fierce storm, but it started raining very hard. The man noticed a crack in the wall. He got up to look at the crack and saw another crack in the ceiling. Just then, a few bricks fell out of the fine custom fireplace. The man went into other parts of the house. The bathroom floors started to buckle. The base of the sink was coming out of the floor! The plumbing was backed up. The roof started leaking. The man didn't understand why his beautiful house was falling apart. He called the building inspector. The inspector said he was not responsible for the house. The man called the state home builder's office to get help. The woman who answered told him that they could only help if the man gave them the house. While he was on the phone, the water pipes burst and water poured into every room in the house. The carpets got soaked and the wood floors warped.

The man called his friends to help. A friend brought a truck to help the man save some of his furnishings. While they were moving the furniture into a truck, the electricity went out. The man was close to tears. He had no idea what was wrong with his home. His friend started looking through the house with a flashlight. He soon discovered the problem. He told the man, "This house has shifted. It has a weak foundation. It cannot survive this storm." Before he could finish his sentence, the entire house crashed down around them.

The house was built on sandy ground. All the fine fixtures and furnishings—indeed, the entire house was worthless. The man was very sad.

The shrewd guess, the fertile hypothesis, the courageous leap to a tentative conclusion-these are the most valuable coins of the thinker at work. But in most schools guessing is heavily penalized and is associated somehow with laziness.

-Jerome Bruner, *The Process of Education*, 1960.

I'll take the standards, warnings and solutions God gave to Moses or King David, King Solomon or the Prophets, over anything that Bill Clinton, Ted Kennedy or a pagan Supreme Court could ever offer.

-Terry Randell

This parable parallels the building of a home to the training of a child. The fact that you bought this book indicates you are interested in building a home—training your child. I know you have high goals and expectations for your home (child). The purpose of this book is to get the focus off the tools and materials and keep your focus on the:

I told this story at a workshop in Tennessee. A parent later told me he knew of a brand new fine house that was destroyed due to a bad foundation. I mentioned I'd like to have a photo of it. He was kind enough to send me these photographs.

- Builder
- Blueprints
- Foundation

The man in the story had a goal to build a fine house (raise a child). His focus was on what would make the house look good to the world (a successful, self-reliant student). The man took the easiest route to have the home built (state). It demanded no time or effort on the part of the man. There was nothing wrong with the basic building materials (knowledge) if the builder used them correctly (curriculum). The man did not know the builder. The builder did not care about the man or the house. The builder used the state's blueprints (curriculum) to provide a foundation of sand (humanism). The man provided the building materials but the blueprints called for the builder to bend and distort the materials. The inspector (test examiner) compared the house to the other homes in the area. He focused on the surface results, not the foundation. This book may be able to point you in the right direction to keep your house (child) from destruction. With the right Builder, Foundation, and Blueprints, you can build a strong fine home.

In spite of God's urgent plea to protect and nurture the mind in accordance to His ways, millions of Christians separate the heart from the mind of their children by sending them to public schools. The reason many Christians allow this to happen is because they have a dualistic view of humans that goes back to ancient Greece and has lasted to this very day. Plato believed that man had a spiritual and material dimension and the two should not be combined. That is why Christians, even to this day, have departmentalized their Christianity. For example, the concept of "going to worship" is based on Christianity being something we do rather than what we are. Surely we would not send our children to a state church on Sunday, where the god of humanism is served. Yet we do allow our children to go to the place of humanistic worship five days a week.

- Kevin J. Pierce, *Worldview Ministries*

First you must get to know the right builder. An experienced builder who personally knows and cares for you will help you build a fine home. I know of a wonderful Builder. He is the architect who designed the Blueprints for the world's most stable home. He is known for providing the strongest foundation available guaranteed to weather any storm. This home will last for eternity. The builder is God through His Holy Spirit leading you through life. The blueprints are the Bible, God's Word, giving instructions for every step of the process. The foundation is Jesus Christ, the Rock of Salvation.

God will provide the foundation and build the house as a free gift to you. You and your child only have to ask Him to take over. God expects you to provide the tools and He will show you the best materials for your home (academic training). He will use the materials wisely if, by faith, you allow God to shape the materials according to His will. This book includes a check list of the basic materials.

	House on the Sand	House on a Rock
Builder	State	God
Blueprints	State Curriculum	Bible
Foundation	Humanism, false gods	Jesus
Building Materials	Basic Achievement Skills	Basic Achievement Skills

The Check List in this book is only a list of basic building materials. You, the child's parent, must decide on the more important foundation and choose whom you want to build the house.

Definition of Education

A look at the different definitions of education from different sources can be quite revealing.

Education is that which remains, if one has forgotten everything he learned in school.
-Albert Einstein, *Out of My Later Years*, 1950.

Webster's 1828 Dictionary

This was the original dictionary by Noah Webster, reflecting the thoughts and values of the early American Christian culture.

EDUCATION, n. [L. education.] The bringing up, as of a child, instruction; formation of manners. Education comprehends all that series of instruction and discipline which is intended to enlighten the understanding, correct the temper, and form the manners and habits of youth, and fit them for usefulness in their future stations. To give children a good education in manners, arts and science, is important; to give them a religious education is indispensable; and an immense responsibility rests on parents and guardians who neglect these duties.

The papers today say that illiteracy has decreased. The more that learn how to read the less learn how to make a living. That's one thing about a little education. It spoils you for actual work. The more you know the more you think somebody owes you a living.
-Will Rogers, *September 4, 1931*, in Donald Day, ed., *The Autobiography of Will Rogers*, 1949.

ED'UCATE, v.t. [L. educo, educare; e and duco, to lead.] To bring up, as a child; to instruct; to inform and enlighten the understanding; to instill into the mind principles of arts, science, morals, religion and behavior. To educate children well is one of the most important duties of parents and guardians.

To know what is meant by "religious education," one must examine the definition of the word religion.

RELIGION: 1. Religion, in its most comprehensive sense, includes a belief in the being and perfections of God, in the revelation of His will to man, in man's obligation to obey His commands, in a state of reward and punishment, and in man's accountableness to God... 2. ...the performance of all known duties to God and our fellow men, in obedience to divine command, or from love to God and His law. [The phrases "divine command" and "His law" are synonymous with what is contained in the Bible.]

"The humanism that is being taught in our schools, media, and intellectual circles will ultimately lead people to the Antichrist, because he will be the consummate figure of humanism"
- Pat Robertson, 1989

God's Word was an essential part of American education in the eighteenth and early nineteenth centuries. Three vital elements contained in the 1828 Webster definition were:

1. The future station (occupation or calling) of the child
2. Religious training
3. Parental responsibility

Compare the 1828 definition to today's Webster's Dictionary (the name Webster was kept, but the new dictionaries bear no relation to Noah Webster):

Today's Webster's New World Dictionary
EDUCATION: 1. The process of training and developing the knowledge, skill, mind, character, etc., especially by formal schooling 2. knowledge, ability, etc. thus developed 3. formal schooling at an institution of learning 4. systematic study of the methods and theories of teaching and learning.

Today's definition is totally void of the three principles listed above.

One Thing is Needful

When Martha was too busy preparing her home to learn from Jesus, He said to her, "Martha, Martha, you are worried about so many things, when there is *one* thing that is needful." He was not saying that Martha should never tend to housework. Just as we should not ignore the basic skills. But the basic skills are a fraction of a weight on a scale compared to what Jesus said is the *one* needful thing—sitting at His feet learning the paths of God—the *one* thing your child needs to prepare him for life!

Christians are commanded to be anxious for nothing. The achievement test and standards are only tools. Proper use of them will allow us to better evaluate our children—as long as we keep the right perspective.

Remember the Primary Purpose of Education

The primary purpose of education should be to train the whole person for lifelong, obedient service, just as it was in Bible times (home was the center for education then). God never changes. He still has the same desire for us to know Him.

Our first goal must be to teach our children God's ways and His paths. We home schoolers cannot be so worried about fractions or spelling that we skip the one needful thing: sitting at the feet learning from our Master, through Bible study and prayer. We can prepare our children for whatever direction their gifts and talents lie; however, God may take your child in another direction. A Christian who is striving to find God's Will for his life will be equipped in the important traits, prepared for anything in life.

Knowing the facts and scoring high on achievement tests is not a formula for success. The education required by the state is not true education. Christians' questions should not be, "What score did she get on the achievement test?" or "What job or college is he prepared for?" The questions should be, "Is my child prepared to use the gifts and talents God has given her to carry out His Will in her life? Is this child seriously directed toward holiness, right relationships, and fruitfulness?"

"Today our state supported public schools are humanistic schools. Actually, they are religious institutions teaching, with public funds, an alien faith. The public schools ARE AN ESTABLISHMENT OF RELIGION: the religion of humanism. No Christian child should go to public school."

-Rousas John Rushdoony, *a prominent Christian theologian.*

Wisdom According to God

God's Word promises that wisdom can be attained by all who seek and follow it. Those who keep God's moral and ethical laws will be rewarded with long life, health, possessions, respect, security, and self-control. (Proverbs 3:2-4).

This wisdom begins when man humbles himself before God in reverence and worship and is obedient to His commands. This is quite different from the Greek and American views of wisdom sought through philosophy and man's rationale as a way of explaining the mysteries of existence and the universe.

Christian wisdom appears to be foolishness to the people of the world. But it is wiser than the philosophy of this age, which comes to nothing. The foolishness of God is wiser than men; and the weakness of God is stronger than men. Wisdom is revealed through God and received through His Spirit. Christians have the highest and most complete wisdom in Christ.

"For Christians to deliberately send their children to such schools makes no more sense than to send them to Buddhist monasteries or Shiite Muslim academies or more to point out, to Nazi schools! Christian children did not become "witnesses" when they donned the brown shirt and joined the Hitler movement and attended Nazi schools: the Nazis brainwashed and converted them into brutal instruments of the state. Similarly, today we do not make "witnesses" by sending them to seminaries of rival religious creeds, nor do we straighten their beliefs by indoctrinating them during the most impressionable years of their lives in the values of a religious system antagonistic to Christianity."

-From the book *Wisdom's Children* by Blair Adams.

Satan's primary tactic in opposing God is not to foster atheism but religion; not to prove there is no God but to be worshipped as God.

- "Dangerous Deceptions," *Jeremiah Home Page*

For it is written, I will destroy the wisdom of the wise, and will bring to nothing the understanding of the prudent. Where is the wise? where is the scribe? where is the disputer of this world? hath not God made foolish the wisdom of this world? For after that in the wisdom of God the world by wisdom knew not God, it pleased God by the foolishness of preaching to save them that believe.

For the Jews require a sign, and the Greeks seek after wisdom: But we preach Christ crucified, unto the Jews a stumbling block, and unto the Greeks foolishness; But unto them which are called, both Jews and Greeks, Christ the power of God, and the wisdom of God. Because the foolishness of God is wiser than men; and the weakness of God is stronger than men. For ye see your calling, brethren, how that not many wise men after the flesh, not many mighty, not many noble, are called: But God hath chosen the foolish things of the world to confound the wise; and God hath chosen the weak things of the world to confound the things which are mighty; And base things of the world, and things which are despised, hath God chosen, yea, and things which are not, to bring to nought things that are: That no flesh should glory in his presence. But of him are ye in Christ Jesus, who of God is made unto us wisdom, and righteousness, and sanctification, and redemption: That, according as it is written, He that glorieth, let him glory in the Lord. (1 Corinthians 1:19-31).

Requirements for Receiving Wisdom

The requirement for wisdom is a desire to follow and imitate God as He has revealed Himself in Jesus Christ, without self-reliance and especially not in a spirit of pride: *A wise man will hear, and will increase learning; and a man of understanding shall attain unto wise counsels: To understand a proverb, and the interpretation; the words of the wise, and their dark sayings. The fear of the Lord is the beginning of knowledge: but fools despise wisdom and instruction.* (Proverbs 1:5-7).

The person who seeks wisdom diligently will receive understanding: *For the Lord giveth wisdom: out of his mouth cometh knowledge and understanding.* (Proverbs 2:6). He will benefit in his life by walking with God: *That thou mayest walk in the way of good men, and keep the paths of the righteous.* (Proverbs 2:20).

Fruits of True Wisdom

The fruits of wisdom are many, and the Book of Proverbs describes the characters of wisdom. In New Testament terms the fruits of wisdom are the same as the fruits of the Holy Spirit. *But the fruit of the Spirit is love, joy, peace, longsuffering, gentleness, goodness, faith, Meekness, temperance: against such there is no law.* (Galatians 5:22-23). *But the wisdom that is from above is first pure, then peaceable, gentle, and easy to be entreated, full of mercy and good fruits, without partiality, and without hypocrisy. And the fruit of righteousness is sown in peace of them that make peace.* (James 3:17-18).

Author David Mulligan said it so appropriately in his book *Far Above Rubies: Wisdom in the Christianity Community:*

> We must do more than rail against Godless education. We must identify a distinctly Christian curriculum—one that takes its identity, its motion, from the reality of our redeemed condition—one that begins with authority of the risen Christ speaking through His Word. It is not enough to know what we are against; we must know what we are for. Dismantling the world is one work; building the Kingdom is another. If we fail to make a positive contribution to education, if we keep the same old public school agenda packaged in Christian dress, our children will not prosper as they should. Without fundamental changes, we are only straining out the gnat while swallowing the camel. We cannot let the wolf of antichrist values in because he is wearing sheep's clothing.

The gains of education are never really lost. Books may be burned and cities sacked, but truth, like the yearning for freedom, lives in the hearts of humble men.

-Franklin D. Roosevelt, speech, Democratic National Convention, June 27, 1936.

Every child in America entering school at the age of five is mentally ill, because he comes to school with certain allegiances toward our founding fathers, toward elected officials, toward his parents, toward a belief in a supernatural being. It's up to you teachers to make all of these sick children well by creating the international children of the future.

-A Harvard Professor of Education and Psychiatry at a childhood education seminar for public schools

Conclusion

Dedicate your children to God at the beginning of their lives (1 Samuel 1:28; Luke 2:22). Teach your children to fear the Lord and turn away from evil, to love righteousness and to hate sin. Instill in them an awareness of God's attitude and judgment towards sin (Hebrews 1:9). Instruct your little ones daily in God's Word, both in conversation and family devotions (Deuteronomy 4:9; 6:5-7; 1 Timothy 4:6; 2 Timothy 3:15).

Teach your children to obey through biblical discipline (Deuteronomy 8:5; Proverbs 3:11-12; 13:20; 23:13-14; 29:15, 17; Hebrews 12:7). Protect your children from ungodly influences by being aware of Satan's attempts to destroy them spiritually through attraction to the world or through immoral comparisons (Proverbs 13:20; 28:7; 1 John 2:15-17). Make them aware that God is always observing and evaluating what they do, think, and say (Psalms 139:1-12). Bring them early in life to a personal faith, repentance, and water baptism in Christ (Matthew 19:14). Establish your child in a spiritual church where God's Word is proclaimed, His righteous standards honored, and the Holy Spirit manifested. Teach them the motto, *I am a companion to all of them that fear thee...*(Psalms 119:63). Encourage your children to remain separated from the world and to witness and work for God (2 Corinthians 6:14; 7:1; James 4:4). Teach them they are strangers and aliens on this earth (Hebrew 11:13-16), and that their real home and citizenship is in heaven with Christ (Philippians 3:20; Colossians 3:1-3). Through example and exhortation, encourage your children to live lives devoted to prayer (Acts 6:4; Romans 12:12; Ephesians 6:18; James 5:16). (Stamps, note on Colossians 3:21.)

If our American way of life fails the child, it fails us all.
-Pearl S. Buck, *Children for Adoption*, 1964

Education is to get where you can start to learn.
-George Aiken, *New York Times*, January 29, 1967.

CHAPTER 2
WORLD VIEWS
Choosing a Carpenter

The importance of world view cannot be overstated. To provide a Christian education you need to have a Christian philosophy. Philosophy is the way of looking at our experience in the world—a world view.

Major world religions are based on world views. Hinduism is a world view based upon many deities, an endless life-death cycle, and the inevitability of human suffering. Islam, on the other hand, is a religion of martyrdom, conquests by force, and state-enforced modesty. Thus, to understand any of these movements and religions, we must understand the world view upon which they are founded. (Auvil n.d.)

What *your child* needs to know depends on your world view. Let me repeat, it's *your* world view (not the state's world view, not your mother-in-law's view, not the neighbor's view, and not Susie's view from your support groups).

Everyone has a world view. You may not have written it down, but you have one. Your world view determines your values. It separates what is important from what is not.

Walsh and Middleton in *Transforming a Vision* suggest there are four questions that identify a person's world view.

1. **Who am I?**
2. **Where am I?**
3. **What is wrong? Why am I often frustrated, disappointed and defeated?**
4. **How can it be fixed? How can I solve my problems and satisfy my desires?**

Before you turn the page, take this opportunity to spend a few minutes to answer each of these questions on paper. Save your answers and compare them with the two world view answers.

The majority of Americans tend to answer the questions in one of two ways—from a secular view (without God) or from a Christian world view.

SECULAR WORLD VIEW

The World View Taught in America's State Schools:

1. Who am I?

I am a human being, an accident. My species evolved from a monkey.

2. Where am I?

I am on earth, a planet that just happened by accident. The accident is called "The Big Bang."

3. What is wrong?

There is a lack of education and a lack of money; therefore, people are frustrated, disappointed, and defeated.

4. How can it be fixed?

By providing money and education. The more money and education one has, the happier his life will be.

Those who do not believe in God have to find a way to explain the universe. They have twisted and tortured the limits of both nature and psychology in an effort to escape God's natural law (Mulligan p. 58).

Humanism, for example, is a world view which states that the universe is centered on man and his achievements. Marxism is a world view which believes in the inevitability of class struggle based on economic factors.

A secular world view does not always value human life. If the only thing a child has ever been taught is that we are all accidents—is it really so unusual that there are so many abortions, murders, and suicides? Let's look at the answers from a Christian world view. What value does a Christian place on life? On education? On material gain?

CHRISTIAN WORLD VIEW

Look again at these four questions from a Biblical view.

1. Who am I?

I am a human being created by an awesome, wonderful, loving God. He especially put me here for a specific reason.

2. Where am I?

I am on the earth created by God. This earth is so marvelously created that if it were hung differently in the universe, one degree more or less, it would not be in existence.

3. What is wrong?

Sin. Our disobedience to God. When sin entered the world it severed our relationship with God, our Creator. We need our relationship with God restored.

4. How can it be fixed?

Jesus Christ, God's only begotten Son, came into the world in human form and gave His life as a sacrifice for our sins. Accepting His sacrifice and making Him Lord of our lives is our only hope.

The public system teaches a secular world view. Children are taught that the answers to all of life's problems are money and education. Much of this philosophy has crept into the church; so much so, that many Christians value education to the extent that they will choose a "good education" over God's command to "be not unequally yoked." Or they will choose curriculum because it is equivalent to the academic requirements of a traditional education.

Developing a Christian world view is of extreme importance in order to advance Christ's kingdom. False systems will collapse under their own corrupted weight. One reason for the decline of Christianity in western culture is the lack of a Bible-based world view. Instead, the cultural world view of materialism, selfishness and greed has become the predominant vision.

In education, a Christian world view seeks knowledge, wisdom, and understanding as outlined by God's Word. A secular world view focuses on SAT testing and rote memorization with no thought to character, morals and values.

Thus, if we were to properly understand the role of the world view, we would understand it as a set of rules that reside at the very core of our beings. If our set of values is earthly, carnal, and debased, then our actions will reflect such rot; however, a change in this set of values will bring a change in our actions. If we are

"[Jesus] is the image of the invisible God, the firstborn over all creation. For by him all things were created: things in heaven and on earth, visible and invisible, whether thrones or powers or rulers or authorities; all things were created by him and for him. He is before all things, and in him all things hold together. And he is the head of the body, the church; he is the beginning and the firstborn from among the dead, so that in everything he might have the supremacy. For God was pleased to have all his fullness dwell in him, and through him to reconcile to himself all things, whether things on earth or things in heaven, by making peace through his blood, shed on the cross." "In Christ are hidden all the treasures of wisdom and knowledge. I tell you this so that no one may deceive you by fine-sounding arguments." (COLOSSIANS 1:15-20; 2:3-4).

-Francis A. Schaeffer

We demolish arguments and every pretension that sets itself up against the knowledge of God, and we take captive every thought to make it obedient to Christ." (2 CORINTHIANS 10:5).

"The Christian belief system, which the Christian knows to be grounded in divine revelation, is relevant to all of life."

-Carl F. H. Henry, *Toward a Recovery of Christian Belief,* (Westchester, IL: Crossway Books, 1990), p. 113.

And just knowing that our children really love the Lord is a faithful parent's passion and reward.

-Jon Mohr

taught a Bible-based world view, radical change will take place. Believers the world over will experience revival, and evangelism will become more effective than ever.

Jesus came to declare the Kingdom of God. A kingdom is far-reaching and broad. People have many vocations and occupations involved in a kingdom, and we are called to serve in various places. The gospel gives man only one vocation: evangelism, but from the perspective of the kingdom there is a multitude of vocations. All our work is sacred before God; thus, evangelism takes on new forms. It is revealed in how we conduct ourselves, in how we steward what is entrusted to us, and how we view the world. All of life is lived out before God, not just certain parts (i.e. gospel proclamation, church, etc.) All science, art, literature, philosophy, theology, business, and culture must be conformed to Scripture. Salvation of individuals is not the primary theme of Scripture, and to interpret it as such is to squeeze Scripture into the hyper-individualism of this age. There is a reason why people interpret the Bible strictly from the gospel, but it is not a noble, well-contemplated Biblical reason. (Noebel)

The principles listed below are a small portion from *Seven Principles of Effective Biblical Worldview* by Kevin J. Price, President of Worldview Ministries.

The principles are discussed in detail in the Worldview Ministries book, *Understanding God's Worldview* and summarized in the booklet *Seven Principles of Effective Biblical Worldview* (ordering information at the end of this chapter). They are not the only principles that are important; in fact, they may not be the most important, but they are useful in understanding how the Christian is to relate to the world.

1. Worship is a twenty-four-hour-a-day activity.

In John 4:20-24, Jesus said people should worship God in spirit and in truth. In essence, Jesus was saying that worship should not be isolated to a time or place, but that our whole lives were to be acts of worship. This differs from the modern view of "going to worship." In God's view, we become worship ourselves (Romans 12:1,2). On a practical level this means Christians are called by God to be an influence in everything we do and that we should not limit ourselves to areas which are religious.

Because God is considered irrelevant in the classroom, there is no longer any basis from which to form opinions on morality, ethics and religion. Our society's motto has become, "Hey, it doesn't make any difference what you believe, as long as you believe it." Our society has become a little schizophrenic, thinking that right answers exist for any area of life except religion and morality. Again, if God exists and spoke, then absolutes exist and we have a basis for deciding right from wrong. Yet, people reject Christianity, not because they researched the historical evidence and found it lacking, but because they simply don't like what it says. That's a classic bias.

We are to respect authority because God, the ultimate authority over all He has created, has called us to do so. A teacher has legitimate authority over his students because the parents have delegated authority to him by enrolling their child in the school. A student who does not respect the authority of his teacher will be hindered in what he can learn from his teacher due to this lack of submission. A submissive spirit is a teachable spirit, but contentiousness blockades the path to true knowledge and wisdom.

"The basic problem of the Christians in this country in the last eighty years or so, in regard to society and in regard to government, is that they have seen things in bits and pieces instead of totals."

2. Biblical world view is crucial in maintaining a stable, healthy society.

In Colossians 1:16-17, Paul noted that Jesus Christ holds all things together. The reason why much in our society is chaotic and confused is because of the lack of a Christian influence.

3. There are two forces: life and death.

This isn't some New Age concept; it is scriptural. In John 10:10 we are informed that Satan comes to kill, steal, and destroy, whereas Jesus came to give life. This view transcends virtually everything. For example, in the realm of economics, Satan's pro-death views have led to population control, abortion, wealth redistribution, and other policies which have harmed the economy and the people these policies were supposed to help.

4. Exercising biblical world view requires recognizing God's authority.

Everything, including the government, is subject to God's authority (Romans 13:1-4; Acts 4:16-20; Acts 5:27-29). When you live in a country where Christians are allowed to be involved, it is imperative that you work to keep your nation in submission to God.

5. History supports Christianity rather than humanism.

In government schools throughout America there has been a divorce of Christianity from history, although all of the founders of this nation argued that America's success was contingent on its relationship with God. They knew that America would eventually collapse without sound policies based on God's law.

6. Be bold in the fact that Christianity is intellectually, as well as spiritually, superior to humanism.

The prophets of humanism—Marx, Rousseau, Darwin, and others—often lived immoral lives and their philosophies contributed to genocide, racism, and slavery. God's world view is superior to any of the immoral ideas of the philosophers.

7. Think and behave with a biblical world view.

Christians must learn to test all things, study God's Word, focus on the cause and not the symptoms of problems, and strive for consistency in their thinking (1 John 4:17; Psalms 40:8; Ephesians 4:14-15). Furthermore, Christians need to strive to solve

"Do not conform any longer to the pattern of this world, but be transformed by the renewing of your mind. Then you will be able to test and approve what God's will is-his good, pleasing and perfect will."
-(ROMANS 12:2)

"Once a Christian discovers that there is a total divorce between mind and spirit in the schools and universities, between the perfection of thought and the perfection of soul and character, between intellectual sophistication and the spiritual worth of the individual human person, between reason and faith, between the pride of knowledge and the contrition of heart consequent upon being a mere creature, and once he realizes that Jesus Christ will find Himself less at home on the campuses of the great universities, in Europe and America, than almost anywhere else, he will be profoundly disturbed, and he will inquire what can be done to recapture the great universities for Jesus Christ, the universities which would not have come into being in the first place without Him."
-Charles Malik,
at the dedication of the Billy Graham Center in Wheaton, Illinois

We believe that "the propitious smiles of heaven can never be expected on a nation which disregards the eternal rules of order and right which heaven itself has ordained."
-George Washington

For other foundation can no man lay than that is laid, which is Jesus Christ.
-(1 CORINTHIANS 3:11)

problems rather than pass them on to the government and others.

The Church is a social institution with a mandate from God to care for the widows, the poor, and the fatherless (orphans). If people would follow God's plan, there would be no need for governmental agencies that work to alleviate poverty and abuse.

The devil has a strategy for the classroom: to drive a deep wedge between education and Christianity, thereby keeping the Christian faith in the churches only. However, our faith is relevant to and deeply affects many disciplines - biology, philosophy, psychology, sociology, religion, business, history, anthropology, etc.

The quest towards education is Christian in its basis and it is one of the few religions [Judaism] that encourages education. Most of the written languages in the world owe some -if not all - of their existence to Christianity.
-Dr. D. James Kennedy

Humanists enjoy pointing out the restrictions Christianity places on cultures, yet the freest countries in the world operate from a biblical perspective. In countries without a moral code (which Christianity provides), oppressive governments rise up to respond to unchecked human behavior.
-Dr. D. James Kennedy

Walk in wisdom toward them that are without, redeeming the time. Let your speech be alway with grace, seasoned with salt, that ye may know how ye ought to answer every man. (Colossians 4:5-6)

But that on the good ground are they, which in an honest and good heart, having heard the word, keep it, and bring forth fruit with patience. (Luke 8:15)

For More Information About World Views

Seven Principles of an Effective World View by Kevin Price. Kevin is an award winning author of several books. To find out more about WorldView Ministries or order their publications, write or call: Worldview Ministries, PO Box 2121, Sugarland, TX 77487, 713-242-8365.

Understanding the Times by David Noebel is a study designed especially for high school and college students. Excellent charts show the difference between the world views of Secular Humanism, Marxism/Leninism and Biblical Christianity in ten categories: theology, philosophy, ethics, biology, psychology, sociology, law, politics, economics, and history. From Summit Ministries available through home school suppliers and Family Christian Academy 1-800-788-0840.

A Christian Manifesto by Francis Schaffer explains how Christians in America tend to see things in bits and pieces instead of the whole picture.This smaller book is a great overview of world views. From Crossway Books available through home school suppliers and Family Christian Academy 1-800-788-0840.

CHAPTER 3
HISTORY OF STATE EDUCATION
Foundation of Sand

HOW DID WE GET HERE?

Greek philosophies are alive and well in today's American educational system. The word philosophy is from the Greek word *philosophia,* which means "love of wisdom" (from *phileo,* "to love," and *sophia,* "wisdom"). As used originally by the ancient Greeks, the term philosophy meant the pursuit of knowledge for its own sake. Every Christian should know about the differences between the pagan Greek philosophies and the education of the Bible. The Greek philosophies are not only in the public school system but are also creeping in our churches.

ANCIENT GREECE: THE ROOTS OF MODERN EDUCATION

The roots of modern America's educational system and traditions come from the Greeks. They were the first to separate education from religious control.

Two contrasting types of education appeared early in ancient Greece: that of Sparta, wholly controlled by the state, and that of Athens, left almost entirely to the home or to private schools. Up to the age of seven, the education of both boys and girls was left to the home; at the age of seven, boys were gathered in barracks, where emphasis was placed upon physical development through games, exercises, and the pentathlon (running, jumping, throwing the discus, casting the javelin, and wrestling) and upon memorizing the laws of Lycurgus, the Spartan lawgiver, and selections from Homer. The whole process was designed to develop endurance, resourcefulness, and discipline. At eighteen, definite training in the use of arms and warfare began; from twenty to thirty, service in the army and guarding the borders of the state were required, and even after thirty, men were required to live in barracks and assist in the training of the boys. Physical training was also emphasized in the education of girls and women, so that they might bear sturdy children. The whole purpose of education was to subordinate the individual to the needs of the state. (Kandel 1996).

The ancient Greeks' interest in learning was evident in their art, politics, and philosophy. They had teachers live in their house-

"The universe and everything in it will someday pass away and be made new by the Creator... Therefore, the events of today that seem so important are not really very significant, except for those matters that will survive the end of the universe, such as securing your own salvation and doing the work of the Lord."

-Bob Biehl, *President, MasterPlanning Associates, Focus on the Family radio interview*

"As man thinketh, so is he, is really most profound. An individual is not just the product of the forces around him. He has a mind, an inner world. Then, having thought, a person can bring forth actions into the external world and thus influence it. People are apt to look at the outer theater of action, forgetting the actor who 'lives in the mind' and who therefore is the true actor in the external world. The inner thought world determines the outward action."

-Francis Schaeffer

Now if any man build upon this foundation gold, silver, precious stones, wood, hay, stubble; Every man's work shall be made manifest: for the day shall declare it, because it shall be revealed by fire; and the fire shall try every man's work of what sort it is. If any man's work abide which he hath built thereupon, he shall receive a reward. If any man's work shall be burned, he shall suffer loss: but he himself shall be saved; yet so as by fire. (1 CORINTHIANS 3:12-15)

The Christian belief system, which the Christian knows to be grounded in divine revelation, is relevant to all of life."

-Carl F. H. Henry, *Toward a Recovery of Christian Belief, (Westchester, IL: Crossway, 1990),* p. 113.

holds. These teachers were often slaves from conquered states. Later, when the Roman Empire was at its height, its citizens also followed the practice of having teacher-slaves, usually Greeks, in their households. Several Greek writers served as the models for the educational systems of ancient Greece, which stressed gymnastics as well as mathematics and music.

Have you ever wondered where we got the subject divisions: literature, history, language? The Greeks divided God's creation into topics. When you divide life into topics, you can separate the topic from the Creator.

The basic divisions of knowledge were grammar, rhetoric, and dialectic. These were meant to help students communicate effectively, and included a study of literature and language, arithmetic, music, geometry, and astronomy. These seven subjects later on became known as the liberal arts. They survive in one form or another in many universities today. Anatomy, biology, and botany were also valid fields of study.

Education, in general, was considered a leisure pursuit only available to the privileged few. The majority of the population that were Greek or Roman received no education. The pursuit of literature was considered the ultimate goal—an idle life of leisure void of manual labor. This pagan goal of the idle rich is in America today.

The Greeks were history's first humanists, believing that man was the measure of all things. The Greek aim was to prepare intellectually well-rounded young people to take leading roles in the activities of the state and society. Greek concepts served as the basis for the liberal arts, the teaching of the various branches of philosophy, the cultivation of the aesthetic ideal, and the promotion of gymnastic training. There is a problem with the education system based on the philosophies of these non-believers!

According to *Microsoft Encarta Encyclopedia,* the intuitive hypotheses of the ancient Greeks foreshadowed many theories of modern science, and many of the moral ideas of pagan Greek philosophers have been incorporated into Christian moral doctrine....With their emphasis on the importance of human perception, Greek philosophers doubted that humanity would ever be able to reach objective truth through reason, and taught that material success rather than truth should be the purpose of life.

GREEK PHILOSOPHERS

The ideas of the Greek had a profound effect on the modern educational system. The way the Greeks interpreted life is how life is studied in the modern educational system. We must understand this thought and compare it to what the Bible says about understanding, knowledge, and wisdom. To the Greek, knowledge was the primary way to goodness.

Greek philosophy formed the basis of all later philosophical speculation in the Western world.

Greek philosophy is divided among those philosophers who sought an explanation of the world in physical terms and those who stressed the importance of non-material forms or ideas. Aristotle, Plato, and Socrates have the prestige of being the most famous of ancient philosophers.

Ionian

The first important school of Greek philosophy, the Ionian or Milesian, was largely materialistic. Thales of Miletus in the sixth century B.C. was considered one of the Seven Wise Men of Greece. Thales became renowned for his knowledge of astronomy after predicting the eclipse of the sun that occurred on May 28, 585 B.C. He is also said to have introduced geometry in Greece. Thales believed that water was the basic substance out of which all matter was created.

Pythagoras

The doctrines held by Pythagoras (sixth century B.C.) strongly influenced Plato. The Pythagoreans adhered to several mysteries. They prescribed obedience and silence, frequent fasting, simplicity in dress, limited possessions, and the habit of frequent self-examination. They believed in immortality and in the transmigration of souls—reincarnation.

Socrates

Socrates (470?-399? B.C.) profoundly affected Western philosophy through his influence on Plato. Socrates believed in the superiority of argument over writing and, therefore, spent the greater part of his mature life in the public places of Athens, engaging in dialogue and argument with anyone who would listen. He

"The classroom must and will become an area of conflict between the old and the new - the rotting corpse of Christianity, together with its adjacent evils and misery and the new faith of Humanism, resplendent in its promise of a world in which the never-realized Christian idea of 'Love thy Neighbor' will finally be achieved."

-John J. Dunphy, "A Religion for a New Age," *The Humanist*, January/February 1983, p. 26.

The leading force behind that state school system was Horace Mann, who was one of the leading humanists of the 19th century. A humanist can be defined as one who wants to place man above everything, including God. Mann once said that he wanted to establish "a new religion, with the state as its true church, and education its Messiah."

-Kevin J. Price, *founder of Worldview Ministries*

For after that in the wisdom of God the world by wisdom knew not God, it pleased God by the foolishness of preaching to save them that believe. (1 Corinthians 1:21)

When God would save the world, he took a way by himself; and good reason, for the world by wisdom knew not God. All the boasted science of the heathen world did not, could not, effectually bring home the world of God. In spite of all their wisdom, ignorance still prevailed, iniquity still abounded. Men were puffed up by their imaginary knowledge, and rather further alienated from God; and therefore it pleased Him, by the foolishness of preaching, to save those that believe. By the foolishness of preaching not such in truth, but in vulgar reckoning.

-Matthew Henry's Commentary

believed in a purely objective understanding of such concepts as justice, love, virtue, and self-knowledge as the basis of his teachings. He believed that all wickedness is the result of ignorance, and that no person was willingly bad; accordingly, virtue is knowledge, and those who know what is right will act correctly.

We believe that our nation's public schools should not be doing things like handing out condoms to our children. Educators should not be allowed to usurp the authority from parents in this and other sensitive areas. Remember, the child is not a ward given to the state for its nurture. The child is a gift of God, given in trust to his parents. And our schools should treat our young people as gifts of God, not as subjects of social experimentation or as young animals in heat.

-William Bennett, *Former Secretary of Education,* 1992

Plato

Plato (428?-347 B.C.) is considered one of the most creative and influential thinkers in Western philosophy. His view of knowledge, his psychology, his concept of the state, and his perspective of art must be understood in terms of his theories. Influenced by Socrates, Plato was convinced that knowledge was attainable. He insisted that knowledge must be certain and infallible. He regarded the objects of the real world as being merely shadows of eternal forms or ideas. Only these changeless, eternal forms could be the objects of true knowledge; all observations made with our senses are changeable and, therefore, not necessarily valid. He believed reason, properly used, resulted in intellectual insights that were certain.

Aristotle

"I never went to school with Plato or Aristotle..."

-Paul Bunyan, *Grace Abounding*

Aristotle (384-322 B.C.) was a philosopher and scientist. Aristotle believed the world was made up of individuals (substances) occurring in fixed natural kinds (species). Each individual had its built-in, specific pattern of development and grew toward proper self-realization as a specimen of its type, thus, growth, purpose, and direction, were built into nature.

Aristotle insisted that something could be better understood when its causes were stated in specific terms rather than in general terms. Thus, it would be more informative to know that a sculptor made the statue than to know that an artist made it; and even more informative to know that Polycleitus chiseled it rather than that a sculptor had done so. (Encarta 1997)

The influence of Aristotle's philosophy has been pervasive; it has even helped to shape modern language and rational thought. His doctrine of the Prime Mover as final cause played an important role in theology. Until the twentieth century, logic meant Aristotle's logic. Until the Renaissance, and even later, astronomers and poets alike admired his concept of the universe. Zoology is based on Aristotle's work.

Greeks Philosophy in a Nutshell

The Greeks sought answers in two different realms, first of all in the areas of *polis* [meaning "city," but referring to the whole society]. The Greeks found that society as society could not give ample meaning [to life]. ...Second, they tried to place particulars in relation to their gods. The difficulty with the Greek gods is they were never big enough to be an infinite reference point...Thus neither society or the gods gave the Greeks a sufficient universal understanding. (Schaffer).

And then shall that Wicked be revealed, whom the Lord shall consume with the spirit of his mouth, and shall destroy with the brightness of his coming- ...And with all deceivableness of unrighteousness in them that perish; because they received not the love of the truth, that they might be saved. And for this cause God shall send them strong delusion, that they should believe a lie.
-(2 Thessalonians 2:8, 10, 11)

The Bible Speaks to the Dangers of Greek Educational Philosophies

True knowledge cannot be gained by unaided human reason. *Canst thou by searching find out God? canst thou find out the Almighty unto perfection?* (Job 11:7) *O the depth of the riches both of the wisdom and knowledge of God! how unsearchable are his judgments, and his ways past finding out!* (Romans 11:33).

Teachers of philosophy give their lives to examining convictions by which people can live in order to develop a consistent world view and way of life based on reliable evidence. The Bible warns against philosophies whose highest realities and concerns are atoms, energy, cosmic laws, or humanity—those founded on the basic principles of the world, and not according to Christ.

Beware lest any man spoil you through philosophy and vain deceit, after the tradition of men, after the rudiments of the world, and not after Christ. (Colossians 2:8).

Christians ought to beware so their minds will not be taken captive by such philosophies as secular humanism, communism, and capitalistic materialism. These philosophies are best fought with spiritual weapons.

(For the weapons of our warfare are not carnal, but mighty through God to the pulling down of strong holds;) Casting down imaginations, and every high thing that exalteth itself against the knowledge of God, and bringing into captivity every thought to the obedience of Christ. (2 Corinthians 10:4-5).

For ye see your calling, brethren, how that not many wise men after the flesh, not many mighty, not many noble, are called: But God hath chosen the foolish things of the world to confound the wise; and God hath chosen the weak things of the world to confound the

..."*for the wisdom of their wise men shall perish, and the understanding of their prudent men shall be hid.* (Isaiah 29:14) All the valued learning of this world was confounded, baffled, and eclipsed by the Christian revelations and the glorious triumphs of the Cross. The heathen politicians and philosophers, the Jewish rabbis and doctors, the curious searchers into the secrets of nature, were all posed and put to a nonplus. This scheme lay out of the reach of the deepest statesmen and philosophers, and the greatest pretenders to learning both among the Jews and Greeks."
-Matthew Henry's Commentary

things which are mighty; And base things of the world, and things which are despised, hath God chosen, yea, and things which are not, to bring to nought things that are (1 Corinthians 1:26-28).

The whole goal of the new Marxist, anti-Western curriculum is to remove today's student from the values of our forefathers. They want to uproot an entire generation of young people from their entrenchment in the "narrow-minded" Western ideas of morality, property, and individual freedom under God. Then, when the operation is complete, they can interject their new, revolutionary ideas. When you eliminate moral values and absolute principles of right and wrong, then you are left with lots of questions and no answers. There is no more room for great books, great ideas, or great men, because there is no longer a means to measure greatness. In terms of the college literature course, that means that the Bible, the U.S. Constitution, and Paradise Lost have no meaning or value for us today.

-Lee Grady, *The Marxist Assault on the Curriculum*

Paul Speaks to the Students of Philosophy

The chief biblical example of how to help students of philosophy who do not accept biblical authority is found in Paul's ministry to the Epicureans and philosophers at Athens. Paul commended their zeal, quoted them favorably on a point of agreement, declared the truth about the living Lord of all, announced their accountability to Christ (not to Socrates, Plato, Aristotle, Epicurus, or Zeno), and called on them to repent and trust Jesus Christ.

Now while Paul waited for them at Athens, his spirit was stirred in him, when he saw the city wholly given to idolatry. Therefore disputed he in the synagogue with the Jews, and with the devout persons, and in the market daily with them that met with him. Then certain philosophers of the Epicureans, and of the Stoicks, encountered him. And some said, What will this babbler say? other some, He seemeth to be a setter forth of strange gods: because he preached unto them Jesus, and the resurrection. And they took him, and brought him unto Areopagus, saying, May we know what this new doctrine, whereof thou speakest, is? For thou bringest certain strange things to our ears: we would know therefore what these things mean. (For all the Athenians and strangers which were there spent their time in nothing else, but either to tell, or to hear some new thing.)

Then Paul stood in the midst of Mars' hill, and said, Ye men of Athens, I perceive that in all things ye are too superstitious. For as I passed by, and beheld your devotions, I found an altar with this inscription, TO THE UNKNOWN GOD. Whom therefore ye ignorantly worship, him declare I unto you. God that made the world and all things therein, seeing that he is Lord of heaven and earth, dwelleth not in temples made with hands; Neither is worshiped with men's hands, as though he needed any thing, seeing he giveth to all life, and breath, and all things; And hath made of one blood all nations of men for to dwell on all the face of the earth, and hath determined the times before appointed, and the bounds of their habitation; That they should seek the Lord, if haply they might feel after him, and find him, though he be not far from every one of us:

For in him we live, and move, and have our being; as certain also of your own poets have said, For we are also his offspring.

Forasmuch then as we are the offspring of God, we ought not to think that the Godhead is like unto gold, or silver, or stone, graven by art and man's device. And the times of this ignorance God winked at; but now commandeth all men every where to repent: Because he hath appointed a day, in the which he will judge the world in righteousness by that man whom he hath ordained; whereof he hath given assurance unto all men, in that he hath raised him from the dead. And when they heard of the resurrection of the dead, some mocked: and others said, We will hear thee again of this matter. (Acts 17:16-34:11).

Most of us had this Greco-Roman education. Modern education tried to change the liberal arts in order to fill the gaps, but ended up destroying the true principles discovered by the Greeks. There were several philosophies in the classical world directed at gaining knowledge about our world. The Greeks wanted to conform to the good and natural things of the world, but without God. This is not possible.

"The United States is attempting to implement major educational changes. There is substantial agreement that other industrialized democracies are doing a better job of educating their students than we are. This holds true not only for their highest achievers but for their middle and lowest tracks as well. Many of these countries differ as much from each other as they do from us. Also, with few exceptions, they are now quite diverse in their student populations."

-Education Reform: What's Not Being Said
Albert Shanker,
President, American Federation of Teachers, Washington, D.C.

Ancient Rome

Rome absorbed the Greek culture in the second century and attempted to establish pagan schools throughout the Empire by way of taxes. The public school during this time period was primarily literal in curriculum and rhetorical in content.

Remember during this time the Hebrews continued educating their children with the foundation of the Torah (first five books of the Bible). The majority of the first church was Hebrew. They taught their children as commanded in Deuteronomy 6—teaching them the commands and statutes of God first and foremost.

During the first three centuries of the Christian church, there was little contact between the believers (later called Christians) and and the pagan educational system. The denial of original sin always leads to disaster. The classical schools, with their intention to produce perfect citizens through education, produced only an artificial and cruel society. Men still look back on the "golden Days" of Greece for personal and cultural inspiration, but they fail to realize that the true nobility that they aspired to was never obtainable on any humanistic premise. True nobility, which the Greek

But were mingled among the heathen, and learned their works. (PSALMS 106:35)

and Roman ideal correctly identified, to some extent, is only available through the obedience to the Gospel of Christ, with its insistence on our recognition and confession of sin and its promise of containing sanctification. This is never attainable though education, but only through the free mercies of Christ our Saviour. (Mulligan)

MIDDLE AGES

The medieval Christian curriculum focus was on study. The medieval scholars used classical learning for Christian purposes. Judaism rejected the world's standards of the pagan culture and education. By this time, the church went from mostly Hebrew to mostly Gentile. Christianity embraced the world views with open arms.

David Mulligan's book *Far Above Rubies: Wisdom in the Christian Community* illustrates how the medieval approach to education used many non-biblical sources—even to the point of neglecting Scripture.

> Two traditions of classical literature and philosophy separated the classical world, but were brought together for the first time in fruitful union by the church and rearranged into an educational method that would be the standard of learning for the next one thousand years.
>
> The joining of the literary and scientific world views in Christ was the unique contribution of Medieval Christianity. The science of grammar and rhetoric were brought into conjunction with the science of dialectic (logic). They were arranged progressively, so that the student could use them to achieve his true goal, which in many cases was the science of theology. This system, known as the Trivium, was the foundation of the seven liberal arts programs that became universal throughout the Middle Ages.
>
> This methodology was kept alive in the West. It used textbooks and examples from the ancient world [Greek and Roman] and never saw a need for writing new ones. That was not because it accepted paganism, but because it believed that in many cases the basic curricula of certain structures had been worked out in the ancient world and did not need to be written again. This explains, for

instance, the medieval emphasis on philosophy.

Natural knowledge became prevalent at the end of the Middle Ages. "Philosophy was discredited, the link between theology and the sciences broken; and man began to work out an approach to life that was independent of religion, independent of God. Secularism was born."

And delivered just Lot, vexed with the filthy conversation of the wicked: (For that righteous man dwelling among them, in seeing and hearing, vexed his righteous soul from day to day with their unlawful deeds;)

2 PETER 2:7-8

During this period the Hebrew people continued to teach their children the ways of God, rejecting pagan culture. Anti-Semitism continued to flourish. Christians believed horrendous lies about the Jews and therefore continued to separate from anything Jewish.

Michael Brown explains the attitude toward the Jews during the later Middle Ages in his book *Our Hands are Stained With Blood*.

> The Black Death that ravaged Europe, wiping out about one-third of Europe's entire population, was blamed on the Jews. Christians believed the lies that the Jews secretly contaminated the wells with a poison mixture made of spiders, lizards, and the hearts of Christians. As a result, thousands of Jews were butchered by angry mobs and Jewish children under the age of seven were baptized and reared as Christians after their families were murdered.

Mulligan's book continues to explain in *Far Above Rubies: Wisdom in the Christian Community* (pp 65-66);

> After the peace of the church, in the reign of Constantine, Christianity began to make converts amid the educated classes. More than ever before, the church was brought into direct confrontation with the dilemma offered by pagan ideals of education and the perfect man. To a large extent the confrontation took place over classical literature. A majority of citizens were of the literary/rhetorical tradition. The issue was over the classical world view. Was the church to discard all pagan culture, or was it to attempt a synthesis between Christian and classical thought? Within the circle of orthodoxy many answers were given. After long trial and debate,

Where was Adam when Satan approached Eve? Satan had the opportunity to ask the innocent weaker vessel, "Yea, hath God said?" when she was all alone. Seeds of doubt planted, questioning the Word of God, false promises and deceit, which the adversary is so good at-when she was all alone.

-Pastor Joseph Cammilleri, *A Generation Which Knew Not the Lord.*[9]

what was finally settled upon has affected our intellectual culture to this day.

By the time the church confronted the issue of education on an institutional level, several important events had already occurred:

1. The Church had transferred from Jewish to Gentile soil.

2. The standard of orthodoxy was moving in a more theological direction.

3. The Judaic roots of Christianity were radically de-emphasized as the Gospel message was universalized.

4. The Biblical wisdom tradition was discarded in exchange for Greek education.

5. Wisdom was redefined in classical terms.

6. As the Church became more and more Gentile, less and less Judaic, an education system arose. The Bible standards that would have caused friction with the classical paideia [education] had retreated into the distance. The Church had undergone a strange transformation.

The Puritans

Let us move rapidly, a few hundred years to the time of the Puritans. We see the Puritans throwing off the lies from the churches and returning to the early church's Hebrew heritage. Marvin Wilson's book, *Our Father Abraham* explains (pp. 127-128):

> During the period of the Protestant Reformation (16th century), some signs of the re-Judaization of the Christian faith began to surface, as certain Hebrew categories were rediscovered. The Reformers put great stress on *sola scriptura* (Scripture as the sole and final authority of the Christian). The consequent de-emphasis on tradition brought with it a return to the biblical roots. Accordingly,

during the two centuries following the Reformation, several groups recognized the importance of once again emphasizing the Hebraic heritage of the Church. Among these people were the Puritans who founded Pilgrim America, and the leaders who pioneered American education. We shall comment briefly on the first of these groups before concentrating on the second.

The Puritans came to America deeply rooted in the Hebraic tradition. Most bore Hebrew names. The Pilgrim fathers considered themselves as the children of Israel fleeing "Egypt" (England), crossing the "Red Sea" (the Atlantic Ocean), and emerging from this "Exodus" to their own "promised land" (New England). The Pilgrims thought of themselves as "all the children of Abraham" and, thus, under the covenant of Abraham. (Feingold p. 46.) The President of Yale College used these words before the Governor and General Assembly of the state of Connecticut in 1783: "Their influence on American society was not soon forgotten: more than a century and a half after the first Puritan settlers reached New England, the American people were referred to in a State Assembly as 'God's American Israel.'" (Feldman p. 5)

Thus saith the LORD, Learn not the way of the heathen,
(JEREMIAH 10:2)

The philosophy of humanism began with Satan and is an expression of Satan's lie that humans can be like God. Scripture identifies humanists as those who have "exchanged the truth of God for a lie, and worshipped and served created things rather than the Creator..."
(ROMANS 1:25)

1600 TO 1800 A.D.

The International Institute for Christian Studies reports:

Just as in Europe with the birth of the earliest universities, "the Christian worldview, more than any other system of thought, dominated American intellectual development during the colonial period.... Regardless of the vocation for which a student was preparing, the colonial college sought to provide for him an education that was distinctly Christian." ..."If colonial higher education operated from a Christian foundation, it did so primarily because such an intellectual framework also characterized the European institutions that served as models for the colonial college founders." ..."Thirty-five of the university men in early New England, including a large majority of the Harvard founders, had attended Emmanuel College of Cambridge University.

Humanism teaches that humanity, the universe, and all that exists consist only of matter and energy shaped into their present form by personal chance. Humanism teaches:

- *God does not exist.*
- *The Bible is not inspired.*
- *Christ is not divine.*
- *There is no life after death.*
- *Biblical account of creation is wrong.*
- *Humans are a product of evolution.*
- *Man has the capacity for self fulfillment and correct ethical conduct,*
- *Moral needs are relative to the needs of society.*
- *Judeo-Christian moral and ethical laws such as the ten commandments are "dogmatic," "outmoded," and a hindrance to human progress.*
- *Moral standards are not absolute, but relative, determined by what makes people happy.*

> The key [Bible] verse of the Puritan educators was, "The fear of the Lord is the beginning of wisdom." ...Education, for them, had to have at its heart the purpose of creating character and producing leaders. The very word *education* comes from a Latin word meaning "to lead out." This meant that what God worked inside a person, got processed out into his daily life and thinking. The professor's role was to draw out that which God was putting into the student. (Millar ed.)

During the 1700s Harvard began moving away from its Puritan roots to become thoroughly Unitarian by the early 1800s.

A Brief History of Christian Influence in U.S. Colleges by Jay Rogers explains:

> Harvard was founded in 1636 by Puritan Calvinists who recognized the necessity for training up a clergy if the new Bible commonwealth was to flourish in the wilderness.
>
> The kind of teaching that Harvard College was to provide was spelled out in its "Rules and Precepts" as follows: "Let every Student be plainly instructed, and earnestly pressed to consider well, the main end of his life and studies is, to know God and Jesus Christ which is eternal life, John 17:3, and therefore to lay Christ in the bottom, as the only foundation of all found knowledge and Learning...."
>
> Secularization of the American university began with the takeover of Harvard by the Unitarians in 1805. Actually, the Unitarian takeover was preceded by a protracted struggle between orthodoxy and liberalism, which began in 1701 when Increase Mather stepped down from the presidency. The liberals, who had obtained a definite majority in the governing Corporation, elected John Leverett as president of Harvard College. Leverett, a religious liberal and a layman, set the college on its course away from Calvinist orthodoxy.
>
> The rebellion against Calvinism was a rebellion against the Biblical view of man and God. For Unitari-

ans, the worship of God depended on His being what they thought He should be, not what He actually was.

TODAY'S HOME SCHOOL IS A RETURN TO THE PAST		
	HEBREW EDUCATION, PURITAN EDUCATION, AND TODAY'S CHRISTIAN HOME SCHOOL	**GREEK EDUCATION AMERICA'S PUBLIC SCHOOL**
GOAL	Prepare individuals to serve God	Prepare individuals to serve the state
HOW ACCOMPLISHED	Teach children to trust God in *all* their ways.	Teach students to trust the state (and the state's requirements).
	Teach children to read the Bible and to understand... the riches both of wisdom and knowledge of God (Job 7:11)	Teach the Bible as a book of myths. Christian are weaklings needing something besides self to believe in.
	Prepare for eternity (God).	Prepare students for the next century (OBE).
	Look at God's world as whole–interconnecting–revealing God in every area. *The heavens declare the glory of God; and the firmaments sheweth his handywork* (Psalms 19:1).	Examine the world by classifying whole things into parts—removing them from the Creator. Redefine knowledge: Final reality is impersonal matter or energy shaped into its present form by impersonal chance.
	Teach children to love learning so they will become self-motivated, lifelong learners.	Limiting students (dumbing down) so they do not think for themselves.
	Discover a child's God-given gifts and talents and develop them to the fullest potential. *Focus on spiritual training–the soul.*	Focus on self-esteem and emotional adjustment the external training—the body.
RESULT	Christ-Centered "Thy will be done" Authority with responsibility Literacy, strong family ties, love of learning, security, independent thinking, high morals, and values.	Self -centered My will be done No restraints Illiteracy, illegal drugs, breakdown of the family, violence, pornography, racial tensions, promiscuity, and abortion.
CURRICULUM SUBJECTS	Bible Creation Science His Story (true history) Character Self-Government (internal obedience to God)	Humanism Evolution Social Studies Values Clarification (no right or wrong)
CURRICULUM CONTENT	Lawful Love one another The last shall be first Deny thyself Obey the Commandments	Lawlessness To each his own Look out for #1 If it feels good, do it There are no absolutes
PHILOSOPHY	Submit yourselves to every ordinance of man for the Lord's sake: whether it be to the king, as supreme; or unto governors, as unto them that are sent by him for the punishment of evildoers, and for the praise of them that do well (1 Peter 2:13-14).	That this is a rebellious people, lying children, children that will not hear the law of the Lord (Isaiah 30:9).

For the time will come when they will not endure sound doctrine; but after their own lusts shall they heap to themselves teachers, having itching ears; And they shall turn away their ears from the truth, and shall be turned unto fables. (2 TIMOTHY 4:3-4)

The Unitarians also rejected the Calvinist view of man as being innately depraved. Man, they were convinced, was not only basically good, but perfectible. For this reason, social action became the principal mode in which Unitarians practiced their religion. They were convinced that evil was caused not by man's sinful nature, but by ignorance, poverty, and social injustice. Thus, by eliminating ignorance (through universal public education), they would eliminate poverty and thereby eliminate social injustice. Once this was done and the happy results observed by all, the Unitarians would have proven that they were right and the Calvinists were wrong. *(A Basic History of the United States).*

While the early Harvard Unitarians believed that their rational form of Christianity was quite scriptural, the newer generation, influenced by the enlightenment and the intoxicating elixir of Hegelian pantheism, saw no reason why they should subject their emotional, spiritual and intellectual aspirations to the stultifying restrictions of the Bible.

The seeds of religious liberty for the American Church did not come from New England leaders such as Roger Williams and Anne Hutchinson—as noble as they and others were. Rather, it came from the Hebrews themselves, whose sacred writings inspired the Puritans. Accordingly, many of the Puritans in seventeenth-century England were learned Hebraists. William Bradford (1590-1657), prominent early American and Governor of Plymouth Colony for more than three decades, maintained an intense interest in Hebrew. Bradford stated that he studied Hebrew so that when he died he might be able to speak in the "most ancient language, the Holy Tongue in which God and, the angels, spake." Cotton Mather (1663-1728), a well-known Puritan minister and scholar from Massachusetts, had a similar deep respect for the Hebrew language. Concerning its importance, Mather once observed, "I promise that those who spend as much time morning and evening in Hebrew studies as they do in smoking tobacco, would quickly make excellent progress in the language." (Rosovsky)

AMERICA'S GODLY HERITAGE

Early American educators are another influential segment that placed a strong emphasis upon Old Testament and Hebrew studies. These people were closely connected to the "olive root" and insisted, in keeping with their Puritan heritage, that Hebrew be central in the realm of higher education. A study of the beginnings and curricula of many of the Ivy League colleges in the East is a case in point. Hebrew inscriptions, for example, are found on the insignias or seals of such schools as Columbia and Dartmouth. Of particular interest for our purposes are the early years of Harvard, Yale, and Dartmouth.

The last three generations of Americans simply have not been told the truth about American history. Active humanists and the liberal media have for years undertaken a concentrated effort to misinform the American public by attacking the "Religious Right" and rewriting America's Judeo-Christian history in a humanistic tone. The motto at the heart of the American expression "In God we trust" has been exchanged for "In man we trust."

Examine the quotes below. Have you heard them before? If so, you did not hear them in an American public history class:

- 1490-1492 - Columbus's commission was given to set out to find a new world. According to Columbus's personal log, his purpose in seeking undiscovered worlds was to "bring the Gospel of Jesus Christ to the heathens. ...It was the Lord who put into my mind...that it would be possible to sail from here to the Indies...I am the most unworthy sinner, but I have cried out to the Lord for grace and mercy, and they have covered me completely ... No one should fear to undertake any task in the name of our Saviour, if it is just and if the intention is purely for His holy service." *(Columbus's Book of Prophecies)*

- 1606 - The Charter for the Virginia Colony read in part: "To the glory of His divine Majesty, in propagating of the Christian religion to such people as yet live in ignorance of the true knowledge and worship of God."

- 1620 - King James I granted the Charter of the Plymouth council. "In the hope thereby to advance the enlargement of the Christian religion, to the glory of God Almighty."

- 1620 - The Pilgrims sign the Mayflower Compact aboard

Obey them that have the rule over you, and submit yourselves: for they watch for your souls, as they that must give account, that they may do it with joy, and not with grief: for that is unprofitable for you. (HEBREWS 13:17)

But the natural man receiveth not the things of the Spirit of God: for they are foolishness unto him: neither can he know them, because they are spiritually discerned.
(1 CORINTHIANS 2:14)

"Sort children by judgments of learning capacity; separate the bright from the dull. This is the fundamental operating principle of our education program, the imperative that drives norm-referenced testing, tracking, ability grouping, gifted and talented programs and all the rest. Practices explicitly designed to exclude millions from rigorous education seem entirely reasonable if you believe the requisite abilities to be unequally distributed. By now five generations have received this treatment; we have come to accept it as a fundamental aspect of 'the way things are.'"

-Jeff Howard,
President, The Efficacy Institute

Humanists are aggressive and evangelistic. They are adept at tearing down traditional faith, even if it means permitting the occult to enter the classroom. They are skilled at pouring their anti-God dogmas into the void.
- Mel and Norma Gabler, *textbook analysts*

the Mayflower, in Plymouth Harbor. "For the glory of God and advancement of ye Christian faith... doe by these presents solemnly & mutually in ye presence of God and one of another, covenant & combine our selves together into a civil body politick[sic]."

- 1623 - "But God gave them health and strength in a good measure; and showed them by experience the truth of the word, Deuteronomy 8:3: 'Man does not live on bread alone but on every word that comes from the mouth of the Lord.'" (William Bradford, in BHOPP, p. 175).

- 1629 - The first Charter of Massachusetts read in part: "For the directing, ruling, and disposing of all other Matters and Thinges, whereby our said People may be soe religiously, peaceablie, and civilly governed, as their good life and orderlie Conversacon, maie wynn and incite the Natives of the Country to the Knowledg and Obedience of the onlie true God and Savior of Mankinde, and the Christian Fayth, which in our Royall Intencon, and The Adventurers free profession, is the principall Ende of the Plantacion...."[sic]

- 1638 - The towns of Hartford, Weathersfield, and Windsor adopt the Fundamental Orders of Connecticut. "To mayntayne and presearve the liberty and purity of the Gospell of our Lord Jesus, which we now professe...." [sic]

- 1639 - The governing body of New Hampshire is established. "Considering with ourselves the holy will of God and our own necessity, that we should not live without wholesome laws and civil government among us, of which we are altogether destitute, do, in the name of Christ and in the sight of God, combine ourselves together to erect and set up among us such government as shall be, to our best discerning, agreeable to the will of God...."

- 1775 - In Patrick Henry's speech: "We shall not fight alone. God presides over the destinies of nations, and will raise up friends for us. The battle is not to the strong alone; it is to the vigilant, the active, the brave... Is life so dear, or peace so sweet as to be purchased at the price of chains and slavery? Forbid it Almighty God! I know not what course others may take, but as for me, give me liberty or give me death!"

- 1787 Article III of the Northwest Ordinance of 1787: "Religion, morality, and knowledge, being necessary to good government and the happiness of mankind, schools and the means of education shall forever be encouraged."

- 1789 - George Washington said "Let us with caution indulge the supposition, that morality can be maintained without religion." (Schroeder ed. p. 106)

- 1794 - John Jay, first Chief Justice of the U.S. Supreme Court, in a letter to his wife, stated "God's will be done; to him I resign—in him I confide. Do the like. Any other philosophy applicable to this occasion is delusive. Away with it." (Johnston ed. vol. 4, p. 7.)

But shun profane and vain babblings: for they will increase unto more ungodliness. (2 Timothy 2:16)

America, founded as a Christian nation, taught children in their own homes. Parents had the sole responsibility for their children's education. The focus from the Puritan Calvinists was on studying God's Word. (See chart on page 43.)

Charles Spurgeon (1834-1892), speaking of education said, "It seemed to me that the preachers of the grand old truths of the gospel, were likely to be found in an institution where preaching and divinity would be the main objects, and not degrees and other insignia of human learning."

A portion of the prospectus for Spurgeon's Pastor's College:

> The College aims at training preachers rather than scholars. To develop faculties of ready speech, to help them to understand the Word of God, and to foster a spirit of consecration, courage, and confidence in God, are objects so important that we put all other matters into a secondary position. If a student should learn a thousand things and yet fail to preach the gospel acceptably, his college course will have missed its true design. Should the pursuit of literary prizes and the ambition of

"If continuous learning is the key to enabling our workers and firms to make their own successful transitions to the new economy, the nature of the challenge to American education must be rethought. Obviously, the challenge is no longer to prepare the majority of citizens for manual labor, whether on the farm, as in 1900, or in the mass production factory, as in 1950. Indeed, it is no longer sufficient just to graduate a majority of youth from high school with basic skills.

-A New Challenge for American Education, Paul R. Dimond, Special Assistant to the President for Economic Policy, The White House.

classical honors so occupy the mind as to divert the attention from his life work, they are perilous rather than beneficial. To be wise, to win souls is the wisdom ministers must possess.

With a few adjustments, this portion of the prospectus for Spurgeon's school for pastors is an excellent outline for a home school family's education statement. For example:

> The Scarlatas' home school aims at training godly men and women rather than scholars. To help them to understand the Word of God, and to foster a spirit of consecration, courage, and confidence in God, are objects so important that we put all other matters into a secondary position. If our students learn a thousand academic things and yet fail to find God's paths, this home school will have missed its true design. Should the pursuit of literary prizes and the ambition of classical honors so occupy the mind as to divert the attention from our children's life work, they are perilous rather than beneficial. To be wise, to follow God's ways is the wisdom that Christian's must possess.

The reason we have lost so many of our religious freedoms is because the liberal educational establishment has worked hard to eliminate our knowledge of the godly heritage of America. The facts, nonetheless, reveal the true convictions of our founders. Without question, they believed that, although no single Christian denomination should dominate the nation, the principles of the Bible and Christianity should underlie our government and the American education system as well.

The Puritans knew the pagan Greek educational system could ruin America. Look at these excerpts written by John Wesley in *The Education Of Children:*

- "And education under Pythagoras or Socrates had no other end, but to teach children to think and act as Pythagoras and Socrates did."
- "And is it not reasonable to suppose that a Christian education should have no other end but to teach them how to think, and judge, and act according to the strictest

rules of Christianity?"

- "At least one would suppose, that in all Christian schools, the teaching them to begin their lives in the spirit of Christianity,—in such abstinence, humility, sobriety, and devotion as Christianity requires,—should not only be more, but a hundred time more, regarded that nay or all things else."
- "Let it be carefully remembered all this time, that God, not man, is the physician of souls; that it is He, and none else, who giveth medicine to heal our natural sickness; that all 'the help which is done upon earth, he doeth it himself;' that none of all the children of men is able to 'bring a clean thing out of an unclean;' and, in a word, that 'it is God who worketh in us, both to will and to do of his good pleasure.' But is generally his pleasure to work by his creatures; to help man by man. He honours men to be, in a sense, 'workers together with him.' By this means the reward is ours, while the glory redounds to him."
- "Ye that are truly kind parents, in the morning, in the evening, and all the day beside, press upon all your children, 'to walk in love, as Christ also loved us, and gave himself for us;' to mind that one point, 'God is love; and he that dwelleth in love, dwelleth in God, and God in him." (Millar ed.)

Because that, when they knew God, they glorified him not as God, neither were thankful; but became vain in their imaginations, and their foolish heart was darkened. Professing themselves to be wise, they became fools, (ROMANS 1:21-22)

John Wesley often quoted William Law. Review the excerpt below from Law's writing, "A Serious Call to a Devout and Holy Life," first published in 1728. In all of the Puritan writings, God—not academics—is the primary source of wisdom.

> Devotion is neither private nor public prayer; but prayers, whether private or public, are particular parts or instances of devotion. Devotion signifies a life given, or devoted, to God.
>
> He, therefore, is the devout man, who lives no longer to his own will, or the way and spirit of the world, but to the sole will of God, who considers God in everything, who serves God in everything, who makes all the parts of his common life parts of piety, by doing everything in the

A declared atheist who sometimes used religious terminology, Dewey was a Hegelian, holding that truth is in process; it never is eternally fixed. Morals change, he believed, as society changed. Students should, therefore, be taught to adjust socially and ethically to change as it occurs.
-Mel and Norma Gabler, *textbook analysts*

Name of God, and under such rules as are conformable to His glory.

We readily acknowledge, that God alone is to be the rule and measure of our prayers; that in them we are to look wholly unto Him, and act wholly for Him; that we are only to pray in such a manner, for such things, and such ends, as are suitable to His glory.

What Happened to America's Godly Education System?

America: The First 350 Years by J. Steven Wilkins is an extraordinary study of the true history of America (the facts left out of the public school system for the last one hundred years). This "must have" for all educators is available on sixteen cassette tapes in a cassette container and a study guide. Wilkins explains in *The Beginning of Public School Movement* (Lecture #29 audio cassette):

> One of the most successful reform movements of the 1830s and '40s was the push for a nationwide, state-supported (and state-controlled) school system. The educational level of our nation was far better than Europe and much higher than the literacy rate today. The male literacy rate at that time ran from 70 to 100 percent. (Blumefield, p. 20.). There were numerous private schools and even charity schools for the poor—all without government assistance. Outside of New England, the country had almost complete educational liberty. This being the case, why a desire for state controlled schools? They were motivated by two things:
>
> 1. The desire to destroy the Christian foundations of the nation; and
> 2. The humanistic belief of salvation through education (Wilkins p. 131).
>
> The public school movement was always more than simply an effort to have schools at taxpayers' expense. Nor was it simply an effort to have educated electorate as the franchise was extended to more people, as sometimes alleged. The most zealous of reformers were determined

to use the power of the state by the way of the schools to break hold of religious traditions and the inherited culture and to change society through the child's training. (*A Basic History of the United States, vol. 3,* pp. 90-91).

Charles Darwin and his colleagues were probably the most influential persons in terms of changing an established way of thinking since Nicolaus Copernicus. Darwin claimed that "natural selection" is what determines life and how it will proceed throughout history. His book, *Origin Of Species,* changed the way scientists, educators, and even the Church, viewed the origin and development of life. Just recently the Catholic Pope announced that Darwin's evolution theory was probably true.

This know also, that in the last days perilous times shall come. For men shall be lovers of their own selves, covetous, boasters, proud, blasphemers, disobedient to parents, unthankful, unholy, Without natural affection, trucebreakers, false accusers, incontinent, fierce, despisers of those that are good, Traitors, heady, highminded, lovers of pleasures more than lovers of God; Having a form of godliness, but denying the power thereof: from such turn away. For of this sort are they which creep into houses, and lead captive silly women laden with sins, led away with divers lusts, Ever learning, and never able to come to the knowledge of the truth.
(2 TIMOTHY 3:1-7)

SOME OF THE LEADERS OF THE "PUBLIC SCHOOL" MOVEMENT

America: The First 350 Years Study Guide, (pp 131-132) gives brief biographical sketches of some of the leaders of the modern school system:

ROBERT OWEN

The father of modern socialism, Owen denounced all religion as the chief cause of human misery. In 1830 he wrote, "Now, when the effects of religion, as it has been hereto taught, and impressed by the human race, shall be followed throughout all their ramifications, it will be discovered that the religion of the world is the sole cause of all disunion, hatred, uncharitableness, and crime which pervade the population of the earth." (Samual Blumfield, Is Public Education Necessary? p 204).

The "salvation" of the world (which in Owen's mind represented embracing of socialism) depended upon the eradication of Biblical education. The populace had to be re-educated. Blumfield observes: "To the Owenites in 1828 it was clear that national public education was the essential first step on the road to socialism and that this would require a sustained effort of propaganda and political activism over a long period of time." Owen was willing to give up on his own generation for socialism. He

But avoid foolish questions, and genealogies, and contentions, and strivings about the law; for they are unprofitable and vain.
(TITUS 3:9)

knew he needed a national school system that could change the nation—that was their vision in 1828. The Owenites knew that public education was the first step on the road to socialism and it would require many years, over a hundred. They had a vision for long term victory. Owen was so outspoken against Christianity that Christians despised him, so he could not be the up front person or the leading man. (He dropped into the background but was still very active. All orders were from him.) Abram Combe replaced him.

ABRAM COMBE

A disciple of Owen, Combe shared along with the others, a revulsion of Biblical faith. Combe was converted from Calvinism to a philosophy of human nature developed by a German physician, Franz Joseph Gall, called Phrenology. He realized his conversion would have to be repeated several times in the lives of other men before a secular, national education system dedicated to the improvement (salvation) of men could be a reality.

HORACE MANN

Like his cohorts, Mann was a Calvinist but rejected it when he was twelve years old. To Mann, inequality was man's great enemy. If man was ever to be equal, there must be equality of education and character. This made public schools with common curriculum necessary. Horrace Mann believed the STATE to be the true parent of the child!

ROBERT DALE OWEN

Son of Robert Owen, Robert Dale Owen followed his father's judgment. He wanted to replace Christian education with a "religiously neutral" education. He and his father felt religion was superstition.

THE MEN THAT BEGAN THE STATE SCHOOL MOVEMENT REJECTED CHRISTIANITY

These men wanted public education to be the "redeemer" or

"regenerator" of this present age. The Owenites later formed a secret society to work toward attaining their goals. They infiltrated other movements, educational groups, political groups and other areas by volunteering or being elected. They spread their ideas among those groups. Orestes Brownson (later a leader in their society) wrote:

> The great object was to get rid of Christianity, and not to convert our churches into halls of science. The plan was not to make open attacks on religion, although we might belabor the clergy and bring them into contempt where we could; but to establish a system of state—we said—national schools, from which all religion was to be excluded and to which all parents were to be compelled by law to send their children. (ibid 95, 96)

They didn't openly attack religion but undermined it any way possible and kept promoting the public school system. Surprisingly, the majority of Christians supported their movement. The reasons were threefold:

1. There was a decline in Calvinism among evangelicals in general. The majority of Christians were in basic agreement with the Unitarians and Owenites in their opposition to Calvinism.

2. There was a great influx of immigrants from Europe, many of whom were Roman Catholic, who had been greatly influenced by rationalism. These people posed a threat to the historic Protestantism consensus, and believed that government schools would ward off their influence.

3. It was the belief of many citizens that public schools would be turned over to the control of Christians once they were established.

These things resulted in the strange coalition of Socialists, Unitarians, and evangelical Christians all supporting a government system for their own reasons. This, coupled with those who

"I am much afraid that schools will prove to be the gates of hell, unless they (schools) diligently labor in explaining the Holy Scriptures, engraving them in the hearts of youth. Every institution in which men are not unceasingly occupied with the Word of God must become corrupt."
-Martin Luther

Standard Eighth Grade Achievement Test in 1907

An excerpt from "Small World Gone: A Family Record of an Era" published by the *Wall Street Journal.* The author talks of the evening she received her eighth grade diploma from a small-town school.

Science

The 'orthography' quiz asked us to spell twenty words, including "abbreviated," "obscene," "elucidation," "assassination" and "animosity." We were also required to make a table showing the different sounds of all the vowels. Among the other eight questions (each subject had ten questions) was one which asked us to divide words into syllables and mark diacritical, defiance, priority, remittance and propagate.

Math

Two of Arithmetic's ten questions asked us to find the interest on an 8 percent note for $900 running two years, two months, six days; and also to reduce three pecks, five quarts, and one pint into bushels.

Reading

In reading we were required to tell what we knew of the writings of Thomas Jefferson and, for another of the ten questions, to indicate the pronunciation and give meanings to the following words: zenith, deviated, coliseum, misconception, panegyric, Spartan, talisman, eyre, triton, crypt and others.

Geography

Among Geography's ten questions were these two: "Name two countries producing large quantities of wheat, two of cotton, two of coal, two of tea." and "Name the three important rivers of the U.S., three of Europe, three of Asia, three of South America, and three of Africa."

Physiology

As one of Physiology's ten we were asked to write 200 words on the evil effects of alcoholic beverages. Another directed us to define boards of health and what their duties were.

Grammar

In Grammar's ten were two directing us to analyze and diagram: "There is a tide in the affairs of men, which, taken at the flood, leads on to a fortune," and then to parse tide, which, taken, leads.

History

In History we were to "give a brief account of the colleges, printing and religion in the colonies prior to the American Revolution," to "name the principal campaigns and military leaders of the Civil War," and to "name the principal political questions which have been advocated since the Civil War and the party which advocated each."

Aavis Carlson took and passed that standard eighth grade test when she was eleven years and eight months old. So much for a one-room school in Kansas, 1907.

PUBLIC SCHOOL TODAY

Let us move from the primitive one-room schoolhouse to the bright and better future of 1986, where our tax dollars were hard at work educating tomorrow's leaders.

Reading

In 1990, Secretary of education Cavazos released the results of two nationwide tests. Fifty-eight percent of seventeen-year-olds cannot understand a twelfth grade textbook or articles in the *Wall Street Journal, Time* or *Newsweek.* Ninety-five percent do not have the reading skills to understand a college textbook. Forty two percent of thirteen-year-olds and fourteen percent of seventeen-year-olds cannot read at an eighth grade level.

History and Literature

In 1986, 7,812 eleventh graders took a national test of their knowledge of history and literature. This was a multiple choice affair, in which there was no penalty for skipping a question altogether. Even so, of all the answers given to the 141 questions on history, only 54.5 percent were correct. The results in literature were even more depressing. As a group, these seventeen-year-olds demonstrated no sense of chronological history. Almost 25 percent thought the Civil War was before 1800. One third thought Columbus discovered the new world after 1750. Three out of four could not place Lincoln within twenty years. Forty-three percent guessed wrong on which half century included World War I. Not even half could identify Patrick Henry.

Math

In 1987 the *News/Sun Journal* in Fort Lauderdale stated, "New evidence ranks the mathematical ability of American primary and high school students among the lowest of any country."

Geography

The Monitor, McAllen, Texas, ran an article titled, "Study: One fifth of students can't find the U.S.A. on a map." A report from the National Council for Geographical Education found that in a 1983 test on geography, American twelve-year-olds often confused Brazil on the map for the United States. American youngsters placed fourth among an international field of eight. Their median scores were 42.9 of a possible 101.

Composition

A study by Educational Writers in Sioux Falls, South Dakota in 1986 stated: "76 percent of seventeen-year-olds could not write an adequate piece of creative writing, 62 percent could not write a satisfactory piece of prose, and 80 percent could not write a persuasive letter."

Our future leaders?

wanted to make money from the system (textbook publishers, professional educators and others), brought tremendous pressure in favor of government financed schools. The pro-school propaganda became increasingly vicious and outrageous. Opponents of the school were labeled the "enemies of light and knowledge" and of the betterment of mankind.

By the year 1850 it was a foregone conclusion that this country would have a system of government-supported schools. They were not to be schools of learning, but engines of change and "reform." Schools were no longer extensions of parental authority but, instead, powerful instruments for state control over the population. The reformers sought to deny parents' authority over the education of their children. Children increasingly became "wards of the state" The public schools would become the chief instrument in implementing the revolution the enemies of Christianity desired.

The schools became the new temples of the new religion of man, and teachers became the new priests. Man, or more precisely "humanity," as incorporated in the state, became the new god and has remained so to this day.

Today denouncing the public school system in this country offends more people than denouncing God. Why? Because people believe education is salvation. Survival from poverty comes from education. If you don't have formal education, you are a low life. (God's word tells us that this is the world's view, not God's. The Bible clearly states wisdom and knowledge come from God.) Christians believe in education, and we will educate our children as God commands, but education is not considered salvation. Education is still to the world—and to Christians who have believed the lie—the great thing that will save the state.

When Prayer was Taken Out of School

David Breese, author of *Seven Men Who Rule the World From the Grave,* explains that through the teachings of John Dewey's humanism, his atheism, his autonomous man, amorality, evolution, and one-world socialism, permeated our educational system and excluded from our textbooks the moral and Biblical teachings which were the bedrock of our American culture. Thus, our American youth have been disenfranchised from our Christian heritage. Now two generations of graduates have been subjected to these godless philosophies through our schools. What are the results?

The results are a spiritually apathetic society that hardly murmured when, in 1962, citing no precedents, a liberal Supreme

Court abolished prayer from the public schools and the next year abolished Bible reading from the schools.... *Because iniquity shall abound, the love of many shall run cold.* (Matthew 24:12).

From that time on, there was a startling rise in teenage pregnancies, up 556 percent; venereal disease, up 226 percent (now thirty-five thousand new cases per day!). Family divorce had declined for fifteen years, then tripled each year since. SAT scores had previously been stable. Now they've declined remarkably.

A recent statistical analysis by David Barton graphically illustrates how America has plummeted from righteous living, prosperity and success in the last quarter century. Consider the following chart compiled from his publication, *America: To Pray or Not to Pray:*

In 1962, the Court examined a simple twenty-two word prayer, first used to negate prayer in schools:

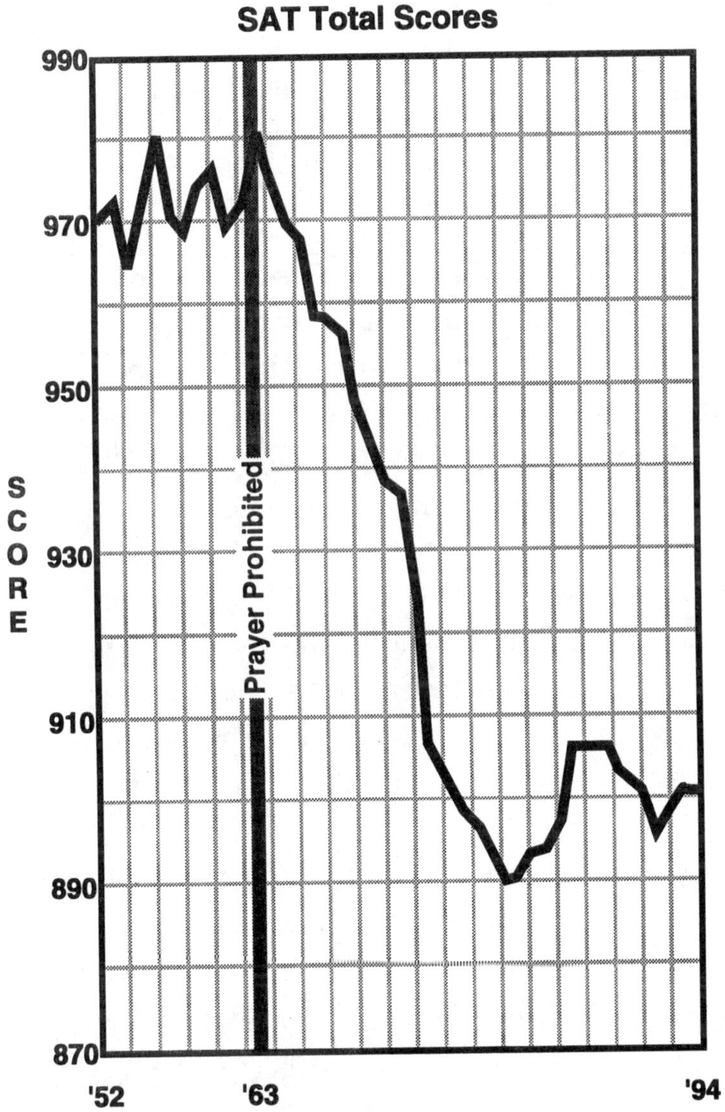

"If you subsidize rice, you get more rice; if you subsidize wheat, you get more wheat. The state subsidizes irresponsible parenting and now we are reaping the whirlwind of this irresponsibility and dependence."

-Milton Friedman

"Almighty God, we acknowledge our dependence upon Thee, and we beg Thy blessings upon us, our parents, our teachers, and our country."

This simple prayer, said by children, acknowledged God. American's indifference allowed the removal of prayer from our schools. This is but one of the steps toward complete destruction of America's original Judeo-Christian education system. The value-free environment has resulted in chaos. Since the 1962 removal of prayer:

- SAT scores have declined dramatically.
- Birth rates of unwed teens have increased over 400 percent.
- Sexually-transmitted diseases have increased almost 400 percent.
- Violent crime has greatly increased.
- The divorce rate has increased 120 percent.
- Couples living together has increased 600%.
- Abortions have become legal and frequent.

Education in the 1990s

Moving to the '90s education systems we see the tragic results of pagan education—immorality and illiteracy.

Don Feder explains in the Introduction of his book *A Jewish Conservative Looks at Pagan America:*

> By Pagan America, I mean this is no longer a Judeo-Christian Nation, animated by the ethical vision of the Bible, with its special emphasis on honesty, hard work, caring, and self discipline. Instead we are evolving into the type of Canaanite culture (unrestrained hedonism, ritual prostitution, child sacrifice and the civic virtue of Sodom), which my ancestors encountered at the dawn of moral history.
>
> ...The gods of the late twentieth century America include the doctrines of radical autonomy, of absolute rights divorced from responsibilities, of gender sameness, of self expression which acknowledges no higher purpose, of moral relativism and sexual indulgence. Their templates are courtrooms, legislative chambers,

> classrooms, news rooms, and the executive suites of entertainment conglomerates and publishing firms. We are one nation under God no more.
>
> ...Ideas have consequences. First the elite, then to a lesser extent the masses embrace certain toxic notions. The consequences fill our prisons, drug rehab centers, divorce courts, shelters for battered and abused, rape crises centers, mental hospitals, mental hospitals, singles bars, and the roster of guests on the *Oprah Winfrey Show.*

We have enormous problems with illiteracy today. Almost 72 million American adults are functional illiterates (*Education Week,* June 13, 1985, p.28.). People find that life is easier, that they can get along without the "sweat" of reading, and so they choose instead to watch the television and view the cartoons. You don't have to read, except to fill out a form. We assume today's people are far superior than those who lived before us; however, the literacy rate was much higher in early America than today. In the fifteenth, sixteenth, and seventeenth centuries there were more people who wanted to learn to read than there were people to teach them.

The right principles that made America great were lost, not just among the lower classes, but in the highest offices in the land. There's no longer any connection between character and destiny. Moral teaching, proper standards, and respect for rules have been removed from our schools. Meaningless courses in "values clarification" and the tenets of secular humanism (classified as a religion by the Supreme Court in 1961) have been substituted. People claim that morals have changed. God makes morals, and He didn't change His mind. God hates wickedness.

The children from this background have now become the parents, teachers, political leaders, and news media of today. Ignorant of the great moral and religious strengths of our country, they were unable to impart these to the new generation.

Now that you have had a brief look at the history of the state's education system, let us examine and compare the history of Biblical education.

CHAPTER 4
HISTORY OF BIBLICAL EDUCATION
Solid Foundation

EDUCATION IN BIBLE TIMES

A Christian's roots are in the Bible, not in the Greeks' Hellenistic paganism. We need to look at the history of our patriarchs, Abraham, Isaac, and Jacob, the faithful followers of God, to find out how they taught their children the enduring, deep-rooted faith.

EDUCATION IN THE HOME

A study of education in Bible times can be very encouraging to home schoolers because the focus is on the home. The Hebrews called the Temple *miqdash.* After the destruction of the Temple, they called the home "*miqdash me`at*. The root of *miqdash* is *qadash* (Strong's 4720, 6942) meaning "to be set apart," a consecrated thing or place, a sanctuary. The family home was put apart for something special. The Hebrew word *me`at* (*meh-at´*) (Strong's 4592) means "little" (Ezekiel 11:16). God made the home the "little sanctuary." The home was a house of prayer, worship and study—all study—academics and spiritual.

Today's Christians have it backwards. The primary sphere of religious activity should be in the home, not the church. The dinner table was a place to gather—not just for food (Dueteronomy. 8:3)—but also to study God's Word, pray, praise, and worship. The home was more important than the synagogue. The center of all training—religious, education, and family—was the home.

The Hebrew word for *parent* is similar to teacher. It is *horeh,* which is from the root word *yarah,* meaning "to cast, throw or shoot." The Bible commands the father, the priest of his little sanctuary, to instruct the children (Deuteronomy 6). The father is to impart wisdom and knowledge diligently to his children.

We can learn much from the weekly worship in the early church. The entire family prepared each week for the Sabbath. The Sabbath was a special day of worship, prayers, singing, and Bible reading. The men of the home went to the Temple (each man prepared to speak) for worship, prayer, and sacrifice, but then he returned home for worship with his family. The father blessed the children as he prayed for them one by one. I recently heard a very sad statement. The observation was made that, "One could walk into a Jewish unbeliever's home today and see the people's love for God, but what would one see in a believer's home?" Would we even be eating together around the table?

Teaching the Whole Child

Collier's Encyclopedia explains that education during Abraham's times taught the whole child:

> The keynote of Jewish education appears as early as Gen. 18:19 in the revelation made to Abraham: *"For I know him that he will command his children and his household after him, and they shall keep the way of the Lord, to do justice and judgment...."* This same note runs throughout the Old Testament in various injunctions: *"Train up a child in the way he should go; and when he is old, he will not depart from it"* (Proverbs 22:6) and *"Fear of the Lord is the beginning of wisdom"* (Proverbs 9:10). The aim of education was ethical and religious. The education of youth was an obligation of the parents, and was intimately associated with the performance of ritual observances and with learning the Mosaic law, both of which were regarded as essential to the survival of the Jews as a people. In the educative process, both father and mother were equally concerned, and both were to be equally honored (the Fifth Commandment). The method of instruction in the home was for a long time oral, and learning by practice, and these methods were continued outside the home in gatherings and assemblies, held for both worship and instruction. Corporal punishment was regarded as an essential element in training.
>
> *"He that spareth the rod hateth his son: but he that loveth him chasteneth him betimes"* (Proverbs 23:24) is a precept frequently repeated both in Proverbs and in Ecclesiastes. Visual aids, including monuments as records of history, were employed. The setting up of "great stones" with inscriptions on them implies an early knowledge of writing (Deuteronomy 27:2, 3, 8, and elsewhere). The scribes were not only copyists but also teachers and interpreters of the Law of Moses. There existed a knowledge of arithmetic and astronomy; music, dancing, games, and sports were cultivated, and moral

instruction was an essential part of education.

STUDY OF WORSHIP

Marvin Wilson explains in *Our Father Abraham*:

> People seek education for many worthy reasons: some desire to broaden horizons; others wish to develop skills; still others want to satisfy their intellectual curiosity. The Bible, however, teaches that study ought to be, above everything else, an act of worship, one of the highest ways by which a person can glorify God.
>
> As a Pharisee, Paul was a learned product of Judaism, a man well versed in Jewish thought and biblical theology. (Philippians 3:4-6) Paul made no distinction between the so-called sacred and secular areas of life. He taught—as his Hebrew forebears did—that all of life was God's domain of activity. Every detail of life therefore, must be set aside and consecrated to the glory of God. So, Paul wrote to the Corinthians, *"Whether therefore ye eat, or drink, or whatsoever ye do, do all to the glory of God."* (1 Corinthians 10:31). He later wrote to the Colossians, *"And whatsoever ye do in word or deed, do all in the name of the Lord Jesus, giving thanks to God and the Father by him."* (3:17). As David Hubbard reminds us, "There is an intimate connection between work and worship. For to work is to give glory to God...We work with God's goods, and we use God's talents to perform the work, and we serve God's people through our work."

Wilson also explains in chapter 14:

> Since the Bible period, Jews have considered the quest for knowledge to be one of the great desiderata [desires] of life (Philippians 3:4-11) Learning—learning—learning that is the secret of Jewish survival. (Hacker, ed. P.21.). ...So strongly did the early rabbis feel about the priority of education that they said it may not be interrupted even for the rebuilding of the Temple... Israel was to acknowledge the Lord's authority in every circumstance and turn of the way. (Psalms 16:8, Proverbs 3:5-6). The ultimate prophetic

vision was that "all the peoples of the earth know that the Lord is God and there is no other." (1 Kings 8:60).

From early in history the center of education was the home. Both parents shared responsibility in this task (Proverbs. 1:8; 6:20), though the Father bore the chief responsibility for the instruction of the children (Deuteronomy 11:9).... In Bible times it was the Father—not textbooks, audiovisuals, or brightly colored classrooms—the main instruction was the learning process. As teacher of his children, the father served as a living dynamic communicator of divine truth. A Bible could not be substituted—there were no Bibles.

There is no shortcut method to a sound education. If someone wants to make spiritual training a priority, one must make a major commitment of time. Thus the Psalmist says, "...*His delight is in the law [instruction] of the Lord; and in His law* [instruction] *doth he meditate day and night."* (Psalms 1:2).

Ancient Israel had no formal system of schooling; however, learning and knowledge were considered one of the greatest goals of life.

A careful study of the Hebrew Bible will reveal what Martin Luther called a "special energy" in its vocabulary. Luther discovered what many Hebraists of the twentieth century have recently come to affirm with him: it is impossible to convey so much so briefly in any other language. Luther concluded the following: "The Hebrew language is the best language of all, with the richest vocabulary.... It has therefore been aptly said that the Hebrews drink from the spring, the Greeks from the stream that flows from it, and the Latins from a downstream pool." (Lapide p. x.)

EDUCATION DEFINED

The 1915 *International Bible Encyclopedia* gives this fascinating information about education during Bible times:

> Religious education among ancient and modern peoples alike reveals clearly this twofold aspect of all education. The first aspect consists in the transmission of religious ideas and experience by means of the of imitation and example; each generation, by actually participating in the religious activities and ceremonies of the social

group. Formal religious education begins with a systematic effort on the part of the mature members of a social group teach the younger members by means of solemn rites and ceremonies, or patient training, or both.

All education is at first religious in the sense that religious motives and ideas predominate in the educational efforts of all peoples. The degree to which religion continues over in the educational system of a progressive nation depends upon the vitality of its religion and upon the measure of efficiency and success with which from the first that religion is instilled into the very bone and sinew of each succeeding generation. The secret of Israel's incomparable influence upon the religious and educational development of the world. The religion of Israel was a vital religion and it was a teaching religion (Kent, GTJC).

Education in Early Israel (from Patriarchal Times to the Exile)

The nomads and shepherds in the early Old Testament period held interests centered in the flocks and herds from which they gained a livelihood. The settlement of the Hebrew tribes in Palestine and their closer contact with Canaanitish culture resulted in changes in social and religious institutions. A permanent dwelling-place made possible, as the continual warfare of gradual conquest made necessary, a closer federation of the tribes, which ultimately resulted in the establishment of the monarchy under David. (Smith)

Education in Nomadic and Agricultural Periods

In these earliest cultural periods, there was no distinct separation between religion and ordinary life. The relation of the people to Yahweh [God's name in Hebrew] was conceived by them in simple fashion as involving on their part the obligation of obedience and loyalty, and on Yahweh's part reciprocal parental care over them as His people. The family was the social unit and its head the person in whom centered also religious authority and leadership, The tribal head or patriarch in turn joined in the functions which later were given to those of priest and prophet and king. Education was a matter of purely domestic interest and concern. The home was the only school and the parents the only teachers. But there was real instruction, all of which, moreover, was given in a spirit of devout religious earnestness and of reverence for the common religious ceremonies and beliefs, no matter whether the subject of instruction was the simple task of husbandry or of some useful art, or whether it was the sacred history and traditions of the tribe, or the actual performance of its religious rites.

According to Josephus (Ant, IV, viii, 12), Moses himself had commanded, "All boys shall learn the most important parts of the law since such knowledge is most valuable and the source of happiness"; and again he commanded (Apion, II, 25) to teach them the rudiments of learning (reading and writing) together with the laws and deeds of the ancestors, in order that they might not transgress or seem ignorant of the laws of their ancestors, but rather emulate their example. Certain it is that the earliest legislation, including the Decalogue, emphasized parental authority and their claim on the reverence of their children: "Honor thy father and thy mother, that thy days may be long in the land which Yahweh thy God giveth thee" (Exodus 20:12); "And he that smiteth his father, or his mother, shall be surely put to death. And he that curseth his father or his mother, shall surely be put to death" (Exodus 21:15,17); while every father was exhorted to explain to his son the origin and significance of the great Passover ceremony with its feast of unleavened bread: "And thou shalt tell thy son in that day, saying, It is because of that which Yahweh did for me when I came forth out of Egypt." (Exodus 13:8).

Education During the Monarchical Period

The period of conquest and settlement developed leaders who not only led the allied tribes in battle, but served as judges between their people. In time, sufficient cooperation was obtained to make possible the organization of strong intertribal union and, finally, the kingship. The establishment of the kingdom and the beginnings of city and commercial life were accompanied by more radical cultural changes, including the differentiation of religious from other social institutions, the organization of the priesthood, and the rise and development of prophecy.

Elijah, the Tishbite, Amos, the herdsman from Tekoa, and Isaiah, the son of Amoz, were all champions of a simple faith and ancient religious ideals as over against the worldly-wise diplomacy and sensuous idolatry of the surrounding nations. Under the monarchy also a new religious symbolism developed. Yahweh was thought of as a king in whose hands actually lay the supreme guidance of the state: "Accordingly the organization of the state included provision for consulting His will and obtaining His direction in all weighty matters" (W. R. Smith, Revue semitique, 30). Under the teaching of the prophets, the ideal of personal and civic righteousness was moved to the very forefront of Hebrew religious thought, while the prophetic ideal of the future was that of a time when "the earth shall be full of the knowledge of Yahweh, as the waters cover the sea" (Isaiah 11:9), when all "from the least of them unto the greatest of them" shall know him (Jeremiah 31:34). Concerning the so-called "schools of the prophets" which, in the days of Elijah, existed at Bethel, Jericho and Gilgal (2 Kings 2:3,5; 4:38), and probably in other places, it should be noted that these were associations established for the purpose of mutual edification rather than education. The Bible does not use the word "schools" to designate these fraternities. Nevertheless, religious training occurred.

Deuteronomic Legislation

Shortly before the Babylonian captivity, King Josiah gave official recognition and sanction to the teachings of the prophets, while the Deuteronomic legislation of the same period strongly emphasized the responsibility of parents for the religious and moral instruction and training of their children. Concerning the words of the law Israel is admonished: "Thou shalt teach them diligently unto thy children, and shalt talk of them when thou sittest in thy house, and when thou walkest by the way, and when thou liest down, and when thou risest up." (Deuteronomy 6:7; 11:19). For the benefit of children as well as adults, the law was to be written "upon the door-posts" and "gates" (6:9; 11:20), and "very plainly" upon "great stones" set up for this purpose upon the hilltops and beside the altars (Deuteronomy 27:1-8). From the Deuteronomic period forward, religious training to the Jew became the synonym of education, while the word *Torah,* which originally denoted simply "Law" (Exodus 24:12; Leviticus 7:1; 26:46), came to mean "religious instruction or teaching," in which sense it is used in (Deuteronomy 4:44; 5:1), "This is the law which Moses set before the children of Israel: ...Hear, O Israel, the statutes and the ordinances which I speak in your ears this day, that ye may learn them, and observe to do them"; and in (Proverbs 6:23),

"For the commandment is a lamp; and the law is light;
And reproofs of instruction are the way of life."

Reading and Writing

With the development and reorganization of the ritual, priests and Levites, as the guardians of the law, were the principal instructors of the people, while parents remained in charge of the training of the children. In families of the aristocracy the place of the parents was sometimes taken by tutors, as appears from the case of the infant Solomon, whose training stems to have been entrusted to the prophet Nathan (2 Samuel 12:25). There is no way of determining to what extent the common people were able to read and write. Our judgment that these rudiments of formal education in the modern sense were not restricted to the higher classes is based upon such passages as (Isaiah 29:11-12), which distinguishes between the man who "is learned" (literally, "knoweth letters") and the one who is "not learned," and (Isaiah 10:19), referring to the ability of a child "to write," taken together with such facts as that the literary prophets Amos and Micah sprang from the ranks of the common people, and that "the workman who excavated the tunnel from the Virgin's Spring to the Pool of Siloam carved in the rock the manner of their work" (Kennedy in *Hastings, Dictionary of the Bible*). It should be added that the later Jewish tradition reflected in the Talm, Targum and Midr, and which represents both public, elementary and college education as highly developed even in patriarchal times, is generally regarded as altogether untrustworthy.

Education in Later Israel
(from the Exile to the Birth of Christ)

The national disaster that befell the Hebrew people in the downfall of Jerusalem and the Babylonian captivity was not without its compensating, purifying, and stimulating influence upon the religious and educational development of the nation. Under the pressure of adverse external circumstances, the only source of comfort for the exiled people was in the law and covenant of Yahweh, while the shattering of all hope of immediate national greatness turned the thought and attention of the religious leaders away from the present toward the future. Two types of Messianic expectation characterized the religious development of the exilic period. The first is the priestly, material hope of return and restoration reflected in the prophecies of Ezekiel. The exiled tribes are to return again to Jerusalem; the temple is to be restored, its ritual and worship purified and exalted, the priestly ordinance and service elaborated. The second is the spiritualized and idealized Messianic expectation of the Second Isaiah, based on teachings of the earlier prophets. For the greatest of Hebrew prophets, Yahweh is the only God, and the God of all nations as well as of Israel. For him, Israel is Yahweh's servant, His instrument for revealing Himself to other nations, who, when they witness the redemption of Yahweh's suffering Servant, will bow down to Yahweh and acknowledge His rule. "Thus the trials of the nation lead to a comprehensive universalism within which the suffering Israel gains an elevated and ennobling explanation" (Ames, Hauck-Herzog, *Realencyklopadie fur protestantische Theologie und Kirche,* 185). In the prophetic vision of Ezekiel, we must seek the inspiration for the later development of Jewish ritual, as well as the basis of those eschatological hopes and expectations which find their fuller expression in the apocalypse of Daniel and the kindred literature of the later centuries. The prophecies of the Isaiahs and the Messianic hope which these kindled in the hearts of the faithful prepared the way for the teachings of Jesus concerning a Divine spiritual kingdom, based upon the personal, ethical character of the individual and the mutual, spiritual fellowship of believers.

Educational Significance of the Prophets

The educational significance of the prophetic writings of this as of the preceding periods is that the prophets themselves were the real religious leaders and representative men (Kulturtrager) of the nation. In advance of their age they were the heralds of Divine truth; the watchmen on the mountain tops whose clear insight into the future detected the significant elements in the social and religious conditions and tendencies about them, and whose keen intellect and lofty faith grasped the eternal principles which are the basis of all individual and national integrity and worth. These truths and principles they impressed upon the consciousness of their own and succeeding generations, thereby giving to future teachers of their race the essence of their message, and preparing the way for the larger and fuller interpretation of religion and life contained in the teachings of Jesus. The immediate influence of their teaching is explained in part by the variety and effectiveness of their teaching method, their marvelous simplicity and directness of speech, their dramatic emphasis upon essentials and their intelligent appreciation of social conditions and problems about them.

The Book of the Law

The immediate bond of union, as well as the textbook and program of religious instruction, during the period of the captivity and subsequently, was the Book of the Law, which the exiles carried with them to Babylon. When in 458 B.C. a company of exiles returned to Palestine, they, along with their poorer brethren who had not been carried away, restored the Jewish community at Jerusalem, and under the suzerainty of Persia, founded a new nationalism, based, even more than had been the earlier monarchy, upon the theocratic conception of Israel's relation to Yahweh. During this period it was that writings of poets, lawgivers, prophets, and sages were brought together into one sacred collection of scrolls, known later as the Old Testament canon, of which the Torah (the law) was educationally the most significant. The recognized teachers of this period included, in addition to the priests and Levites, the "wise men," or "sages" and the "scribes" or *copherim* (literally, "those learned in Scriptures").

Wise Men or Sages

Whether or not the sages and scribes of the later post-exilic times are to be regarded as one and the same class, as an increasing number of scholars are inclined to believe, or thought of as distinct classes, the wise men clearly antedate, not only the copherim but in all probability all forms of book learning as well. Suggestions of their existence and function are met with in earliest times both in Israel and among other nations of the East. Isaiah 29:10, 2 Samuel 14:1-20, and 1 Kings 4:32 may be cited as illustrations of their pre-exilic exixtence. It is no lesser personage than King Solomon who, both by his contemporaries and later generations as well, was regarded as the greatest representative of this earlier group of teachers who uttered their wisdom in the form of clever, epigrammatic proverbs and shrewd sayings. The climax of Wisdom-teaching belongs, however, to the later post-exilic period. Of the wise men of this later day an excellent description is preserved for us in the Book of Ecclesiastes 39:3-4,8,10.

He seeks out the hidden meaning of proverbs,
And is conversant with the subtitles of parables,
He serves among great men,
And appears before him who rules;
He travels through the land of strange nations;
For he hath tried good things and evil among men.

He shows forth the instruction which he has been taught,
And glories in the law of the covenant of the Lord.

Nations shall declare his wisdom,
And the congregation shall tell out his praise.

The Book of Proverbs

Of the instructional experience, wisdom, and learning of these sages, the Book of Proverbs forms the biblical compartment. Aside from the Torah, it is thus the oldest handbook of education. The wise men conceive of life itself as a discipline. Parents are the natural instructors of their children:

My son, hear the instruction of thy father,
And forsake not the law of thy mother.
—(Proverbs 1:8).

The substance of such parental teaching is to be the "fear of Yahweh," which "is the beginning of wisdom;" and fidelity in the performance of this parental obligation has the promise of success:

Train up a child in the way he should go,
And even when he is old he will not depart from it.
—(Proverbs 22:6).

In their training of children, parents are to observe sternness, not hesitating to apply the rod of correction, when needed (compare 23:13,14), yet doing so with discretion, since wise reproof is better than "a hundred stripes" (17:10). Following the home training there is provision for further instruction at the hands of professional teachers for all who would really obtain "wisdom" and who can afford the time and expense of such special training. The teachers are none other than the wise men or sages whose words "heard in quiet" (Ecclesiastes 9:17) are "as goads, and as nails well fastened" (12:11). Their precepts teach diligence (Proverbs 6:6-11), chastity (7:5), charity (14:21), truthfulness (17:7) and temperance (21:17; 23:20-21,29-35); for the aim of all Wisdom-teaching is none other than *"To give prudence to the simple, To the young man knowledge and discretion: That the wise man may hear, and increase in learning; And that the man of understanding may attain unto sound counsels."* —(Proverbs 1:4-5).

Scribes and Levites

The copherim, or "men of book learning," were editors and interpreters as well as scribes or copyists of ancient and current writings. As a class, they did not become prominent until the wise men, as such, stepped into the background, nor until the exigencies of the situation demanded more teachers and teaching than the ranks of priests and Levites, charged with increasing ritualistic duties, could supply. Ezra was both a priest and a copher (Ezra 7:11; Nehemiah 8:1), concerning whom we read that he "set his heart to seek the law of Yahweh, and to do it, and to teach in Israel statutes and ordinances" (Ezra 7:10). Likewise the Levites often appear as teachers of the law, and we must think of the development of sopherism (scribism) as a distinct profession as proceeding very gradually. The same is true of the characteristic Jewish religious-educational institution, the synagogue, the origin and development of which fell within this same general period. The pupils of the copherim were the Pharisees (*perushim* or "separatists") who during the Maccabean period came to be distinguished from the priestly party or Sadducees.

Greek and Roman Influences

The conquest of Persia by Alexander (332 B.C.) marks the rise of Greek influence in Palestine. Alexander himself visited Palestine and perhaps Jerusalem (Josephus, Ant, X, i, 8), befriended the Jews and granted to them the privilege of self-government, and the maintenance of their own social and religious customs, both at home and in Alexandria, the new center of Greek learning, in the founding of which many Jews participated. During the succeeding dynasty of the Ptolemies, Greek ideas and Greek culture penetrated to the very heart of Judaism at Jerusalem, and threatened the overthrow of Jewish social and religious institutions. The Maccabean revolt under Antiochus Epiphanes (174-164 B.C.) and the reestablishment of a purified temple ritual during the early part of the Maccabean period (161-63 B.C.) [the reason for the Hanukkah celebration today] were the natural reaction against the attempt of the Seleucidae forcibly to substitute the Greek gymnasium and theater for the Jewish synagogue and temple (Felten, NZ, I, 83 f; compare 1 Macc. 1, 3, 9, 13 and 2 Macc. 4-10).

The end of the Maccabean period found Phariseeism and strict Jewish orthodoxy in the ascendancy [power] with such Hellenic tendencies as had found permanent lodgment in Judaism reflected in the agnosticism of the aristocratic Sadducees. The establishment of Roman authority in Palestine (63 B.C.) introduced a new determining element into the conditions under which Judaism was to attain its final distinguishing characteristics. The genius of the Romans was practical, legalistic, and institutional. As organizers and administrators, they were preeminent. But their religion never inspired to any exalted view of life, and education to them meant always merely a preparation for life's practical duties. Hence, the influence of Roman authority upon Judaism was favorable to the development of a narrow individualistic Phariseeism, rather than to the fostering of Greek idealism and universalism. With the destruction of Jerusalem by the Romans a little more than a century later (70 A.D.) and the cessation of the temple worship, the Sadducees as a class disappeared from Judaism, which has ever since been represented by the Pharisees devoted to the study of the law. Outside of Jerusalem and Palestine, meanwhile, the Jewish communities at Alexandria and elsewhere were much more hospitable to Greek culture and learning, at the same time exerting a reciprocal, modifying influence upon Greek thought. It was, however, through its influence upon early Christian theology and education that the Hellenistic philosophy of the Alexandrian school left its deeper impress upon the substance and method of later Christian education.

Education in New Testament Times (from the birth of Christ to the end of the 1st century) Elementary Schools

Jewish education in the time of Christ was of the orthodox traditional type and in the hands of scribes, Pharisees and learned rabbis. The home was still the chief institution for the dispensation of elementary instruction, although synagogues, with attached schools for the young, were to be found in every important Jewish community. Public elementary schools, other than those connected with the synagogues, were of slower growth and do not seem to have been common until some time after Joshua ben Gamala, high priest from 63-65 A.D., ordered that teachers be appointed in every province and city to instruct children having attained the age of six or seven years. In the synagogue schools, the *chazzan,* or attendant, not infrequently served as schoolmaster.

Subject Matter of Instruction

As in earlier times the Torah, connoting now the sacred Old Testament writings as a whole, though with emphasis still upon the law, furnished the subject matter of instruction. To this were added, in the secondary schools (colleges) of the rabbis, the illustrative and parabolical rabbinical interpretation of the law (the haggadhah) and its application to daily life in the form of concise precept or rule of conduct (the halakhah). Together the haggadhah and halakhah furnish the content of the Talmud (or Talmuds), as the voluminous collections of orthodox Jewish teachings of later centuries came to be known.

Method and Aims

As regards teaching method, the scribes and rabbis of New Testament times did not improve much upon the practice of the copherim and sages of earlier centuries. Memorization, the exact reproduction by the pupil of the master's teaching, rather than general knowledge or culture, was the main objective. Since the voice of prophecy had become silent and the canon of revealed truth was considered closed, the intellectual mastery and interpretation of this sacred revelation of the past was the only aim that education on its intellectual side could have. On its practical side it sought, as formerly, the inculcation of habits of strict ritualistic observance, obedience to the letter of the law as a condition of association and fellowship with the selected company of true Israelites to which scribes and Pharisees considered themselves to belong. The success with which the teachings of the scribes and rabbis were accompanied is an evidence of their devotion to their work, and more still of the psychological insight manifested by them in utilizing every subtle means and method for securing and holding the attention of their pupils, and making their memories the trained and obedient servants of an educational ideal.

Valuable Results of Jewish Education

Jewish education, achieved four valuable results:

it developed a taste for close, critical study.

it sharpened the wits.

it encouraged a reverence for law and produced

desirable social conduct.

it formed a powerful bond of union among the Jewish people.

To these four points of excellence enumerated by Davidson must be added a fifth which, briefly stated, is this:

Jewish education by its consistent teaching of lofty monotheism, and its emphasis, sometimes incidental and sometimes outstanding, upon righteousness and holiness of life as a condition of participation in a future Messianic kingdom, prepared the way for the Christian view of God and the world, set forth in its original distinctness of outline and incomparable simplicity in the teachings of Jesus.

The Preeminence of Jesus as a Teacher

Jesus was more than a teacher; but He was a teacher first. To His contemporaries he appeared as a Jewish rabbi of exceptional influence and popularity. He used the teaching methods of the rabbis; gathered about Him, as did they, a group of chosen disciples (learners) whom He trained and taught more explicitly with a view to perpetuating through them His own influence and work. His followers called Him Rabbi and Master, and the scribes and Pharisees conceded His popularity and power. He taught, as did the rabbis of His time, in the temple courts, in the synagogue, in private, and on the public highway as the exigencies of the case demanded. His textbook, so far as He used any, was the same as theirs; His form of speech (parable and connected discourse), manner of life, and methods of instruction were theirs. Yet into His message and method He put a new note of authority that challenged attention and inspired confidence.

Breaking with the traditions of the past, He substituted for devotion to the letter of the law an interest in men, with boundless sympathy for their misfortune, abiding faith in their worth and high destiny, and earnest solicitude for their regeneration and perfection. To say that Jesus was the world's greatest and foremost example as a teacher is to state a fact borne out by every inquiry, test, and comparison that modern educational science can apply to the work and influence of its great creative geniuses of the past. Where His contemporaries and even His own followers saw only "as in a glass, darkly," He saw clearly; and His view of God and the world, of human life and human destiny, has come down through the ages as a Divine revelation vouchsafed the world in Him. Viewed from the intellectual side, it was the life philosophy of Jesus that made His teachings imperishable; esthetically it was the compassionate tenderness and solicitude of His message that drew the multitudes to Him; judged from the standpoint of will, it was the example of His life, its purpose, its purity, its helpfulness, that caused men to follow Him; and tested by its immediate and lasting social influence, it was the doctrine, the ideal and example of the human brotherliness and Divine sonship, that made Jesus the pattern of the great teachers of mankind in every age and generation. With a keen, penetrating insight into the ultimate meaning of life, He reached out, as it were, over the conflicting opinions of men and the mingling social and cultural currents of His time backward to the fundamental truths uttered by the ancient prophets of His race and forward to the ultimate goal of the race. Then with simple directness of speech He addressed Himself to the consciences and wills of men, setting before them the ideal of the higher life, and with infinite patience sought to lift them to the plane of fellowship with Himself in thought and action.

Educational Work of the Early Disciples

It remained for the disciples of Jesus to perpetuate His teaching ministry and to organize the new forces making for human betterment. In this work, which was distinctly religious-educational in character, some found a field of labor among their own Jewish kinsmen, and others, like Paul, among the needy Gentiles (Galatians 1:16; 2:7; 1 Timothy 2:7). As regards a division of labor in the apostolic church, we read of apostles, prophets, evangelists, pastors, and teachers (1 Corinthians 12:28; Ephesians 4:11). The apostles were the itinerant leaders and missionaries of the entire church. Their work was largely that of teaching, Paul insisting on calling himself a teacher as well as an apostle (2 Timothy 1:11; 1 Corinthians 4:17). The prophets were men with a special message like that of Agabus (Acts 21:10-11). The evangelists were itinerant preachers, as was Philippians (8:40), while the pastors, also called bishops, had permanent charge of individual churches.

The professional teachers included both laymen and those ordained by the laying on of hands. Their work was regarded with highest honor in the church and community. In contrast with the itinerant church officers, apostles and evangelists, they, like the pastors, resided permanently in local communities. With this class the author of the Epistle of James identifies himself, and there can be little doubt that the epistle which he wrote reflects both the content and form of the instruction which these earliest Christian teachers gave to their pupils. Before the close of the first century the religious educational work of the church had been organized into a more systematic form, out of which there developed gradually the catechumenate of the early post-apostolic period. In the Didache, or Teachings of the Apostles, there has been reserved for us a textbook of religious instruction from this earlier period (Kent, GTJC). Necessarily, the entire missionary and evangelistic work of the apostolic church was educational in character, and throughout this earliest period of church history we must think of the work of apostles, evangelists, and pastors, as well as that of professional teachers, as including a certain amount of systematic religious instruction.

SECTION II
STATE ACHIEVEMENT TESTS

CHAPTER 5

ACHIEVEMENT REQUIREMENTS

Construction Materials

BASIC ACADEMIC REQUIREMENTS

We all need to seek God's Will in our lives, especially in regard to what we teach our children. This does not mean we should not teach basic skills and school subjects. God forbid. We are stewards of what God has given us. God gave us our children. We are responsible for developing their minds to their fullest potential. We want our children to learn academics, but more importantly, to learn about life. We want them to be prepared to face challenges of the world. We want them to learn all about God's great creations, not merely to pass a test, but for a greater motive.

We want them to learn:

- Science—all about God's creation
- Math—about God's order
- History—about His-Story, His plan for the world and the redemption of His people
- Government—how God has established government for specific purposes
- Language Arts—how to tell others about God's truth (writing and speaking)
- Literature—to read of how He affected other lives
- Economics—to understand stewardship, God's rules
- Arts—to appreciate God's gifts of music, drama, dance, and art, as forms of worship to Him
- Health—to learn of God's plan for nutrition and health

It is our personal responsibility to teach our children to read, study, research and reason. We must teach them how to read, understand, analyze, and apply the Bible in a way that does not compromise or distort the intentions of the biblical author, or the real meaning of the biblical text. We, ourselves, need to learn to, and teach our children to learn to, ground our understanding of why we do what we do in a clear and sober analysis of what Scripture actually teaches. Otherwise we will lack judgment, "blown about by every wind of doctrine."

Why worry About the State's Requirements?

Other subjects (besides Bible) can help us in our study of Scripture. It is a good reason, but it is doubtful whether that is the real reason we include them in the curriculum. We include them because they mean school to us—learning, education. That assumption—that we automatically know without pondering it—of what real education is constitutes the intellectual barrier we traverse to get to a wisdom-centered curriculum.

We are not working for the school board or even for the children but for God. Our first desire should be to inspire students to become "hearers and doers" of God's Word and to encourage students to search the Scriptures and apply them to everyday situations.

The Evaluation Check Lists in this book are intended to reflect common activities and expectations that are structured around developmentally appropriate activities, based on national curriculum standards.

The basic skill standards are generally non-biased. Facts such as math and spelling are safe. There is no opinion involved within establishing spelling rules. There are no secret messages in when to add *es* or *s* to a word.

The achievement standards aren't all bad. It's how the State plans on enforcing the standards that concern us.

It is one thing to write a set of goals and quite another thing to write, design, and complete a series of lessons to reach those goals. Christians and non-believers can agree on basic academic goals, such as what to strive for: phonics, handwriting, grammar, the scientific method, arithmetic, and drawing. The problems take place when a secular, politically-correct curriculum twists the facts in order to be politically-correct.

It is the content, not the goals, that is the problem. For instance, Christians and the state schools agree that children should understand the scientific method. The disagreement comes when the public school teaches that the scientific method can solve all of mankind's problems or it twists the results from the scientific method to present a theory as fact, such as evolution.

Christians and the state schools agree that children should read a variety of classical literature. In fact, it is a wonderful standard! We should hope all our children would read the classics. So what is the concern?

The state's definition of good classical literature and a Christian's view of good classical literature are quite different. Authors are teachers. They educate, motivate, touch the imagination, and indoctrinate students. What great literature does the state schools require? Would it be Henry Wadsworth Longfellow or Edgar Allen Poe? Ruth Norse wrote an article contrasting the lives of two men. Look at just a portion:

> Henry Wadsworth Longfellow's work was for over fifty years considered classic. Today, Longfellow's work has been excluded from the required reading. Apparently, those who select great literature to be studied by students feel American literature must be filled more with passion and less with sentiment.
>
> Henry Wadsworth Longfellow was a man who pursued happiness in the traditional American way. He was born in Portland, Maine, in 1807, and became the best known and best loved American poet at home and abroad. His father was a Harvard graduate and attorney who would later be elected to the Massachusetts legislature and then to congress. The piety and patriotism of his mother, Zilpah, did honor to six Mayflower pilgrims named among her ancestors. Puritan and pilgrim faith merged in the shaping of the poet's character and worldview. Threads of truth from the King James Bible strengthen Longfellow's poetry. Frequent notations and commentaries on Sunday sermons are sprinkled through all the years of his letters and journals. They reflect his lifelong pursuit of reality in the practice of the Christian faith. Longfellow was freely enjoyed by American school children for 50 years.
>
> Edgar Allan Poe was born in Boston in 1809. Poe's articles appeared in the several magazines he wrote for or edited between 1835 and 1845. Poe was quoted as saying, "I love fame: I dote on it: I idolize it." And in another place, "My whole nature utterly revolts at the idea that there is any Being in the universe superior to myself!" The poet's mental and emotional state was displayed in

several drunken sallies. He and his friends drank with such abandon that the sheriff was called to bring order to the campus. Most biographers tell us that he accumulated more than $2000 in gambling debts. One who knew him wrote: "He walked the streets, in madness or melancholy, with lips moving in indistinct curses, or with eyes upturned in passionate prayers, (never for himself, for he professed that he felt already damned), but for the happiness of those who were at the moment the object of his idolatry." (Nourse)

To which author—which teacher—would you have your child listen? The state schools require students to read literature by Edgar Allen Poe. Most Christians are offended by Poe's writings. A Christian standard for good literature is spelled out in God's Word: *Finally, brethren, whatsoever things are true, whatsoever things are honest, whatsoever things are just, whatsoever things are pure, whatsoever things are lovely, whatsoever things are of good report; if there be any virtue, and if there be any praise, think on these things. Those things, which ye have both learned, and received, and heard, and seen in me, do: and the God of peace shall be with you.* (Philippians 4:8-9). Poe's books are anything but true, pure, virtuous, and lovely.

What is a Standardized Achievement Test?

Standardized tests are usually created by commercial test publishers and are designed to give a common measure of students' performance. Because large numbers of students throughout the country take the same test, they are said to give educators a common yardstick or "standard" of measure. Educators use these standardized tests to tell how well school programs are succeeding or to give themselves a picture of the skills and abilities of today's students.

Standard-That which is established by sovereign power as rule or measure by which others are to be adjusted; that which is established as a rule or model, by the authority of public opinion, or by respectable opinions, or by general consent.

Achieve-To perform, or excite; to accomplish; to finish or to carry to a final close. To gain or obtain by means of exertion.

Test-To compare with a standard; to try; to prove strength or genius anything by experiment or by some fixed principle or standard.

Some popular tests include the California Achievement Tests (the CAT), the Stanford Achievement Test, the Iowa Test of Basic Skills (the ITBS), and the Stanford-Binet Intelligence Scale.

Are Standardized Test Scores Accurate Evaluations of a Child's Skills?

The use of standardized tests by schools is commonly criticized by parents, school teachers, and school officials. The tests do not necessarily test what students have learned. They do not reveal what the student has achieved. Critics have suggested that alternatives to standardized tests be developed and used for more effective student evaluation.

Tests are powerful only if we attach high value to them and relinquish our judgment about how to educate children (Meisels, 1992). Some tests are less informative than others, and some are hopelessly biased, narrow, or unrealistic; but any test can be misused, just as any idea can be distorted.

The pressure to demonstrate effectiveness through children's performance on standardized tests not only changes how teachers teach and what children study, but it also seems to be changing our very understanding of the nature of learning and achievement (McGill-Franzen and Allington, 1993). The public schools are actually pushed into being test-preparation organizations.

Group-administered tests focus on the acquisition of simple facts, low-level skills, superficial memorization, and isolated evidence of achievement. The tests hold great power, and that power can be abused. Of greatest concern is that they rob teachers of their sense of judgment about how to help children develop to their optimal potential.

This loss of judgment is often observed in the use of readiness and early school achievement tests. The appropriateness of using standardized, group-administered achievement tests for children below third grade is highly dubious and questionable. The content of these tests is generally abstract, verbally mediated, and potentially biased against children unfamiliar with or uncomfortable with test-like activities and with middle class manners and mores

(Stallman and Pearson, 1990). Even more problematic is how little can be learned from the results of standardized tests administered to young children; the data may tell us a child's percentile ranking on a subtest, but they cannot tell us whether the child's performance reflects an inability to follow the complex test directions or whether the child did not have mastery of the information or skill.

Have the Achievement Tests Helped the Public System?

Standardized tests are problematic at all ages and levels of schooling. They are especially questionable in primary grades. In these years, children's growth is most uneven, and in large measure, personal skills needed for school success, are in their most fluid stages.

The last thirty years have brought a dramatic decline in the quality of education in this country. In October, 1993, the U.S. Department of Education admitted that nearly 50 percent of all adults are "functionally illiterate" and cannot handle anything more than the simplest mathematical tasks. SAT scores have fallen almost 80 points since 1960. How these tests are being adjusted to change these scores to ensure that less achievement will get higher scores. We are not increasing the knowledge required on these students' tests, but are lowering the results and expectations—with higher scores for equal or less knowledge.

Schools began handing out higher grades much more freely in the 1970s—at the same time standardized test results showed scholastic achievement was actually dropping. Often this has led to a false security. In an extreme, but not an isolated case, a valedictorian of a school was denied admission to college because his SAT math test results were in the bottom 5 percent and SAT verbal test results were in the bottom 13 percent. After a repeat test (without a time limit), the admissions dean said, "My feeling is that a kid like this has been conned. He thinks he's a scholar. His parents think he's a scholar. He's been deluded into thinking he's gotten an education." (Adams)

The National Commission on Excellence in Education reported that "Each generation of Americans has outstripped its parents in education, in literacy, and in economic attainment. Now for the first time in the history of our country, the educational skills of one generation will not surpass, will not equal, will not even approach those of their parents."

Home Educated Students Score Higher on Achievement Tests

A nationwide study (Ray, 1990) using a random sample of 1,516 families from one organization's membership, found home educated students to be scoring, on average, at or above the 80th percentile in all areas on standardized achievement tests. Note: The national average on standardized achievement tests is in the 50th percentile.

Wartes (1989) found that home school students in Washington consistently score at the 66th percentile on the Stanford Achievement Test, with their strongest scores in science, listening, vocabulary, and word reading.

Home education students in Montana scored at the 72nd percentile on standardized achievement tests (Ray, 1990).

The state of Tennessee (1988) reported that home educated students in that state averaged about 83rd percentile in reading and about 77th percentile in math on standardized achievement tests.

The state of Oregon (1988) found that 73 percent of the home school students who were tested scored above average.

Dr. Howard Richman and his colleagues have found that the home-educated students in Pennsylvania score, on average, at the 86th percentile in reading and the 73rd percentile in math.

Repeatedly, across the nation, the home-educated students score as well as or better than those in conventional schools.

Dr. Gary Knowles of the University of Michigan explored adults who were home educated. None were unemployed and none were on welfare. Ninety-four percent said home education prepared them to be independent persons. Seventy-nine percent said it helped them interact with individuals from different levels of society, and they strongly supported the home education method. (National Home Education Research Institute).

Understanding Achievement Tests Scores

The percentile level equates scores to any other nationally-validated test. When using it, we are comparing the student's performance to that of the national sample of students at that grade level who were used to standardize the test. In order to get the most accurate comparison to these national norms, the test is administered in April, since that is when the students in the national samples were tested. The percentile score shows where the student ranked relative to the rest of the population. For example, a percentile score of 70 means the student scored higher than 70 percent of the students in the tested population. The 50th percentile is often referred to as the national norm or median.

Scores Are Estimates

No score on any abilities or achievement test should be treated as a precise measure. Test scores are subject to measurement error. That is, if a student gave equal effort to two perfectly equivalent forms of the same test on successive days, corresponding scores would not likely be the same. Thus, we must recognize that differences of 5 to 10 percentile points or possibly more do not necessarily mean there are real differences in levels of achievement. This is true regardless of whether we are comparing scores for two students, the same student in different subject areas, or year-to-year scores in the same subject area. On the other hand, actual performance levels can differ by more than the percentile scores indicate.

A student's pattern of nationally-referenced test scores over time is more revealing than a single set of scores. You should also consider other achievement measures such as the Writing Assessment, state tests, special projects or performance assessments, as well as results of abilities tests in conjunction with achievement scores.

Nationally-referenced test scores, particularly a single set, should never be the only criteria by which a student's educational progress is assessed.

NCE Scores

Group averages are reported in normal-curve-equivalent (NCE) scores rather than percentile ranks. This is because percentile scores are unevenly spaced and cannot legitimately be averaged. NCE scores are more difficult to interpret and would be a poor choice for evaluating a student's scores.

Group Scores

Average scores for classrooms or grade levels are much more stable than those for individual students. Assuming a test has been administered under standard conditions to a fairly large group, we can be relatively confident that the average scores are fairly close to the group's actual achievement levels in areas measured by the test.

Absolute and Gain Scores

When interpreting scores, two dimensions to be considered are (a) the absolute values of the scores and (b) any changes in the scores.

Consider the example of School A in which eighth graders had an average NCE of 53, a drop of 3 points from the previous year's mean eighth-grade score of 56. In School B the current year's average of 38 is 5 points above that of 33 for the past year's eighth graders. If other factors are fairly comparable, the results for School A are clearly superior to those for School B. Students in School A have an average slightly above the national median (NCE of 50), whereas those in School B are well below the national average, despite the gain of 5 NCEs.

However, other factors may warrant consideration. If School A served only gifted students, a mean score of 56 would not be impressive, and the further loss of 3 NCEs would reflect even more negatively on the results. If in School B, major reforms had been taken to address the previous poor performance of students, the gain of 5 NCEs may be viewed positively despite the fact that students are still achieving at less than desirable levels.

Extreme Scores

School administrators should investigate cases where either absolute or gain scores are extreme. Group gains or losses of 10-20 NCEs are possible, but unusual. Similarly, when a group of students show dramatic increases one year followed by sharp losses the following year, causes should be assessed. Consistently low scores (e.g., NCE under 30 or well below the general performance for students at that school) should be a cause for concern. One general exception to score deviations is at the kindergarten level where average scores tend to be higher than at other grade levels. This appears to be a function of the test and/or its norms. Finally, the discussion of extreme scores does not imply that these are the only scores worthy of attention. The tests, combined with other sources of data, can be valuable tools for improving educational outcomes.

What You Can Infer From Test Scores

William A Mehrens, in his article "Preparing Students To Take Standardized Achievement Tests," states: "The only reasonable, direct inference you can make from a test score is the degree to which a student knows the content that the test samples. Any inference about why the student knows that content to that degree...is clearly a weaker inference...."

Teaching to the test alters what you can interpret from test scores because it involves teaching specific content. Therefore, it also weakens the direct inference that can be reasonably drawn about students' knowledge. Rarely would you want to limit your inference about knowledge to the specific questions asked in a specific format. Generally, you want to make inferences about a broader domain of skills.

Further complicating matters, many people wish to use test scores to draw indirect inferences about why students score the way they do. Indirect inferences can lead to weaker and possibly incorrect interpretations about school programs.

Indirect inferences cannot possibly be accurate unless the direct inference of student achievement is made to the correct domain. Rarely does one wish to limit the inference about knowledge to the specific questions in a test or even the specific objectives tested. For example, if parents want to infer how well their children will do in another school next year, they need to make inferences about the broader domain and not about the specific objectives that are tested on a particular standardized test. For that inference to be accurate, the instruction must not be limited to the narrow set of objectives of a given test. Thus, for the most typical inferences, the line demarking legitimate and illegitimate teaching of the test must be drawn between Points 3 and 4.

While, in my view, it is inappropriate to prepare students by focusing on the sample of objectives that happen to be tested, you can undertake appropriate activities to prepare students to take standardized tests.

Standardized Tests Have Limitations

The tests are not perfect measures of what individual students can or cannot do or of everything students learn. Also, your child's scores on a particular test may vary from day to day, depending on whether your child guesses, receives clear directions, follows the directions carefully, takes the test seriously, or is comfortable in taking the test.

How Can I Help My Child Do Well On Tests?

Spend some time teaching your children general test-taking skills. These skills would help students answer questions correctly if they have mastered the objectives. Without some level of test-taking skills, even knowledgeable students could miss an item (or a set of items) because they did not understand the mechanics of taking a test.

Veteran home school mothers can tell you how their children will perform on an achievement test. They have been working with the children on a one-to-one basis for a while and know just what their strengths and weaknesses are. If a home school mother tells me her son does not do well in math, odds are he'll score low in math. If for some reason, a mother says her child is an excellent reader and the child scored low in reading, I would look over the test to be sure there was not another reason for such a score. You can usually depend on the mother's observations more than the test results.

Test preparation activities should not be additional activities, they should be incorporated into the regular, ongoing instructional activities such as:

- Immersing your children in a rich print and story environment by having a variety of books and magazines at home to encourage your child's curiosity;
- Using these books to find out any learning gaps;
- Making sure your child is well-rested and eats a well-rounded diet;
- Not being anxious about test scores, but encouraging your child to take tests seriously;
- Memorizing Philippians 4:6 (*Be careful for nothing; but in every thing by prayer and supplication with thanksgiving let your requests be made known unto God*).

States That Require Testing for Home School Students

Alaska	Nevada	Pennsylvania
Arkansas	New Mexico	South Carolina
Georgia	New York	South Dakota
Hawaii	North Dakota	Tennessee
Minnesota	Oregon	Virginia

Taking the Achievement Test: Avoid Test Anxiety

It's good to be concerned about taking a test. It's not good to have "test anxiety." This is excessive worry about doing well on a test, and it can mean disaster for a student.

Students who suffer from test anxiety tend to worry about the future and are self-critical. Instead of feeling challenged by the prospect of success, they become afraid of failure. This makes them anxious about tests and doubtful of their own abilities. Ultimately, they become so worked up that they feel incompetent about the subject matter or the test.

It does not help to tell the child to relax, to think about something else, or to stop worrying, but there are ways to reduce test anxiety.

Encourage your child to do these things:

- Space studying over days or weeks. (Real learning occurs through studying that takes place over a period of time.)

- Understand the information and relate it to what is already known. Review it more than once. (By doing this, the student should feel prepared at exam time.)

- Don't "cram" the night before—cramming increases anxiety, which interferes with clear thinking.

- Get a good night's sleep. Rest, exercise, and eating well are as important to test-taking as they are to other schoolwork.

- Read the directions carefully when the teacher hands out the test. If you don't understand them, ask the teacher to explain.

Look quickly at the entire examination to see what types of questions are included (multiple choice, matching, true/false, essay) and, if possible, the number of points for each. This will help with pacing the various parts of the test.

If you don't know the answer to a question, skip it and go on. Don't waste time worrying about it.

Mark it so you can identify it as unanswered. If you have time at the end of the exam, return to the unanswered question(s).

Do's and Don'ts

You can be a great help to your children if you will observe these do's and don'ts about tests and testing:

- Don't be too anxious about a child's test scores. If you put too much emphasis on test scores, this can upset a child.

- Do encourage children. Praise them for the things they do well. If they feel good about themselves, they will do their best. Children who are afraid of failing are more likely to become anxious when taking tests and more likely to make mistakes.

The more effort and energy a child puts into learning, the more likely he or she will do well on tests.

CHAPTER 6
ANSWERS TO FREQUENTLY ASKED QUESTIONS

Q. How Do I Find Out if My Child is Required to Take The Achievement Test?

A. Home schooling laws regulate home schooling differently in each state. You should get a copy of your state's home schooling law. Contact the Home School Legal Defense Association at (703) 338-5600, Box 159, Paeonian Springs, VA 22129.

Q. How Do I Know if I Am Meeting State Standards?

A. The second section of this book contains the Evaluation Check Lists. These check lists represent an overall picture of general content of the most widely used achievement test according to category and grade level.

Q. How Do I Know If My Curriculum Covers Everything on the Test?

A. How do we know if the public school curriculum covers everything on the test? *The American Federation of Teachers (AFT)* reports that only 13 of 49 state standards are specific enough to be used effectively by teachers. Take a look at the public schools' scores—an average of 30 percentile points below the home school scores. Currently, each of the fifty states has a different academic requirement for each grade. There are thousands of curriculum choices and dozens of teaching methods. No one curriculum covers everything on the achievement test and no one test includes everything in any given curriculum. One curriculum covers an objective in the third grade that another curriculum covers in second grade. One curriculum taught by one teacher will focus on an entirely different aspect of the subject compared to that taught by another teacher. Some children are stuck in a drill-and-practice curriculum for basic skills, and other kids have an enriched literature-based curriculum, which will easily get them to the standards. Some children have teachers who care and who are well-trained in the curriculum, while other teachers simply don't care.

One child, whose father was in the military, attended five different schools in six years. Because of the different state standards, she was never taught basic cursive writing. She had missed basic cursive in second grade in one school, went to third grade in a school that taught cursive in the fourth grade, then transferred to fourth grade in a school that taught cursive writing in second and third grades.

Home-schooling parents have the advantage of teaching their children an individual plan on different levels. The Evaluation Check List will guide you to any gaps, and you can take the time to get the basics mastered before going on to another level.

For more about the way the state teaches, see the book, *The Right Choice: The Incredible Failure of Public Education* and the *Rising Hope of Home Schooling* by Christopher J. Klicka, or the book by the New York Teacher of the Year, *Dumbing Us Down* by John Taylor Gatto.

Q. Shouldn't I Use Textbooks like the schools?

A. Textbooks don't work with all students. The public school achievement test scores speak for themselves. Seventy-five percent of students using textbooks require more motivation (hands-on practice, presentations, etc.) to retain the material.(McCarthy)

The easiest way for the state to teach is to divide everything into subjects (from the Greeks' philosophy). They then divide each subject into 180 hours—thirty-six weeks of five days of forty-five to sixty minute classes. In this manner they can teach from textbooks, somewhere between thirty to fifty children at a time. Surprise! Not all children will learn a subject to the same degree in 180 hours. Some need much more time; others need much less. Some children can learn the material two to four times as fast using a different method. Instead of measuring 180 hours, we should be measuring the end result.

A few of my favorite books explaining alternatives to textbooks are: *You Can Teach Your Child Successfully* by Ruth Beechick, *The Language Wars and Other Writings for Homeschoolers* by Ruth Beechick (anything written by Dr. Beechick is profitable), and *The Whole Hearted Child Home Education Handbook* by Clay and Sally Clarkson.

Home-schooling parents have the advantage of choosing the curriculum that suits their children. They can use a variety of approaches and levels if necessary.

These books are recommended to explain the different approaches and different materials available: *The Christian Home Educators Manual: Elementary Edition, The Christian Home Educators Manual: Jr. And Sr. High Edition,* and *The Big Book of Home Learning* by Mary Pride available in four manuals: *Getting Started, Elementary, Jr. Sr. High,* and *After School.*

Q. What About College?

A. Most colleges and universities have entrance exams, but many of them place much more weight on an individual student's ability and aptitude. Home schooled students are welcomed at local community colleges, Ivy League universities, vocational institutes, or other avenues of higher education. Most of these institutions value ability and attitude over formal transcripts, diplomas, or GEDs. Home schooled children have encountered little difficulty continuing their education.

Before you place extreme importance on a college education, remember a college degree is worthless if one does not know Christ. It is of little value for our children to master chemistry and algebra if they don't know how to get along with their spouses or cannot learn how to discipline their children. It is of little value for one to be fluent in several foreign languages if he doesn't have tongue control. It is of little value for one to diagram a sentence if one cannot communicate true feelings. Are you sure college is God's plan for your child?

If you are planning for college or are interested in higher education alternatives, an excellent seminar by Inge Cannon will answer all your questions. The seminar titled *Apprenticeship Plus: Preparing Lives Unto Service* is available on tapes and in workbooks. This and many other excellent educational helps are available through Education Plus, P.O. Box 1029, Mauldin, SC 29662, (803) 281-9316. Call or write for a free brochure.

Q. What About Algebra, Higher Math, and Lab Sciences?

A. With all the excellent self-teaching materials, manuals, CD Roms, and videos available, you can learn much of what is needed to teach as you prepare for each day, or even while your child learns. Home schoolers all over the country have formed small classes, hired tutors, and "swapped" teaching roles with experienced home schoolers for higher math and lab sciences. There are excellent self-teaching courses, videos, and other alternative teaching methods available to those who want to go beyond the basic skills.

Both *Senior High: A High School Formula* and *Lab Science* by Barb Shelton include an abundance of information for those interested in college preparatory courses.

Q. How will Goals 2000, Outcome Based Education (OBE) and the new national standards affect the achievements tests?

A. The new government programs such as Goals 2000, National Standards, School-to-Work, and their successors should set off blaring alarms to all Christians. This question would take an entire book to answer, and thankfully these questions have been answered in Cathy Duffy's well-researched book *Government Nannies.* All parents should educate themselves concerning the new government educational reforms.

In the next few years, Goals 2000 will bring about major changes in the state standards. Eventually the tests will be re-written to affect the national standards and other agendas from the government. The tests direct the curriculum. parents have no control over the curriculum; therefore, no control over what their children are being taught. We can only wait and see the results.

Goals 2000 will greatly expand power of government over educational matters. To receive monies from the $400-million funds, each state must produce plans that conform to the national standards. This act will shift the control of the curriculum and management from local communities and states to the federal government. Goals 2000 appears to be more of an application for funds than an educational program.

Forty-three states used some sort of statewide assessment in 1994-96; most have not developed or adopted assessments that are connected to the new standards. One of the reasons most often cited by states is that the cost of developing these better forms of assessments is high. Reform requires a sustained, long-term commitment. As state standards are changed, there is the need to develop new materials, upgrade curricular materials, and provide teachers with training to update their knowledge bases and teaching skills. At the time of this writing (1997 edition), the national standards have not affected the conventional achievement tests. The Evaluation Check List will be revised to reflect the new tests, standards, subject categories, benchmarks, and frameworks as they change.

Q. How Do I Know if I am Teaching the Material that will Apply to My Child's Future?

A. Who decided the educational goals should consist of particular subjects, some of which are only used by a very small percent of the population? You can't make everyone the same by forcing them all to learn the same thing. No one person can learn everything there is to know. God gave us all different gifts and talents. Jesus' whole story about the church being a part of the body illustrates this. Is the goal of education to make everyone the same?

Biology is a required subject because the student may choose a career in which he will need the skills taught in biology class. However, if the student chooses to become a businessman, many of the facts he spent time learning and memorizing in biology class [the ability to label the digestive system of a grasshopper] would probably be useless. Learning about any subject is always useful even if one is just learning to learn. However, most students are frustrated with learning and memorizing what they consider boring because it has no relevance to their lives.

The state's reasoning that children need to "learn skills for a possible goal" does not motivate learning. Students are told to learn algebra without ever being told when they may use algebra in real life. If the child doesn't know what the goal is, or if he will ever even be interested in such a goal. learning the skills is boring to the child. Adults learn the other way around—we choose a goal, then find out what skills are needed. When our eyes are on the goal, we are automatically motivated to learn the necessary skills.

Teaching all the children all the skills to prepare them for whatever path they may choose does not work. First of all, it is impossible to foresee all the pieces of knowledge a child will need in the future. Secondly, if a student is trying to be good at all the options, he will not have time enough to prepare for the specific path that God has chosen for him.

This story illustrates my point: Once a man had three horses: a racehorse, a plow horse, and a pony. The man made a schedule to get the most work out of his horses. On Mondays, Wednesdays, and Fridays, all three horses worked in the fields hooked to a plow. On Tuesdays and Thursdays, he took all three horses to the racetrack so each horse would learn to run fast. On the weekends, he used the three horses to give pony rides to children. At the end of the week the man complained that not one of the horses met his expectations.

The racehorse turned to the man and said, "I could not run properly when my back ached from plowing. If you had let me stay at the racetrack all week, I could have spent time doing and improving at what I do best."

The plow horse said, "If my feet were not so swollen from racing, I could have pulled the plow straighter and farther. If you had allowed me to stay in the fields all week, I could have spent time doing and improving at what I do best."

The pony said, "I have had it! If I didn't ache all over from doing things I am not made for, I wouldn't have been so grumpy to the children who rode me. If you had allowed me to give children rides all week, I could have spent time doing and improving at what I do best."

Christians should teach the skills established by God. The Bible does not command us to learn basic academic skills. It does not say "thou shall learn to read." Neither does the Bible tell us to learn to drive a car, but we know that anyone living in America in the '90's should know how to drive. Common sense tells us our children need to learn the three R's to function in this world. God's Word does tell us to teach our children His Word. His Word is full of wisdom for practical daily living. As children learn the Bible, they are learning how to learn. If we teach a child to study God's word— reasoning, relating, researching, and recording— then he will know how to learn. When it is time, he will be prepared to learn the skills necessary to meet his goals. By the way, most of the higher level critical thinking skills can be learned from reading, studying, and interpreting God's Word.

God knows more than the public school system! We can trust Him with our children's futures. God's Word promises that if we acknowledge God in all our ways, He will direct our paths. We know God has made each of our children for a specific purpose. If we teach them what He commands us to teach them, He will guide us to prepare them for the plan He has for them—knowingly or unknowingly. God can prepare us for the future in many ways. Just think about your life now. What happened in your past to prepare you for what God is calling you to do now? Did you learn it from school? From your parents? From church? From different situations? God uses all things for His good. Life is a classroom. He can and often does use bad situations to help us turn a weakness into a strength. Do you have an evaluation check list consisting of all the things that you have learned in your life to bring you to a place to do God's will? If you do, I venture it's a prayer list–not the state standards.

Q. How Do I Motivate an Unmotivated Child to Learn?

A. The answer to this question depends on the child. Is he not interested in the subject, not interested in learning, or not interested in obeying you—the parent?

IF A CHILD DOES NOT WANT TO OBEY

A child must be disciplined to learn. Depending on maturity levels, external discipline is necessary until he develops internal discipline. Younger children need supervision and guidance to complete projects until they are trained to work alone efficiently. Rules and consequences for breaking rules should be established in every home. If there is a discipline problem in the home, you may need to forgo school for a few days until the child understands who is in authority. If you need motivation or instruction in discipline, run, don't walk, to get What the Bible Says about Child Training by Richard Fugate (available in book, video, or audio forms).

IF A CHILD DOES NOT WANT TO LEARN ANYTHING

Children love to learn naturally. Even children attending a traditional school setting enjoy learning—at first. Especially when a kindergarten class is full of neat things to learn about—goldfish, hamsters, seeds sprouting, math manipulatives, play areas, etc. Sometime around the second grade when textbooks and workbooks are introduced and a child must sit in a one-square-foot desk area for six or more hours, most children decide that school is boring and their interest in learning declines. Many books are available describing different learning styles and methods to meet your child's needs. See Cathy Duffy's book *The Christian Home School Curriculum Manual* or Mary Pride's *Big Books of Home Learning* for hundreds of suggestions.

Learning can be fun, but there are times when learning requires diligent work. These types of situations are also training in character. For example, children are not usually thrilled to memorize the multiplication tables. There are fun games to reinforce learning, but actual memorizing must be applied. Some learning is an opportunity to teach diligence, patience, longsuffering (no grumbling and complaining), kindness, etc.

If a Child Does Not Want to Learn a Specific Subject

Working with a child almost always gives a child incentive. Most children enjoy the attention of talking and sharing with their parents. Please don't throw workbooks at a young child, assign pages, and think learning has occurred. Workbooks are great—some of the time, but not all of the time. Children can be motivated by changing the instruction method. Some children are simply bored to tears working in textbooks. When's the last time you curled up by a fire with a good textbook? Provide "living books": historical novels, biographies, and classics that cover the material you want your children to know.

If you spend the time explaining why the child will need to know the material you are teaching, you will see a world of difference in your teaching. Examine your own learning motivations by answering the questions for each of the following scenarios:

1. Your support group decides to go to on a field trip to a sheep farm in nearby Sheep Town. You have a large van, so you volunteer to drive. You are not familiar with Sheep Town. When you get home, you pull out your map to find out just where Sheep Town is. You call a friend who has been to Sheep Town to double check the directions. The day of the field trip, you drive to Sheep Town. After the field trip, you drive home. Even if you made a wrong turn, you eventually found your way to Sheep Town. On the way to and from the location, you observe new surroundings. You have learned the route from your home to Sheep Town. A month lat-

er someone asks directions to Sheep Town. You can accurately give him the directions to Sheep Town.

2. You and your husband are at a support group meeting. The group decides to go to Sheep Town. Your husband offers to drive and proceeds to get directions. You proceed to talk about curriculum with a friend. Your husband plans the trip to Sheep Town. You, your children, and friends all ride to Sheep Town together. You return home. A month later someone ask directions to Sheep Town. Can you give them the directions? You didn't pay much attention to the subject because you depended on someone else to know the directions.
3. You are at a support group meeting and someone asks you how to get to Sheep Town. You've never heard of the town and don't know the directions. Are you less intelligent than the person that does know the directions to Sheep Town? Of course not. You have never needed to know that information. Knowing information you will never use does not make you intelligent.
4. You're in a support group meeting. The leader announces a field trip to Sheep Town on Thursday. You have plans; your dentist is going to give you a root canal on Thursday. The leader asks anyone interested to stay after the meeting so she can show a map and explain the directions to Sheep Town. Would you stay after the meeting to learn the directions to Sheep Town? If you had no reason to have to know how to get there, you wouldn't stay.
5. Suppose someone came to you during the support group meeting in the scenario above to tell you that all the stores in Sheep Town were having a 70 percent off sale the week after your dental appointment. Would you reconsider staying after the meeting for directions? Most of the time, if we spend the time giving children a reason for having to know material, they respond favorably. Children, like adults, need to know that material they are learning is relevant to their lives.
6. You are at home teaching your child. The geography book has a chapter titled "Sheep Town." You read this

chapter to your child. Four months later, your child takes the achievement test. There is a question asking how far your town is from Sheep Town. Your child forgot what he learned about Sheep Town, so he guesses at the answer. How would you feel if he got the answer wrong? If he got the answer right?

If your child guessed wrong does it mean you failed as a teacher? Does it mean your child is learning disabled? Are you both a success if he guessed right? Are you both wrong because he had to guess? If you are teaching your child, I will assume sometime before the fifth or sixth grade you will have taught him to read a map. Chances are your child will never have a question like "How far is it to Sheep Town?" unless a map of the area is provided. A nationwide achievement test will not evaluate specific things, like knowing where Sheep Town is, because children in other parts of the country will not be exposed to Sheep Town. Achievement tests evaluate basic skills such as map reading because it is a basic skill needed to get along in the world

Q. What About Grades?

A. If a student is grade-oriented, he will spend more time and effort trying to find out the criteria for getting an A before he tries to learn the material. A college professor told me students frequently ask how long a term paper needs to be to get an A—as if it is graded by the pound. Are you grade-oriented? Do you teach your children to make sure they pass tests? If so, you are thinking like the majority of today's American parents, with a "school mentality." The "school mentality" is a belief that making a high grade means learning, and that retention has taken place. You need to change your thinking. Change your goals to motivate children to learn and to enjoy learning—not to worry about grades and percentiles.

New home schoolers often fret over report cards and grades. This is another area in which we think that it must be profitable if the schools do it. Spend a moment and re-think these two issues—do home schoolers need report cards and grades? Could these items even be damaging? Are they scriptural? To determine if something is scriptural, look at the motives. Why do teachers give report cards?

- To tell parents how the children are progressing?
- So the teacher can keep everyone straight because she has thirty students?
- To brag about how well the child is doing or how well the teacher is instructing?
- To compare the child with the other children? (see Proverbs 16:18.)
- To keep a record of a child's progress?
- To evaluate the child?

You will know how your child is progressing by working with him daily. You evaluate the child by checking the work or listening to the child, not by giving the grade. What does God's Word say about comparing?

For we dare not make ourselves of the number, or compare ourselves with some that commend themselves: but they measuring themselves by themselves, and comparing themselves among themselves, are not wise. But we will not boast of things without our measure, but according to the measure of the rule which God hath distributed to us, a measure to reach even unto you. (2 Corinthians 10:12-13).

We, as Christians, have a responsibility to do the best we can in all circumstances, not comparing ourselves to anyone but comparing only to the individual gifts and talents God has given to us.

Dr. George Reavis wrote a delightful story about an Animal School. It explains how we've been conditioned by yet another "school-mentality" concept, and it is an excellent illustration the different gifts and talents of children.

THE ANIMAL SCHOOL

Once upon a time, the animals decided they must do something heroic to meet the problems of a "new world." So they organized a school.

They adopted an activity curriculum consisting of running, climbing, swimming, and flying. To make it easier to administer the curriculum, ALL the animals took all the subjects.

The duck was excellent in swimming, in fact, better than his instructor, but he made only passing grades in flying and was very poor in running. Since he was slow at running, he had to stay after school, *and* drop swimming in order to practice running. This was kept up until his webbed feet were badly worn and he was only average in swimming. But average was acceptable in school so nobody worried about that—except the duck.

The rabbit started at the top of the class in running, but had a nervous breakdown because of so much makeup work in swimming.

The squirrel was excellent in climbing until he developed frustration in the flying class, where his teacher made him start from the ground up instead of from the tree down. He also developed a charley horse from over-exertion, and then got a C in climbing and a D in running.

The eagle was a problem child and was disciplined severely. In the climbing class he beat all the others to the top of the tree, but insisted on using his own way to get there.

At the end of the year, an abnormal eel that could swim exceedingly well, and also run, climb, and fly a little, had the highest average, and was valedictorian.

Should you grade and give report cards? You decide. What are your motives? Be concerned about learning and retaining the material—not to get a letter grade on a paper. If letter grades are fun and motivational for your child, use them. If he doesn't know the material, keep teaching it until he does. If he was not applying himself, discipline measures should be taken.

Grading math quizzes and spelling tests is easy. If a child gets three out of ten wrong, then he reworks or reviews the problem word or lesson until he grasps the concept. Writing assignments and abstract work are more difficult to grade. Imagine you have a set of twins. Twin 1 has a writing gift. He retains information easily, and expresses himself well. Twin 2, though a hard worker, consistently struggles with simple sentences. You assign both a passage to write about. Twin 1 glances at the books and haphazardly writes a few paragraphs. Twin 2 studies for several hours and struggles though each word, writing and re-writing his paragraphs. Twin 1's summary is written much better than Twin

2's. Do you reward 1 with an A, when you know he could do better work, and discourage 2 with a C when he obviously did his best?

Different Gifts and Talents

What if a child is unable to learn the material? Do you grade ability or effort? A special child that cannot grasp a certain concept or several concepts can try again next year or learn a method of getting along in the world without that concept. Should a child who learns easily receive a higher mark than a child who struggles with a subject?

The state of Louisiana has a strange law: If a child scores below a certain level on the achievement test for a certain time, he must go to public school. The irony is that many Louisiana public-schooled children score below the national norms—why don't they send the children home to school?

I know of a child who has struggled through spelling for many years. He doesn't get a grade. He and his mother both understand that spelling is a problem area, and continually work on it. What is the alternative? Should she give him an F and put him in public school? Should she keep him in the eighth grade for five years, giving D's in spelling? Should he fail because he has a weakness in spelling? This boy is so busy building and repairing computers, he hasn't had much time to work on spelling. By the way, who made these standards anyway? I wonder if they can put a computer together? Sometimes, it is OK for the duck to be an average runner, especially if he loves to swim. God made him that way.

Q. How do I really know if I'm doing enough?

A. The school system evaluates a student by grades. This is due to the belief that, if a student makes a superior grade, it means that learning and retention have taken place. This mentality teaches that the way to get along in the world is to learn to play the game—understand and provide correct answers to the "authorities." There is the appearance of learning from filling in blanks in a workbook or making a high grade on a school test, but is the material retained? Can the student use the material?

Many things we know we have learned without trying to learn. Grammar is a good example. Most children can speak and carry on a conversation without knowing how to diagram a sentence.

Should you teach your child diagramming? Will he need it? When was the last time you diagrammed a sentence? Children do not have to learn grammar to speak well. A child will speak correctly by reading good grammar, hearing the English language spoken correctly, and being corrected when he uses incorrect grammar. Memorizing vocabulary words usually has no purpose except to increase a test score. People use the words that they acquired naturally by being exposed to large vocabularies in books and conversations.

Pray for wisdom and ask God to show you what His Will is for your child. Observe your child's gifts and leanings. The Bible says: Train up a child in the way he should go: and when he is old, he will not depart from it. (Proverbs. 22:6). "The way he should go" in Hebrew comes from the word *peh,* which means specific edge, portion, or side; with the preposition "according to," meaning according to the child's God-given gifts. It assuredly does not mean to train him up according to the secular, state standards.

Your child will learn more than enough if you will:

- Study God's Word daily (most important).
- Teach the basic skills—the three **R's**: **R**eading, w**R**iting, and a**R**ithmetic.
- Teach how to do the three **R's** of learning: **R**esearch, **R**eason, and **R**ecord.
- Use the Evaluation Check Lists (in this book) to evaluate and plan.
- Instill a love for learning by making subjects interesting.
- Provide good literature (home library or library card).
- Find out your child's God-given gifts and his aspirations. Motivate him to follow those desires and supply the necessary provisions to find out more.

THE PURPOSE OF EDUCATION

We must ask ourselves what are our goals? When educating our children. "The end of learning," wrote John Milton, "is to repair the ruin of our first parents by regaining to know God aright, and out of that knowledge to love Him, to imitate Him, to be like Him. If this be so—and the Bible says it is so—then the aim of American education is all wrong."

Gordon Clark explains in his book *A Christian Philosophy of Education:*

- The purpose of education is not to enable a student to earn a good income.
- The purpose of education is not to preserve our American system of government and political freedom.
- The purpose of education is not world unification.
- The purpose of education is not to teach young people a trade.
- The purpose of education is not to encourage the never-ending search of truth.
- The purpose of education is not to put the student in harmony with the cosmos.
- The purpose of education is not raise the consciousness of the students and train them for world revolution.
- The purpose of education is not to prepare the student for productive careers.
- The purpose of education is not the social adjustment of the child.
- The purpose of education is not to create good citizens.
- The purpose of education is far more noble than any of these things. The purpose of education is to make Christian men (and women), transformed by the renewing of their minds after the image of He who created them.
- The purpose of education is not for a job, diploma, or college. Abraham, Elijah, Moses, John the Baptist, and Jesus received much of their training in the desert, not in a college.

CHAPTER 7
EVALUATION
Inspection

TESTS ARE NOT THE ONLY WAY TO EVALUATE YOUR CHILD

Think about the achievement test and the different ways children learn. Can we really believe that a child's intelligence, achievement, and competence can be represented adequately by standardized tests? Do we believe that any distribution curve is capable of classifying all children? Such beliefs would defy almost everything we understand about children's growth and responses to educational encounters.

Achievement testing is certainly not the best way to evaluate your child. We can evaluate our children using a variety of methods: by observing them, evaluating their day-to-day work, listening to them retell what they have learned, keeping records of how they mature throughout the year, and partially, by administering tests.

We must understand that standardized tests give only part of the picture of your child's strengths and weaknesses. The results of many methods will gain well-rounded insights into the skills, abilities, and knowledge of the child.

Studies by the education systems show that evaluation is best made by working closely with the child, observing his reactions and work. Sound familiar? Home schooling is the ultimate way to evaluate your child. If you think about it, it is amazing that we home school parents would place any value on an achievement test score over our own experience (another sign of "school mentality"). You have been there with your child, side by side, through writing, math problems, and spelling quizzes. How could one achievement test tell you how your child is doing?

SHOULD MY CHILD TAKE THE ACHIEVEMENT TEST?

The home schoolers who test usually do so because their state requires testing. Testing is not necessary for evaluation purposes. If your state does not require testing, the Evaluation Check List in this book will give you the basics.

If you have been home schooling and your child is not doing well in a subject, you will know it—you don't need the test to tell you he's having trouble with fractions—you work with him daily. You know he's having trouble with fractions because you have been frustrated teaching him fractions. Or you know that you have not yet addressed fractions.

If your child is doing well in a subject and an achievement test score indicates he is doing poorly, chances are:

1. You haven't covered the material yet.
2. He misunderstood some questions in the form they were given.
3. He missed one question and was one question off for the rest of the answer sheet.
4. He was having a bad day.
5. He was intimidated with the unfamiliar environment.
6. The state's guidelines are different from your guidelines.
7. He was worried about test taking. (One little girl was so nervous she told her mother, "I hope Jesus comes back before I have to take that test.")
8. He doesn't do well with timed tests.
9. Someone or something was distracting him.
10. The teacher told the testing group that they could play on the playground as soon as they were finished. (This happened to my own son. I watched, in horror, as he filled in twenty circles in less than thirty seconds!)

Diagnostic Testing

Diagnostic Testing can be beneficial before you start home schooling or if your child has a trouble area (cannot learn the material). If you're bringing your child home to school in the beginning of fourth grade, you may want to find out if he is really ready for the fourth grade material. He could be at fourth grade level math and second grade level in phonics. We have found that many children are promoted to the next grade level before they have mastered the basics. In these cases we recommend Diagnostic testing. Diagnostic testing is a one-on-one, un-timed test, presented verbally as well as written, that will reveal gaps much more accurately than achievement tests.

Evaluation Checklists

Studies show checklists are powerful substitutes for group-administered achievement tests. Research about this system shows that it provides teachers with reliable and valid data about children's academic performance (Meisels, Liaw, Dorfman, & Fails, in press). This system simultaneously informs, expands, and structures those perceptions while involving children and parents in the learning process. The Check lists provide detailed, observation-based information about the child's skills, accomplishments, knowledge, and behavior.

Combining the"Evaluation Check Lists" with a cumulation of the child's work will give a great deal of information and evidence about children's activities and development that can be used to enhance instruction and to plan future goals.

The "Evaluation Check Lists" create a profile of children's individualized progress. Because of the common structure of the checklists from kindergarten through eighth grade, you can chart your children's progress over a wide span of time and develop or plan a curriculum that reflects individual growth and change.

Portfolios

Portfolios provide a cumulation of your child's work, made with the child's input, in an organized manner. Portfolios highlight and record aspects and progression of a child's quality work. A portfolio is a collection of samples of a child's interest, and evidence of his or her God-given abilities. A portfolio can show others more about your child's learning than any letter grade. Most children absolutely love building portfolios. The portfolios can center on your child, a thematic unit study, or a period of time. This method encourages children to be active learners, learning through a variety of means (living books, audios, videos, field trips, or writing. When children's experiences are rich and diverse, it invites them to display their initiative, and engages their curiosity. This performance assessment will help you learn about your child as you watch him learn about his world. Many schools now require portfolios for graduation requirements.

Portfolios include anything demonstrating what you have learned from a subject (writing, science, etc.), course of study, Bible study, unit study, semester, or other time period of a school year.

For example:

Art Work	Bible Studies	Book Reviews
Brochures	Computer Disks	Computer Printouts
Displays	Essays	Field Trip Reports
Formal Letters	Journal Entries	Maps
Photographs	Play Dialog	Poetry
Projects	Recipes	Research Papers
Songs	Writing Samples	

If you could only teach your children one thing in your life, what would it be?

The most important thing you can ever teach your child is the Gospel, the good news, the best that ever came from heaven to earth. If your child is too small to understand, stop now and write a letter to him explaining the plan of salvation. Do you know the plan of salvation well enough to explain it to your child? You must! God's Word commands it. If anything ever happens that you are separated, be sure he has this letter and God's Word. If your child is old enough to memorize, put God's Word in his heart so that he will always have it.

Teach your child that he is a sinner (Romans 3:10-12). The wages of sin is death (Romans 6:23), then hell. God provided a sacrifice for sinners, a gift–His only begotten perfect son. Jesus took all your child's sins, your sins, and the sins of the world upon Himself. Jesus, God in the flesh, suffered and died that our sin would be paid for (Romans 5:8). But death could not conquer Him, and Jesus arose on the third day. He came to save us by pardoning us, that we might not die by the sentence of the law.

For God so loved the world, that he gave his only begotten Son, that whosoever believeth in him should not perish, but have everlasting life (John 3:16). God has given his love to the world: God so loved the world, so completely, so richly. Now we see that He loves us, and wishes us well. Behold, and wonder, that the great God should love such a worthless world! We can accept this gift from God by simply taking it.

And have put on the new man, which is renewed in knowledge after the image of Him that created him. (Colossians 3:10)

Real growth and knowledge can only come from Jesus; in Him we become a new man, and only then can we follow Him and find our created purpose.

SECTION III
TEACHING WISDOM

CHAPTER 8
AIMING FOR A HEART OF WISDOM

Wisdom is the principal thing; therefore get wisdom: and with all thy getting get understanding. (Proverbs 4:7).

To learn true wisdom a curriculum should spend a significant amount of time in God's Word. *For the word of God is quick, and powerful, and sharper than any two edged sword, piercing even to the dividing asunder of soul and spirit, and of the joints and marrow, and is a discerner of the thoughts and intents of the heart.* (Hebrews 4:12).

The home school movement has brought about (or restored) many superior, efficient, exciting teaching approaches. These methods verify, as explained in this book; we need to renew our thinking concerning education. Not only must we renew our thinking about the context of what is taught but also the method of what is taught (Joshua 24:23; Proverbs 3:5-6; Matthew 6:19-21; Romans 12:22). This section of this book explains one approach (based on a combination of several effective approaches) and centers all teaching on God's Word. You can use this approach as explained, or adapt it to the methods and curriculum you are using.

David Mulligan explains the importance of Scripture-centered curriculum book in a chapter of his book *Far Above Rubies: Wisdom in the Christian Community.* He also reveals the surprising hesitancy Christians feel about this approach to curriculum. He states:

> The idea of spending a lot of school time on the study of Scripture may at first be disturbing. We are so used to dividing "religious" activities from the rest of our time it seems as if Bible study just does not fit, except in a minor way, in our regular school day. We think of Bible study as suitable for family devotions, church services, Sunday school classes, and if the study gets "deep," in the seminary. How much Bible can children get without detracting from other studies?
>
> In asking this question we uncover in ourselves something of the tension that exists in the Western world

between learning and religion. We know somehow the question is not right; we should be first giving place to Scripture, but can not quite let go of the other side of things. And rightly so! The other side, God's creation, is vastly important, but still Scripture should come first, and all other studies find their place in relation to it. We should turn the question around: "How many secular studies can a student pursue without detracting from his knowledge of God's Word?!"

...Christian education must be built upon a pattern that maintains Scripture at its center and bring all subordinate studies into the circle of light radiating from thence.

Now these are the commandments, the statutes, and the judgments, which the LORD your God commanded to teach you, that ye might do them in the land whither ye go to possess it: That thou mightest fear the LORD thy God, to keep all his statutes and his commandments, which I command thee, thou, and thy son, and thy son's son, all the days of thy life; and that thy days may be prolonged. And thou shalt teach them diligently unto thy children, and shalt talk of them when thou sittest in thine house, and when thou walkest by the way, and when thou liest down, and when thou risest up.

-DEUTERONOMY 6:1-2,7.

This approach was greatly influenced, and actually a combination of teaching methods, from the Judah Bible Curriculum, Ruth Beechick's language arts teaching methods, Charlotte Mason's philosophy, Marilyn Howshall's Lifestyle of Learning the 4mat System, David Mulligan's writings, and the writing to learn philosophy from Write Source.

The Bible verse home schoolers lean on is not just a mandate to teach our children. It is a command to teach them God's Word!

We also claim a wonderful promise in Malachi 4:6a *And he shall turn the heart of the fathers to the children, and the heart of the children to their fathers...* but often forget verse 4 telling us the promise will happen when we remember God's ways. *Remember ye the law of Moses my servant, which I commanded unto him in Horeb for all Israel, with the statutes and judgments.*

The ultimate desire for Christians should be for their children to have a heart of wisdom—true wisdom from God. The philosophy described throughout this book has progressed into a teaching approach called the Heart of Wisdom (H.O.W.) approach.

Heart of Wisdom Teaching Approach

The Heart of Wisdom teaching approach is centered around reading the Bible through in one year and the creation of a Bible portfolio. This teaching can be the most important undertaking in your child's entire life. In this approach, the Bible is the main focus and the core of the curriculum, with the secondary focus dedicated to developing writing skills using the "writing to learn" method. The H.O.W. approach leads progressively to a renewed mind and to a self-chosen commitment to a life of intellectual and moral integrity. After all, the Bible is instruction for life.

All scripture is given by inspiration of God, and is profitable for doctrine, for reproof, for correction, for instruction in righteousness: That the man of God may be perfect, throughly furnished unto all good works. (2 Timothy 3:16-17).

Parents and students of all ages are active in an ongoing project based on reading through the Bible in one year, every year. This teaching approach does not separate academics and religion. The Bible is studied daily as students compile a chronicle of the concepts and beliefs into a Bible portfolio. All language arts skills are practiced daily while creating the Bible portfolio. (History, science and math are added in a unit study or textbook approach.)

Heart of Wisdom Approach

- The Bible is the textbook.
- The portfolio is a chronicle of the lessons and concepts studied.
- Learning takes place as the portfolio is created.
- God's Word is the thematic focus out of which academics naturally flow
- The lessons include several interrelated aspects:
    - spiritual training.
    - academic training.
    - character training.

Heart of Wisdom Goals

1. Read the Bible daily
2. Read through the Bible with the family once a year
3. Develop the student's writing skills
    a. context b. form c. mechanics
    d. editing and revision
4. Develop student's spelling skills by creating a personal spelling dictionary from student's writings
5. Develop student's handwriting skills by practicing writing Bible verses
6. Develop student's critical thinking skills:
    a. managing and using information to solve problems
    b. interrelating knowledge
    c. effectively communicating learning outcomes.
7. Reinforce phonics instruction using Bible storybooks.
8. Develop student's character through assignment completion. Teach:
    a. attentiveness b. commitment c. confidence
    d. decisiveness e. efficiency f. faithfulness
    g. perseverance h. promptness i. responsibility
    j. self-control
9. Develop excellence in achievement by requiring quality assignments

a. clarity b. accuracy c. relevance
d. prioritizing e. consistency f. depth
g. breadth

H.O.W. is actually a thematic unit study on the Bible. H.O.W. is ongoing and repeated each year while other thematic unit studies are usually completed in a time frame anywhere from one to twelve weeks. Add history, science, phonics, and math for a complete curriculum or add a unit study, phonics and a math program for a complete curriculum. The list below explains the subjects H.O.W. replaces:

SUBJECT	TRADITIONAL	HEART OF WISDOM
Bible	Workbook	Creating the Portfolio
Handwriting	Workbook	Copying Bible Verses
Spelling	Workbook	Misspelled Words from Writing
Creative Writing	Prompts	Summary, Research Writing about Bible Topics
Writing Mechanics	Workbook	Comparing Writing to Writing Handbook
Grammar	Textbook	Comparing Writing to Writing Handbook
Vocabulary	Workbook	Integrated Vocabulary List
Phonics	Workbook	Bible Storybook
Critical Thinking	Workbook	Bible study, interpretation, discernment
Map Skills	Workbook	Map Tracing Related to the Lesson
Economics	Textbook	Studying God's Principles

The family re-reads through the Bible every year; each student creates a new Bible portfolio. Each year, the portfolio will reflect changes in ability, depth, and focus. (Some states require portfolios for graduation.) Writing, spelling, grammar, capitalization and punctuation, handwriting, vocabulary, phonics, and critical thinking skills are learned, not as separate subjects, but integrated into each study. The first year, a younger child's portfolio will contain drawings, handwriting samples, memory verses, dictated summary pages, photos of a play costume, pages from a Bible coloring book, etc., while older students' portfolios will contain character and event summaries, research papers, essays, computer printouts, timelines, maps, sketches, etc.

Reasoning Skills

Studying the Bible is the ultimate lesson in reasoning skills (also termed critical thinking skills). Teaching students to think critically as they confront different information resources is the core of resource-based learning. Ann Bleakley explains: "Resource-based learning is the process by which students acquire these information-handling skills: managing and using information to solve problems, interrelating knowledge, and effectively communicating learning outcomes."

Reasoning skills enable students to assess both their own thought and action and that of others by reference. Considerable emphasis is placed on analogies in light of achievement test and college entrance exams. Some of the highest-level thinking skills are developed by studying analogies. Christians don't need expensive analogy workbooks. We have the depth of God's Word: the parables Jesus taught, the foreshadows in Bible holidays, the significance in numbers, the symbolism, the types, and passages such as Isaiah 53 revealing Christ.

THE WRITING PROCESS

- *Prewriting (collecting and planning)*
- *Write the first draft (use your own words)*
- *Revise (improve writing)*
- *Edit and proofread (correct errors)*
- *Transfer writing onto summary page and place in portfolio.*

WRITING TO LEARN

This project is much more than an accumulation of report writing. Students learn how to:

- assess information
- determine information appropriateness
- evaluate and compare
- analyze and discern
- add their own feelings
- organize information
- communicate conclusions

The concept of "writing to learn" is the second focus of this teaching approach. Students learn about the Bible as they learn the writing process. The Bible characters and events serve as built-in writing prompts.

Parents assess a student's writing and thinking for clarity, precision, accuracy, relevance, significance, and depth until the student has learned internal discipline to assess his own writing. Step-by-step writing process details are included in the Write Source books (described in this chapter.) Students should write a summary for each major event or character (unless you assign alternative writing). If a reading portion covers too much material, read the entire passage, but focus the study on a few major events (as the Holy Spirit leads your family). The following year, you can focus on the other events. Younger children can dictate or "retell" what they have learned as parents write the story with the children.

The writing portion of this project is much more than report writing. Students learn to express themselves by listening to a passage, practicing discernment, evaluating the story, compiling the information, and using the writing to communicate. The reading portions are also used for dictation and copying. Each document entered into the portfolio is the student's final process (developing several character traits). Notes, outlines, drafts, and prewriting can be maintained in a notebook, but only the revised, edited, polished productions enter the portfolio.

TYPES OF THINGS IN THE BIBLE PORTFOLIO	
Event Summary Pages	Character Summary Pages
Letters to Bible Characters	Rewritten Bible Stories
Play Script	Holiday Description
Related Bible Studies	Art Work/Drawings/ Sketches
Maps	Timelines
Photos of Projects	Pages from Coloring Books
Pages from Bible Workbooks	Desk Top Published Creations

Research studies confirm the value of phonics knowledge as a means for identifying printed words. But phonics alone is not enough; there are other highly important aspects in learning to read that cannot be ignored. *Teach a Child to Read with Children's Books* by Mark B. Thogmartin explains how to teach language arts skills using storybooks. H.O.W. takes this approach one step further to combine storytelling, reading, phonics, and writing by using Bible storybooks. To use the Heart of Wisdom approach, reading through the Bible each year, with young children, read the instructions from *Teach a Child to Read with Children's Books* and substitute the early reader books with a set of Bible storybooks such as *Arch© Bible Storybooks.* The *Arch© Bible Storybooks* consists of a set of inexpensive, lively, rhyming poems and colorful illustrations for children preschool to kindergarten.

CHAPTER 9
IMPLEMENTING A H.O.W. APPROACH

There are four basic steps to this approach. The amount of time for each step will vary from a few minutes to few days depending on the activities chosen. Plan on completing all four steps for the selected Bible reading within one week. These four steps teach to all four learning styles and both brain hemispheres. Studies show this four-step method motivates students to comprehend the material better and retain the information longer.

Step 1 Excite: Create an interest. Motivate students by making the lesson meaningful to their lives. Discuss what the children may already know about the passage and what they would like to find out. Brainstorm, make lists, mindmap, outline, etc.

Step 2 Examine: Find out the facts. Read the Bible passages. Refer to commentaries, Bible dictionaries, time lines, and maps pertaining to the material for more information.

Step 3 Expand: Do something with what was learned. Complete handwriting practice and vocabulary words. Dictate a portion of Scripture to your child or have him copy a portion. Reinforce the lesson by creating a project that will be entered into the portfolio. Projects can be simple ten-minute activities or elaborate three-day endeavors. You are only limited by your imagination). All writing assignments are edited and finalized. All projects are prepared for display or photographed. Work is added to the Bible portfolio.

Step 4 Excel: Pull everything together (synthesis). The writing assignment or project is verbally shared and explained to another person (daddy, grandmother, neighbor, home school group, sibling, etc.). When a student can teach someone else what he has learned, he knows the subject.

---

[1] See *Mapping Inner Space* by Nancy Margulies at the end of this chapter.

READING THE BIBLE CHRONOLOGICALLY

The Bible Check List in Section IV arranges the Scriptures chronologically in the order the Bible events occurred. These portion divisions are from *The Narrated Bible: In Chronological Order*. *The Narrated Bible* is not a paraphrase or translation, the central text is composed entirely of Scripture using the New International Version. Narrative commentary is included in a separate and distinct type and color. The narrative commentary is written in such a way as to be part of an unfolding story. The text in *The Narrated Bible* can be used for dictation and copying lessons, (teaching handwriting, grammar, capitalization, and punctuation) because it is written is everyday English. Families with very young children may decide to use Bible storybooks (explained later in this chapter). You can use any Bible version by referring to the chapter and verses listed in the Bible Check List.

Weekly Readings

The Bible Check List is divided into 360 Bible portions listed by verse and by page number for *The Narrated Bible*. Some portions are very short and some are very long. The readings are also divided into fifty-two weekly readings, keeping the amount of daily reading time approximately the same each week. You will read an average of seven or eight pages per day five days a week in *The Narrated Bible.* The Bible Check List is purposely not divided into daily readings so each family can work around their own schedule. The Heart of Wisdom approach is designed to use year round. Math and other subjects can be completed within the school months. Teaching this approach year-round keeps everyone in the Bible daily. It also reinforces reading and writing practice through the summer months, when many lessons are forgotten and must be re-introduced if not re-taught in the fall. You can easily adapt the Bible readings to any time frame suited to your family. Here is a sample of weekly readings:

DAY	BIBLE READINGS	NUMBER OF PAGES
Monday	Creation to Adam to Noah	8
Tuesday	Flood to Dispersion of the Human Family	9
Wednesday	The Beginning of Nations to Abraham and Lot	9
Thursday	Defeat of the Kings to Circumcision	12
Friday	Heavenly Visitors to Scheme of Lot's Daughters	7

LEARNING STYLES--

Be cautious studying learning style theories. As with other truths, non-believers take a discovery, as the secular world often does, and distorts the principle to fit their secular world view. This does not mean we must discount facts because the non-believers discovered them just as we would not discount discoveries such as the automobile, eyeglasses, or other things we use daily that may have been discovered by an unbeliever.

The Bible describes how different people are given different gifts and talents. Anything you read about learning styles should line up with God's Word and never be an excuse for sin or shortcomings.

The 4Mat System Studies have proven the four step system outlined in this book prove:

-Improved Retention
-Higher Achievement
-Increased Motivation
-Improved Thinking Skills
-Lower Remediation

--EXCEL, INC

For further reading see:
-*The 4Mat System, Teaching to Learning Styles with Right and Brain Processing Techniques* by Bernice McCarthy;
-*4Mat in Action* by Susan Morris and Bernice McCarthy,
-*The 4Mat System Workbook; The 4Mation Developer Software* by Excel, Inc.

Unfortunately, many Christian's do not read their Bibles often. Many who do read the Bible usually just read a few verses or a chapter, so reading ten or more Bible chapters a day may seem overwhelming. However, it really is very easy and so interesting that the children may urge you to continue to the next story. The daily readings usually take about thirty to forty-five minutes (less time than a television show, Nintendo, computer game, ball practice, or board game).

Scheduling

All families and schedules differ. There are two sample school days in this chapter to give you a practical idea using the Heart of Wisdom approach. The times listed in this samples are only approximates. The amount of time spent could be anywhere from two to six hours depending on the ages and abilities of the children. The samples show a day for a preschooler or beginner reader and for a family with three children ages eight, nine and fourteen. A school day would be longer for a high school student but much of the work is independent. (See the description of *The Judah Bible Curriculum* at the end of this chapter).

The Heart of Wisdom for Preschoolers and Beginning Readers

Preschool to first grade or second grader combine story telling, reading, phonics, and writing by using Bible storybooks. Bible reading and language arts take one to two hours.

Teach a Child to Read with Children's Books by Mark B. Thogmartin explains how to teach language arts skills using storybooks. Research studies confirm the value of phonics knowledge as a means for identifying printed words. But phonics alone is not enough; there are other highly important aspects in learning to read that cannot be ignored.

Read the instructions from *Teach a Child to Read with Children's Books* and substitute the early reader books with a set of Bible story books. Here Thogmartin explains one simple writing activity:

> One of the single most instructive activities you and your child could participate is writing short stories together. Allow the child to dictate the story as you write down the words. It's fine to correct his language as you

STEP 1 EXCITE
-Brainstorming
-Mindmapping
-Observing a video
-Discussing
-Making lists
-Drawing tentative conclusions.

STEP 2 EXAMINE
-Read the Bible
-Look up items and words in a Bible Handbook
-Refer to a Commentary
-View Bible Maps
-Interview father or pastor

STEP 3 EXPAND
-Write a song
-Write poetry
-Make a poster
-Create illustrations
-Make a salt dough model (lamp, menorah, etc.)
-Play interactive software
-Do a science experiment
-Create a puppet show
-Make a diorama from a shoe box
-Write a letter from a character
-Write a letter to a character
-Write a newspaper article about an event
-Trace a journey on a map
-Create a costumed play
-Make a booklet or pamphlet

STEP 4 EXCEL
Share and Explain a Project:
Writing Activities
Portfolio
Artwork
Oral Stories
Recite poetry
Sing a song

The most important activity for building knowledge and skills eventually required for reading is that of reading aloud to children.
--MARILYN ADAMS, *reading expert*

Reading the Bible each day causes children to come to you all day long with questions. This gives you an opportunity to do what God commands us to do in Deuteronomy 6:7. And thou shalt teach them diligently unto thy children, and shalt talk of them when thou sittest in thine house, and when thou walkest by the way, and when thou liest down, and when thou risest up.

BIBLE VERSIONS
We recommend the 1611 authorized King James Version Bible *for Bible study with lexicons to look up Greek and Hebrew words. However, for daily Bible reading we think of* The Narrated Bible *as a "story book" to read aloud giving the children an overview of the entire Bible. It reads like a novel and is easy-to understand.*

write a s long as it is not done in a discouraging way. Say each word slowly, sound the letters or letter blends as you write, and then spell the word back before going to the next word. Frequently repeat the sentence as you are completing it so the child (and you) don't forget what you are writing. Read each sentence as it is finished, pointing out the word as you read. When you are finished with he story, allow the child to illustrate it, or work together to add some special "pizzazz." You will find that with practice, the child will be able to read the story himself. Encourage him by suggesting he read to any interested person that comes to visit.

SAMPLE SCHOOL DAY (CHILDREN AGES 4 TO 7)

8:00 Prayer, memory verse

8:10 *Explode the Code* phonics lesson (or another phonics program.)

9:00 LESSON ONE, CREATION

Step 1 Create an Interest-- Discuss what the child knows about the creation story.

Step 2 Find Out the Facts--Read the story of creation from a storybook. Point out letter identification, phonics, word families, etc. studied in phonics lesson.

Step 3 Do Something With What is Learned

- The child dictates the creation story to mother (one day of creation per page) to make a booklet.
- The child illustrates the booklet with markers and stickers.

Step 4 Share What was Learned

- The child reads or tells his story to someone else *(Preschoolers and kindergartners stop after lesson one. First and second graders go on to second lesson).*

10:00 LESSON TWO, ADAM AND EVE

Step 1 Create an Interest--Read Adam and Eve from a storybook.

Step 2 Find Out the Facts--Point out letter identification, phonics, word families, etc. studied in phonics lesson.

Step 3 Do Something With What is Learned

- Practice writing letters from the story.
- The child dictates the story of Adam and Eve to mother. (this may only be one or two sentences.)

Step 4 Share What was Learned

- The child reads or tells his story to someone else.

10:30 HISTORY AND SCIENCE LESSONS

Incorporate history and science into the Bible reading by reading aloud related books such as *A is for Adam* (rhyme and coloring book about creation) or one of the easy readers from the God is Good series (small books from Rod and Staff) such as: *God makes a Seed that Grows, God Made Me, God Made the Animals*, etc.

SAMPLE SCHOOL DAY (CHILDREN AGES 8 TO 14)

The Bible reading for this sample day is Genesis chapter 1-5:32 (pages 1-10 in *The Narrated Bible*) consisting of three Bible stories or lessons: 1.) Creation, 2.) The Fall, 3.) The Chronology from Adam to Noah.

8:00 OPEN WITH PRAYER, DEDICATING YOUR DAY AND BIBLE READING TO GOD. RECITE BIBLE MEMORY VERSES TOGETHER.

FIRST LESSON, CREATION

Step 1 Create an Interest: Ask the children to tell what was created on each day of the creation story. Ask them to tell you what they know about Creation and what they would like to know. Make a list or mindmap (about ten minutes).

Step 2 Find out the Facts: Read the creation story (about ten minutes); stop to discuss the story; answer questions. Look up the location on a Bible map. Look up unfamiliar words in a dictionary or Bible dictionary. Oldest child takes notes.

Step 3 Do Something with What was Learned:

- Younger children write and illustrate a verse for each of the creation days. Or complete a puzzle from *Through the Bible in a Year Puzzles.*
- Each child traces the four rivers (mentioned in the creation story) from a Bible map.
- Older child writes the first draft of the creation story in his own words.
- Mother reviews writing and explains errors, reviewing necessary punctuation or grammar rules from *Write Source* book.
- Misspelled words are entered into spelling notebook.
- Icons for creation are added to the time line.

9:00 SECOND LESSON, THE FALL

Step 1 Create an Interest: Discuss with the children what they know about the story of Adam and Eve and what they would like to know. Make a list or mindmap (about ten minutes).

Step 2 Find out the Facts: Read about the Fall in Genesis 3 and 4 (about ten minutes). Stop and discuss. Older children take notes and jot down questions about the story.

Step 3 Do Something with What was Learned:

- Younger children and mother write a story together about Adam and Eve, (a few sentences depending on child's age), reviewing necessary punctuation or grammar rules from *Write Source* book.
- Younger children copy Bible verse for handwriting practice.

HOW JESUS TAUGHT

Step 1

He took the people where they were and made the lesson meaningful to their lives in some way. He spoke to shepherds about sheep, farmers about planting, fishermen about fishing.

Step 2

He brought in the facts shown in Scripture, "It is written, ..."

Step 3

He asked them to do something with what they learned

-to actively respond

-by listening.

"He that hath ears to hear, let him hear;" by showing faith, "Arise, and walk;" by obeying, "Come," "Go sin no more;" etc.

Step 4

He asked them to go and tell others. "Go ye therefore, and teach all nations...."

READING STORYBOOKS CHILDREN LEARN:

-Print contains a message

-Differences between letters and words

-Letter sounds

-Left to right progression of words

-Top to bottom progression of lines on a page

-Expressive and fluent reading

-Practice of correcting oneself when mistakes occur, to maintain meaning

--MARK B. THOGMARTIN

For detailed instructions relating to copying and dictation methods, read chapters six through ten in Ruth Beechick's You Can Teach Your Child Susessfully.

LISTENING TO BIBLE READINGS

If you are reading Bible text to older children the toddlers may not seem to gain much from the reading time but this period is excellent opportunity to teach children to sit still and be quiet.

Sometimes we practice being still and sometimes, I provide a set of wood blocks or coloring books for younger children (only available to them during this reading time).

OUR FAMILY'S SCHOOL DAY

Our day consists of two thematic studies, math, and typing.

A minimum of one-half of each school time is spent in the Bible and language art skills, as the second half of the day is devoted to another unit study (a theme on a specific topic or time period), such as the Middle Ages, Civil War, Ocean, Astronomy, etc., from Far Above Rubies or The Biblical Holidays. Each day, the children work on two portfolios, Bible and a thematic unit study.

- Mother dictates a portion of the story to the older student. Or older student writes a summary titled "The Consequences of Sin" using the word processor.
- Mother reviews all writing and explains errors, reviewing necessary punctuation or grammar rules from Write Source book.
- All misspelled words are entered into spelling notebook.
- Icons (cut out illustrations) for Adam and Eve are added to the time line.

10:00 THIRD LESSON, CHRONOLOGY FROM ADAM TO NOAH

Step 1 Create an Interest: Discuss what the children know about who lived between the time of Adam and Noah.

Step 2 Find out the Facts: Read the chronology from Adam to Noah, Genesis 5 (about five minutes).

Step 3 Do Something with What was Learned

- Make a family tree showing the genealogy from Adam to Noah.
- Make a Family tree showing genealogy from your children to their grandparents.

11:00 REVISE AND COMPLETE WORK

- Older student continues to revise and edit writing assignments. When work is error-free, it is entered into the Bible portfolio.
- Younger children work with Explode the Code work books (or another phonics program). Mother points out phonic lessons learned this day, sounds, word families, etc. from today's Bible readings.

11:30 MATH

- Mother works on math with younger children.
- Older child does math assignments independently.

12:00 LUNCH AND CLEAN UP

12:30 - HISTORY AND SCIENCE

Incorporate other subjects into the Bible stories by reading aloud (or independent reading) portions of related books such as *The Great Dinosaur Mystery and The Bible* (creation science), *Dry Bones and Other Fossils* (creation science), *In the Days of Noah* (history), *Amazing Animals* (biology), *Life Before Birth* (anatomy), etc.

Or work on a non-related unit study such as *Life in the Colonies.* Mother reads the section about trade winds. Children complete a work sheet. Younger child reads aloud a story from *Boy and Girls of Colonial Days.* Older child completes a work page from *Colonies to Constitution* and reads aloud to younger children from *George Washington* biography from the Sower Series.

2:30 OR 3:00 FORMAL SCHOOL TIME IS OVER.

There is time for typing, piano lessons, chores, play, etc.

Step 4: Share What was Learned

- That evening or at a convenient time children share projects and discuss Bible lessons with father (or siblings, grandparents, home school group, etc.).

In just one day you have read nine chapters and look at the portfolios!

Younger Child's Bible Portfolio	Older Child's Bible Portfolio
1. The Creation Story illustrated	1. The Creation Story paraphrased by student
2. Bible Map of four rivers	2. Bible Map of four rivers
3. Adam and Eve Story	3. The Consequences of Sin *(writing assignment)*
4. Family Tree: Adam to Noah	6. Family Tree: Adam to Noah

Using H.O.W. for History and Science Subjects

Using the Heart of Wisdom Approach for a complete curriculum (except math) takes a little more planning but it is "doable." History, geography and science are easily studied, as they each appear, relating to the weekly Bible reading. Reading the story of creation leads to reading a book refuting evolution, explaining carbon dating,and the scientific process. Reading about Moses leads to the study of life in Ancient Egypt and, ultimately, modern Egypt. Reading about Jesus' birth and the wise men who followed a star can lead to an entire unit study of astronomy. Reading about borrowing and lending from the Bible is the best economic lesson available! Reading Paul's letters leads to a study of the life in ancient Rome.

Combining Unit Studies with The Heart of Wisdom Approach

Unit studies are available for every topic imaginable. Each of the subjects mentioned above—creation, ancient Egypt, astronomy, money—are addressed in one or more unit studies available form most home school suppliers. You can use other unit study programs by rearranging the units to follow the Bible Readings. See *A Family Guidebook to the Biblical Holidays* (includes nine unit studies), *Far Above Rubies* (over one hundred unit studies for jr. high and up), *Life in America* (dozens of science and history units for grade 3-6), *Konos* (dozens of science and history units), *Amanda Bennet Unit Study Guides* (dozens of science and history units) and more.

Design Your Own Lessons

Use the academic Check Lists in this book to outline the topics you want to include for the year and find an appropriate place to incorporate each into your Bible study. Design your own lessons

Several Bible storybooks are available in Christian bookstores.

Hear Me Read BIble Storybooks *are available on two levels. Each story consists of 15 to 25 words that are repeated often to help children develop a sight vocabulary. There are currently twenty-six books in the series.*

The Arch© Bible Storybooks *consists of a set of inexpensive, lively, rhyming poems, and the colorful illustrations for children preschool to kindergarten. The books in this series published before in the 1980s include realistic type illustrations. The newer illustrations are too "cartoony" for our family. There are over forty-four books in the series.*

Now You Can Read Bible Stories *are delightfully written and illustrated. The new series (from Thomas-Nelson) consists of nine books; however, we were able to find several books that used to be in this series (originally published by Rourke) from used book stores.*

The Biblearn Series *are good read aloud hardback books with nice illustrations. Currently there are twenty-four books in this series. Books include several stories each.*

MATERIALS TO MAKE THE BIBLE PORTFOLIO
- *A large sturdy three-ring notebook with a clear plastic front (designed to slip a cover sheet under the plastic) for each child.*
- *Three-hole punched plastic protective covers (for photos, artwork and flat collections)*
- *Plastic photo pages (for photos of plays, large projects, etc., in portfolio).*
- *Ten tabbed notebook dividers labeled:*
  1. *Law/Instruction*
  2. *Historical*
  3. *Poetry*
  4. *Major Prophets*
  5. *Minor Prophets*
  6. *Gospels*
  7. *Acts*
  8. *Paul's Letters*
  9. *General Instruction*
  10. *Prophecy*

Optional Supplies
- *Colored pencils and/or washable markers and/or crayons*
- *Ruled and un-ruled paper*
- *Scissors*
- *Construction paper*
- *Three-hole punch*
- *Decorative paper*
- *Decorative stamps*
- *Various art supplies (charcoal, paint, chalk, etc.)*

to use with the Bible readings by referring to reference books and reading literature on the topic. Each Bible story teaches about specific places and time periods. Refer to a chronological history reference book such as *Kingfisher's Illustrated Guide to History* to find out what was going on at the same time in other parts of the world. Science is also easily integrated. When ever a concept comes up such as water, yeast, wind, stars, animals, etc. Look up the topic in a book like *The Kingfisher's Science Encyclopedia* or *Encarta Encyclopedia* (check the listed related topics). Studying the Israelite slavery in Egypt easily leads to studying slavery in America and the Civil War period. Reading about Passover flows into a study on sheep, studying both the wool industry, spinning wool, friction, and animal biology. Examining church government easily leads to a study of American government. Reading the story of Jesus calming the sea proceeds into a study of oceanography.

Detailed information and lesson plans using the Heart of Wisdom Approach are being developed as the Lord leads.

TO USE THE HEART OF WISDOM APPROACH, YOU WILL NEED:

- KJV Bible for Reference
- Bible to read aloud such as *The Narrated Bible*
- Bible Storybooks for younger children
- Write Source Handbook (proper age level)
- Spelling Notebook (spiral bound notebook divided alphabetically)
- Vocabulary Notebook (spiral bound notebook divided alphabetically)
- An art portfolio (Poster board stabled together to protect large artwork.)
- Materials to make the Portfolio (see margin)
- Optional but highly recommended
  - Bible Dictionary
  - Bible Handbook
  - Bible Commentary
  - Bible Map Book
  - Strong's Reference Book
  - Hebrew Lexicon
  - Greek Lexicon

Descriptions of Suggested Resources

The Narrated Bible with narration by F. LaGard Smith is unique in concept and design –a rare combination of clarity, beauty and quality, combining chronological accuracy, typographic innovation. It is neither a translation nor a paraphrase. The central text is composed entirely of scripture. Narrative commentary notes are included to give the story background.The result is an invitation to reading and a guide to understanding. An excellent history text, reads like a beautiful, exciting story. You'll have the children on the edge of their seats!

Through The Bible in One Year is a a fifty-two lesson introduction to the sixty-six books of the Bible by Alan B. Stringfellow. Takes you completely through the Bible book by book, you will learn how to analyze all sixty-six books, which are the most significant chapters, where to find the central purpose, which chief verses to copy and remember.

Judah Bible Curriculum by Bill Burtness is an excellent Bible study curriculum similar to the approach outlined in this chapter, combined with an entry level to the Principle Approach to Education and Christian Self-Government (based on the philosophy of government). This curriculum is especially suited for primary and secondary study level. *The Judah Curriculum* takes you through main events in the Bible concentrating on five themes which describe what is happening governmentally through the Bible.

1.) Creation
2.) Redemption
3.) Kingdom of Israel
4.) Kingdom of God
5.) Early Church

Each "theme" is broken down into "Bible Keys." While studying each time period, students research key individuals, key events, key situations, key institutions, and key documents. Each week parents teach the place of the Bible Key in God's purpose in history, the students study one "Key" in depth. Each year the focus changes to another key in the same theme.

Students fill in the "Key Sheets" and produce a personalized Bible notebook. The teacher teaches the student to research, reason, and record. The student applies these methods to the Bible. The reproducible key sheets go into the student's note book:

- Key Individuals
- Key Events
- Key Institutions
- Key Documents

Writing Prompts

-Write a newspaper article for an event that happened in the Bible story. Include who, what, where, why, when and how.
-Contrast the life of the people in the Bible story with your life today. How are they alike and different?
-Give examples of cause and effect in the event.
-Write about a character that displayed qualities of bravery. Tell what you would have done if you had been in that character's place.
-Write an editorial expressing your opinion about an event
-Choose characters from the Bible reading and give a report on them.

By using the Heart of Wisdom approach, students see the relationship between research, life skills, and language skills. As they read through God's Word, all subjects relate around a specific portion of the Bible (life's instruction) grammar, phonics, spelling, vocabulary, critical thinking skills, language mechanics, etc.

Other programs don't relate. Look what you may have been doing instead:

8:00 Bible Workbook-lesson about a parable of Jesus.
8:30 Spelling workbook- learning unrelated words and using them in unrelated sentences.
9:00 Handwriting workbook- copying various letters in various unrelated sentences.
9:30 Creative writing-My Day at the Park.
10:30 Grammar workbook-diagramming sentences from a story about a dog. Practice homophones in miscellaneous sentences.Underlining parts of speech in various unrelated sentences.
11:00 Vocabulary notebook--learning unrelated words and using them in unrelated sentences.
11:30 Critical Thinking Workbook--Finding the shape that completes the square. Fill in the blank (analogy relationships).

The content in this curriculum recognizes God's sovereignty and is sensitive to His rule personally in every area of life. It develops a character that self governed (godly), self-educating (intelligent), productive, responsible, able to reason based on Biblical understanding (truly literate), and who recognizes servanthood as the basis of true authority (leadership[p).

Creator Bill Burtness has compiled an excellent set of audio tapes to teach parents and teachers. Audio tapes include:

1. Education and Character
2. How God Changes Nations
3. Internal Government: Creation-Flood
4. Internal Government: Abraham to Malachi
5. Internal Government: Matthew-Revelation
6. Methods, Weekly Themes, Notebooks, Key Sheets
7. Internal Government: Pentecost-Present.

An important, exciting concept of this curriculum is that it teaches you and the student to break curriculum dependence and become self educating Christian scholars.

You Can Teach Your Child: Grades 4-8 is written in a clear, friendly, encouraging language, Ruth lays a solid foundation to use the language arts methods mentioned in this chapter, based upon her experience as a teacher, curriculum developer, and professor of education. The basic subjects—reading, writing, and arithmetic—are covered quite thoroughly, as well as history and social studies, science and health, music and art, and the Bible. If you plan on using the Heart of Wisdom approach you really need to read this book (especially chapters six through ten.

Teach a Child to Read with Children's Books by Mark B. Thogmartin is an approach to prepare a child for reading success before lessons begin. Phonics instruction is excellent but, used alone, may bore your child. This book demonstrates how to use literature to promote learning and enjoyment by combining book experiences and phonics. It also teaches you ways to use writing to enhance your child's reading progress and why reading aloud is so important, and suggests hundreds of storybooks for reading aloud on different levels. Author Jim Trelease said, "For home-schoolers, *Teach a Child to Read Using Children's Books* should be a second bible in the family, for it is filled with resources, information, strategies, and inspiration for learning. I highly recommend it." The author is a Christian, and the former headmaster of a private Christian school where he also administered a home education program. However, some his book suggestions were very disappointing (stories about witches, the Easter Bunny, Christmas Elves, etc.) just skip anything that might offend your beliefs. The main reason you'll use this book is to follow the suggested reading and writing activities substituting Bible stories for other stories.

Mapping Inner Space by Nancy Margulies explains a revolutionary way to put ideas onto paper. Mind mapping has proven to be an effective way of brainstorming, pre-writing, sequencing, cause-effect reasoning, describing attributes, comparing and contrasting, and the organization of ideas by drawing and connecting thought on paper in a pictorial form opposed to the traditional outline methods). Mind maps are drawn in many forms: clusters of circles, icons, bridge maps, tree maps, etc. The maps help students with part/whole reasoning. This approach is a comprehensive model for transferring thinking skills directly to content learning. This book teaches you how to pour ideas onto paper with a mindmap, how to practice mapping, and how to teach mindmapping to students. Mindmaps are great Step 1 activities and excellent helps creating unit studies.

The Write Source Books (Writer's Express, Write Source 2000, Writer's INC) are beautifully laid out in full color, illustrated pages jam-packed with information. Write Source asked nationally acclaimed writers, storytellers, performers, and educators to contribute to this project. The handbooks can be used for years to help students whenever they have a question about punctuation, usage, or writing. Each hand book includes:

The Writing Process: Getting Started, Working with the Writing Process, Understanding the Basics of Writing, Improving Your Writing

The Forms of Writing: Journals & Narratives, Newspapers, Reviews, and Letters, Creative Stories, Tales, Poems, Plays, and Riddles, Research, Summaries, Reports

Preparing to Learn: Becoming a Better Reader, Becoming a Better Speaker, and Listener, Becoming a Better Thinker, Becoming a Better Student

Proofreader's Guide: Marking Punctuation, Using Capital Let-

Resources are available though most home school suppliers or call 1-800-788-0840 to order.

Step 3 Activities

- -Tape-record a section of the Bible reading you especially liked. Tell why you chose this part. Add background music to fit the mood of the passage.
- -Create a political cartoon, caricature, or cartoon strip for some event or character in the Bible reading.
- -Create a mural, diorama, 3-dimensional figure, costume, or mobile to depict an event or person in the Bible reading.
- -Make an acrostic using a character in the Bible reading. Tell about the character using each letter from the title.
- -Make a timeline for the events in the story.
- -Create a travel brochure depicting points of interest in the Bible reading. Include transportation used, landforms, kind of housing, natural beauty, etc.

ters, Selecting the Right Word, Understanding the Parts of Speech

Student Almanac: Useful Tables and Lists, All About Maps, Improving Math Skills, Historical Documents, and more!

Through the Bible in One Year Puzzles is a great companion to the the Heart of Wisdom approach. The entire book is packed with reproducible puzzles for students in grades 3-6. The Table of Contents give the puzzle title and Bible reference so it is easy to find the puzzle for that days Bible readings. Consists of over 180 worksheets of puzzles, mazes, hidden words, sign language, sound alike, true or false, secret codes, fill-in-the-blanks, scrambled messages, etc.

Bible Time Crafts for Kids includes all sorts of crafts for preschool through grade 6. It includes instructions to make costumes, jewelry, scrolls, pottery, baskets, musical instruments, and more. Also includes reproducible Bible time puppets, and coloring posters.

The Big Book of Books and Activities Old Testament and *The Big Book of Books and Activities New Testament* are illustrated guides to encourage creativity from expressions through writing, designing, illustration and building. Each book contains dozens of unique, fun, projects.

SECTION IV
EVALUATION CHECK LISTS

CHAPTER 10
BIBLE EVALUATION
The Solid Foundation

True learning, I believe, is learning something to the point at which it becomes second nature. Reading and math are good academic examples. Normally, we can read without thinking of how to sound out letters. Most of us know the multiplication tables without thinking. This applies to all areas of life.

Shouldn't our goal be to instill God's Word into our children, the way God instills the nurturing or protecting instinct into parents? Can we teach them, by word and deed, to the point that they would recognize evil—without thinking—and automatically turn away? Can we teach our precious ones to respond—automatically—in kindness to an unkind deed? Yes, we can.

PRIORITY: GOD'S WORD

If I could only give one piece of advice to a new home schooler, it would be this.

> **Do not get so wrapped up in academics that you leave out the most important thing. The Bible is the only book where true wisdom is found. Teaching your children to apply God's truth will teach them to discern what's right or wrong, true or false, loving or cruel, profitable or foolish, noble or cowardly. Start every morning in God's Word! If you start with other subjects, Bible easily gets pushed out of the way.**

Remember the saying that goes something like this: Give a man a fish and you've fed him for a day, but teach a man to fish and you've fed him for life. The greatest gift you will ever give your child will be to teach him to develop the habit of purposefully reading, studying, and applying God's Word daily. It will affect every area of his life every day of his life.

Bible study is a legitimate subject! Bible reading should be the highest priority in your child's studies. Students study literary forms and cultural background in the books of the Bible and apply the messages to their lives, to their relationships, and to the world.

The Bible is the perfect textbook. *All scripture is given by inspiration of God, and is profitable for doctrine, for reproof, for correction, for instruction in righteousness: That the man of God may be perfect, thoroughly furnished unto all good works.* (2 Timothy 3:16-17).

J. I. Packard writes in the book *Knowing God:*

> A study of the nature and character of God is the most practical project anyone can engage in. Knowing about God is crucially important for the living of our lives....We are cruel to ourselves if we try to live in the world without knowing about the God whose world it is and who runs it. The world becomes a strange, mad, painful place, and life disappointing and unpleasant business for those who do not know about God. Disregard the study of God and you sentence yourself to stumble and blunder through life blindfolded, as it were, with no sense of direction and no understanding of what surrounds you. This way you can waste your life and lose your soul.

Using the Check List

The Check List in this chapter is based on reading the Bible through in one year, reading between thirty minutes to an hour five days a week. (The amount of time for most television programs). Use the Check List according to the selected daily schedule or your own schedule and ignore the suggested schedule. Both verses and *The Narrated Bible* page number are included in the Check List. (A Check List for seven daily readings is included in the back of *The Narrated Bible*).

The previous chapter explains how the daily Bible readings can also be used to teach or reinforce language arts skills.

One Year through God's Word

A STUDY USING

*The Narrated Bible**

**The Narrated Bible* is a narration by F. LaGard Smith using the New International Version (NIV), published by Harvest House Publishers, Eugene, Oregon 97402

WEEK ONE

Beginnings of Early Mankind (Creation to Ca. 2100 B.C.)

The Beginnings	1	Genesis 1:1-2:4	☐
Adam and Eve	3	Genesis 2:4-3:24	☐
First Three Sons of Adam and Eve	6	Genesis 4:1-26	☐
Descendants from Adam to Noah	8	Genesis 5:1-32	☐
Mankind's Degeneration into Wickedness	11	Genesis 6:1-8	☐
Noah and the Flood	12	Genesis 6:9-9:17	☐
Human Condition Remains Sinful	16	Genesis 9:18-29	☐
Dispersion of the Human Family	17	Genesis 11:1-9	☐
Beginning of Nations	18	Genesis 10:1-32	☐
Descendants from Shem to Abram	20	Genesis 11:10-26	☐
Job, the Righteous Sufferer	22	The Book of Job	☐

Period of the Patriarchs (Ca. 2100-1525 B.C.)

The Call of Abram	23	Genesis 12:1-9	☐
Abram Dishonors Himself in Egypt	24	Genesis 12:10-20	☐
Separation of Abram and Lot	25	Genesis 13:1-18	☐
Defeat of the Kings	27	Genesis 14:1-20	☐
God's Covenant with Abram	29	Genesis 15:1-21	☐
Birth of Ishmael Through Hagar	30	Genesis 16:1-16	☐
Names and Circumcision As Signs of Covenant	32	Genesis 17:1-27	☐
Appearance of Heavenly Visitors	34	Genesis 18:1-15	☐
Destruction of Sodom and Gomorrah	35	Genesis 18:16-28	☐
The Scheme of Lot's Daughters	38	Genesis 19:30-38	☐

WEEK TWO

Abraham Deceives Abimelech	39	Genesis 20:1-18	☐
The Birth of Isaac	41	Genesis 21:1-7	☐
Abraham and Abimelech Settle Dispute	42	Genesis 21:22-34	☐
Expulsion of Hagar and Ishmael	43	Genesis 21:8-21	☐
Abraham's Ultimate Test of Faith	44	Genesis 22:1-19	☐
News Regarding Nahor's Family	45	Genesis 22:20-24	☐
Sarah's Death and Burial	46	Genesis 23:1-20	☐
Abraham Arranges Wife for Isaac	47	Genesis 24:1-67	☐
Abraham Marries Keturah	50	Genesis 25:1-6	☐
Death of Abraham	51	Genesis 25:7-10	☐
Last Account of Ishmael	51	Genesis 25:12-18	☐
Esau and Jacob	52	Genesis 25:11-28	☐
A Birthright is Sold	53	Genesis 25:29-34	☐
Isaac Follows in Abraham's Footsteps	53	Genesis 26:1-33	☐
Trouble Between Jacob and Esau	55	Genesis 26:34-35; 27:1-41	☐
Jacob Leaves for Haran	58	Genesis 27:42-46; 28:5-22	☐
Jacob Marries and Has Children	59	Genesis 29:1-35	☐
Laban and Jacob Outsmart Each Other	62	Genesis 30:25-43	☐
Jacob Leaves Laban	63	Genesis 31:1-55	☐
Jacob Returns to Canaan	66	Genesis 32:1-32	☐

WEEK TEN

WEEK SEVENTEEN

Reading	Page	Scripture	Done
Psalms of the Troubled Soul (cont'd)	508	Psalm 70; 71; 77	☐
Psalms About Righteousness and Wickedness	521	Psalm 1; 14	☐
Psalms of Joy and Praise	536	Psalm 8; 9; 16	☐

WEEK EIGHTEEN

Reading	Page	Scripture	Done
Psalms of Joy and Praise (cont'd)	540	Psalm 29; 33	☐
Psalms Expressing a Variety of Sentiments	570	Psalm 4; 12	☐

WEEK NINETEEN

Reading	Page	Scripture	Done
Psalms Expressing a Variety of Sentiments (cont'd)	574	Psalm 42; 53; 58	☐
Psalms of the Messiah	580	Psalm 2; 22; 27	☐
Solomon Becomes King	587	1 Kings 1:1-53	☐
Solomon Secures His Kingship	591	1 Kings 2:13-46	☐
Solomon Blessed with Wisdom	594	1 Kings 3:2-3	☐
Building of the Temple	596	1 Kings 5:1-9; 2 Chronicles 2:1-16	☐

WEEK TWENTY

Reading	Page	Scripture	Done
Dedication of the Temple	602	1 Kings 8:1-1	☐
Construction of Cities and Royal Palace	606	1 Kings 7:1-12	☐
Extent of Solomon's Glory	609	1 Kings 4:29-34	☐
Proverbs of Solomon	613		☐
The Book of Proverbs, Arranged Topically	614	Proverbs 8:1-36	☐
Proverbs of Solomon and Sayings of the Wise	619	Proverbs 22:17-21	☐
Preeminence of God			
Fear of the Lord	620	Proverbs 9:10-12	☐
Trust in God or Self	620	Proverbs 3:5-8	☐
Divine Providence	621	Proverbs 15:3; 16:1, 4, 9, 33	☐
Insight and Ignorance			
Wisdom and Folly	622	Proverbs 13:14; 14:24	☐
Dealing with Fools	622	Proverbs 26:4-11	☐
Discernment and Understanding	623	Proverbs 10:13, 23	☐
Knowledge	623	Proverbs 10:14; 13:16	☐
Sharing and Responding to Wisdom			
Advice and Rebuke	624	Proverbs 3:1-2; 9:7-9	☐
Value of Advisors	625	Proverbs 11:14	☐
Discipline	625	Proverbs 3:11-12	☐
Lawkeeping	626	Proverbs 28:4, 7	☐
Repentance	626	Proverbs 14:9	☐
Good and Evil			
Righteousness and Wickedness	627	Proverbs 10:6-7	☐
Integrity and Perversion	629	Proverbs 10:9; 13:6	☐
Appropriate Consequences	629	Proverbs 3:33-35	☐
Sincere Motivation			
Motive and the Heart	630	Proverbs 15:11; 16:2	☐
False Worship	631	Proverbs 15:8	☐
Duplicity	631	Proverbs 6:12-15	☐
Concern for Others			
Love and Faithfulness	632	Proverbs 3:3-4	☐
Love, Hatred and Compassion	632	Proverbs 10:12	☐
Kindness and Mercy	633	Proverbs 11:16-17	☐
Overstaying Welcome	633	Proverbs 25:16-17	☐

Concern for Self			
Pride and Humility	633	Proverbs 11:2; 12:9	☐
Selfishness	634	Proverbs 18:1	☐
Jealousy	634	Proverbs 27:4	☐
Envy	634	Proverbs 14:30; 24:19-20	☐
Greed	634	Proverbs 28:25	☐
Control of Self			
Self-Control	634	Proverbs 25:28; 29:11	☐
Rashness	634	Proverbs 20:25; 21:5	☐
Temper and Patience	635	Proverbs 12:16; 14:16-17	☐
Drunkenness and Gluttony	635	Proverbs 20:1	☐
Adultery	636	Proverbs 5:1-6	☐
Prostitution	639	Proverbs 23:26-28	☐

WEEK TWENTY-ONE

Control of the Tongue			
Wise and Foolish Talk	639	Proverbs 15:2, 7	☐
Righteous and Wicked Talk	640	Proverbs 10:20-21	☐
Appropriate Speech	640	Proverbs 15:23	☐
Maintaining Silence	640	Proverbs 10:19; 12:23	☐
Controlled Speech	641	Proverbs 15:1; 17:27	☐
Flattery	641	Proverbs 26:28	☐
Slander and Gossip	641	Proverbs 10:18; 11:13	☐
Hurtful Talk	641	Proverbs 11:12; 12:18	☐
Quarreling	642	Proverbs 17:14, 19	☐
Lying	642	Proverbs 12:19, 22	☐
Power of Tongue	642	Proverbs 18:20-21	☐
Disharmony and Strife			
Solicitation to Evil	643	Proverbs 1:10-19	☐
Violence	643	Proverbs 3:31-32	☐
Murderers	643	Proverbs 28:17	☐
Causing Others Harm	644	Proverbs 3:29-30	☐
Revenge	644	Proverbs 20:22	☐
Dissension and Strife	644	Proverbs 6:16-19	☐
Meddling	644	Proverbs 26:17	☐
Honesty			
Truthfulness	644	Proverbs 12:20	☐
Accurate Weights	645	Proverbs 11:1	☐
Boundary Stones	645	Proverbs 22:28	☐
Wrongfully Obtained Gains	645	Proverbs 10:2	☐
Bribery	645	Proverbs 15:27	☐
Justice			
False Witnesses	645	Proverbs 12:17	☐
Open-Mindedness	646	Proverbs 18:17	☐
Judicial Justice	646	Proverbs 17:15, 26	☐
Economic Well Being			
Wealth and Poverty	647	Proverbs 3:9-10	☐
Benevolence and Generosity	648	Proverbs 3:27-28	☐
Oppression of the Poor	649	Proverbs 13:23	☐
Conservation	651	Proverbs 21:20	☐
Surety for Another	651	Proverbs 6:1-5	☐

Week Twenty-Six

The Prophecies of Micah	803	Micah 1:1-16	☐
Early Beginnings of Captivity	813	2 Kings 15:29	☐
War Between Syria, Israel and Judah	814	2 Kings 15:37	☐
Isaiah Prophesies About a Savior	815	Isaiah 7:1-25	☐

Week Twenty-Seven

Isaiah Prophesies Against Nations	825	Isaiah 34:1-4	☐
More of Isaiah's Prophecies Against Nations	834	Isaiah 14:28-32	☐
The Reforms of Hezekiah	839	2 Chronicles 29:3-36	☐
Isaiah Tells of "Last Days"	844	Isaiah 24:1-23	☐
Isaiah Warns Against Relapse	850	Isaiah 28:1-15	☐
The Fall of Israel	859	2 Kings 17:3-5	☐

Week Twenty-Eight

Judah After Israel's Fall (Ca. 725-525 B.C.)

Isaiah Warns About Egypt and Ethiopia	863	Isaiah 18:1-7	☐
Last Years of Hezekiah's Reign	870	2 Kings 18:13-16	☐
Spiritual Decline Under Manasseh	877	2 Kings 20:21	☐
Isaiah's Prophecies About Restoration and the Messiah	878	Isaiah 40:1-31	☐

Week Twenty-Nine

Spiritual Renewal Under Manasseh	928	2 Kings 19:37	☐
Nahum's Prophecy Against Nineveh	929	Nahum 1:1-15	☐

Week Thirty

From Manasseh to Josiah	934	2 Kings 21:17-18	☐
Zephaniah Prophesies About the Day of the Lord	935	Zephaniah 1:1-18	☐
Josiah's Reforms	941	2 Chronicles 34:3-7	☐
Jeremiah the Weeping Prophet	941	Jeremiah 1:1-19	☐
Jeremiah Rebukes an Unfaithful Nation	943	Jeremiah 2:1-37	☐

Week Thirty-One

Jeremiah Rebukes an Unfaithful Nation	968	Jeremiah 13:1-27	☐
Effect of Jeremiah's Preaching	983	2 Kings 22:3-7	☐
Assyria Falls and Babylonia Emerges	987	2 Kings 23:29-37	☐
Jeremiah Faces Charges	989	Jeremiah 26:1-23	☐
Jeremiah's Judgment Against Egypt	991	Jeremiah 46:1-28	☐
Habakkuk's Questioning Prophecy	994	Habakkuk 1:1-12	☐

Week Thirty-Two

First Deportation from Judah	999	2 Kings 24:1	☐
Jeremiah Tells Length of Captivity	1000	Jeremiah 25:1-38	☐
Jehoiakim Burns Jeremiah's Scroll	1003	Jeremiah 36:1-4	☐
Daniel the Faithful Captive	1006	Daniel 1:3-20	☐
Nebuchadnezzar's Dream	1007	Daniel 2:1-49	☐
Jehoiakim's Last Years	1010	2 Kings 24:1-4	☐
The Great Deportation	1018	2 Kings 24:6, 8	☐
Reign of Zedekiah	1019	2 Kings 24:17, 18	☐
Jeremiah's Prophecies Under Zedekiah	1020	Jeremiah 24:1-10	☐

Week Thirty-Three

Ezekiel, Prophet in Exile	1038	Ezekiel 1:1-28	☐
Ezekiel's Denunciations of Judah	1045	Ezekiel 8:1-18	☐

Week Thirty-Four

Ezekiel's Denunciations of Judah (cont'd)	1067	Ezekiel 23:1-13	☐

Siege of Jerusalem	1070	2 Kings 24:20	☐
Siege Announced to Ezekiel	1070	Ezekiel 24:1-27	☐
Jeremiah's Prophecies During Siege	1072	Jeremiah 21:1-14	☐
Jeremiah Sees Spiritual Restoration Under Messiah	1082	Jeremiah 23:1-8	☐
Ezekiel's Prophecies During Siege	1085	Ezekiel 25:1-17	☐

WEEK THIRTY-FIVE

Jeremiah Escapes Death	1097	Jeremiah 37:3-21	☐
Fall of Jerusalem	1100	2 Kings 28:2-4	☐
Gedaliah and Jeremiah	1102	2 Kings 25:22	☐
Jeremiah's Lamentations	1103	Lamentations 1:1-22	☐
A Remnant Flees to Egypt	1115	2 Kings 25:23-24	☐

WEEK THIRTY-SIX

The Exiled Nation (Ca. 585-535 B.C.)

Ezekiel's Restoration Prophecies	1121	Ezekiel 33:21-33	☐
Shadrach, Meshach, and Abednego	1134	Daniel 3:1-30	☐
Ezekiel's Great Temple Vision	1136	Ezekiel 40:1-49	☐
End of Ezekiel's Ministry	1150	Ezekiel 29:17-21	☐

WEEK THIRTY-SEVEN

Nebuchadnezzar's Temporary Insanity	1151	Daniel 4:1-37	☐
End of Jeremiah's Ministry	1154	Jeremiah 52:31-34	☐
Job and the Problem of Suffering	1155	Job 1:1-22	☐

WEEK THIRTY-EIGHT

Job and the Problem of Suffering (cont'd)	1202	Job 38:1-41	☐
Psalms of a People in Exile	1209	Psalm 44, 74	☐
Daniel's Apocalyptic Visions	1221	Daniel 7:1-28	☐
The Writing on the Wall	1225	Daniel 5:1-31	☐
The Seventy "Sevens"	1227	Daniel 9:1-27	☐
Daniel in the Lion's Den	1230	Daniel 6:1-28	☐

Period of Restoration (Ca. 535-425 B.C.)

First Return to Jerusalem	1233	Ezra 1:1-11	☐

WEEK THIRTY-NINE

Daniel's Last Vision	1238	Daniel 10:1-20; 11:1-45	☐
Opposition to Temple's Construction	1243	Ezra 4:6-24	☐
Preaching of Haggai and Zechariah	1247	Haggai 1:1-15	☐
Zechariah's Visions	1250	Zechariah 1:7-21	☐
The Meaning of Restoration	1255	Zechariah 7:1-14	☐
Completion of the Temple	1257	Ezra 6:14-22	☐
Psalms of a Nation Restored	1258	Psalm 78	☐

WEEK FORTY

Zechariah's Futuristic Prophecies	1269	Zechariah 9:1-17	☐
Esther and the Feast of Purim	1276	Esther 1:1-22	☐
Prophecies of Malachi	1286	Malachi 1:2-14	☐
Ezra and the Second Return	1290	Ezra 7:1-28	☐
Problem of Intermarriage	1293	Ezra 9:1-15	☐

WEEK FORTY-ONE

Nehemiah Rebuilds the Wall	1297	Nehemiah 1:1-11	☐
Redistribution of Population	1304	Nehemiah 7:1-73	☐
Law and Covenant	1309	Nehemiah 8:1-18	☐
Nehemiah's Religious Reforms	1315	Nehemiah 13:4-31	☐
Dedication of the Wall	1317	Nehemiah 12:27-47	☐

Official Records of Israel	1318	1 Chronicles 1:1-54	☐

WEEK FORTY-TWO

Historical Interlude (Ca. 425-5 B.C.)

End of Old Testament Record	1337		☐
Writings of the Apocrypha	1339		☐
Influences on a Dispersed People	1343		☐
Hellenism and the Jews	1345		☐
Judaism Under Roman Rule	1346		☐

Jesus the Christ (Ca. 5 B.C. – A.D. 30)

The Coming of the Messiah	1349		☐
The Gospel Accounts	1350		☐
Introductions by the Gospel Writers	1351	Mark 1:1; John 1:1-18	☐
The Genealogies of Jesus	1353	Matthew 1:1-17	☐
The Births of Jesus and John the Baptist	1355	Luke 1:5-80	☐
Visit of the Magi and Flight into Egypt	1361	Matthew 2:1-18	☐
From Infancy to Manhood	1362	Matthew 2:19-23	☐

WEEK FORTY-THREE

The Ministry of John the Baptist	1364	Matthew 3:1-3	☐
Jesus Faces Temptations	1366	Matthew 4:1-11	☐
Jesus' Early Work in Judea, Samaria, and Galilee	1367	John 1:35-51	☐
Beginning of the Great Galilean Ministry	1373	Matthew 4:12-17	☐
The Rise of Opposition	1376	Matthew 9:9	☐
The Sermon on the Mount	1381	Matthew 5:1-12	☐
The Ministry Continues	1386	Matthew 8:5-13	☐

WEEK FORTY-FOUR

Teaching Through Parables	1394	Matthew 13:1-43	☐
Performing Miracles	1397	Matthew 8:18-22	☐
Sending Out Apostles	1400	Matthew 9:35-38	☐
Miracles and Multitudes	1403	Matthew 14:14	☐
Extensive Tour Throughout Galilee	1408	Matthew 15:21-39	☐
Preparation of Apostles for the End	1410	Matthew 16:13-28	☐

WEEK FORTY-FIVE

In Jerusalem for Feast of Tabernacles	1415	John 7:2-53	☐
Ministry from Galilee to Judea	1422	Matthew 19:1-2	☐
In Jerusalem for Feast of Dedication	1426	John 10:22-42	☐
The Perean Ministry	1427	Luke 13:22-35	☐
Return to Judea to Raise Lazarus	1433	John 11:1-54	☐
The Final Journey	1435	Matthew 19:3-30	☐
The Triumphant Entry—Sunday	1440	John 12:12-13	☐
Final Week—Monday	1442	Matthew 21:18-19	☐
Final Week—Tuesday Morning	1443	Matthew 21:20-22	☐

WEEK FORTY-SIX

Discourse on Future Events	1449	Matthew 24:1-51	☐
Final Week—Tuesday Afternoon	1453	Matthew 26:1-16	☐
Final Week—Wednesday	1454	Luke 21:37-38	☐
The Upper Room	1457	Luke 22:14-30	☐
Final Discourse	1462	John 15:1-18	☐
Betrayal and Arrest	1465	Matthew 26:36-56	☐
Trial Before Sanhedrin	1467	John 18:12-23	☐
Trial Before Pilate	1470	Matthew 27:2-32	☐
The Crucifixion of Jesus	1473	Matthew 27:33-56	☐
The Burial of Jesus	1476	Matthew 27:57-66	☐

WEEK FORTY-SEVEN

Jesus' Resurrection and Appearances	1477	Matthew 28:2-15	☐
Final Instructions and Ascension	1482	Matthew 28:16-20	☐
Conclusion to the Gospel Accounts	1484	John 20:30-31; 21:25	☐

Christ's Church and the Apostles (Ca. A.D. 30-100)

Acts of the Apostles	1485	Acts 1:1-5	☐
Power of the Holy Spirit	1485	Acts 2:1-47	☐
Growth of the Early Church	1488	Acts 3:1-26	☐
Martyrdom of Stephen	1493	Acts 6:8-15; 7:1-54	☐
Persecution and Preaching	1496	Acts 8:1-40	☐
Conversion of Saul	1499	Acts 9:1-31	☐
First Gentile Converts	1500	Acts 9:32-43	☐
Persecution by Herod Agrippa I	1505	Acts 12:1-25	☐
First Missionary Journey	1506	Acts 13:1-52	☐
The Jerusalem Conference	1510	Acts 15:1-35	☐

WEEK FORTY-EIGHT

Letter to the Galatians	1513	Galatians 1:1-24	☐
Second Missionary Journey	1519	Acts 15:36-41; 16:1-40	☐
First Letter to the Thessalonians	1524	1 Thessalonians 1:1-10	☐
Second Letter to the Thessalonians	1527	2 Thessalonians 1:1-12	☐
Third Missionary Journey	1530	Acts 18:23-28	☐
First Letter to the Corinthians	1531	1 Corinthians 1:1-31	☐

WEEK FORTY-NINE

Second Letter to the Corinthians	1550	2 Corinthians 1:1-23	☐
Letter to the Romans	1561	Romans 1:1-32	☐

WEEK FIFTY

Paul's Arrest and Trial	1583	Acts 21:17-40	☐
Paul Before Felix, Festus, and Agrippa	1587	Acts 24:1-27	☐
Voyage to Rome	1592	Acts 27:1-44	☐
House Arrest in Rome	1592	Acts 28:16-31	☐
Letter to the Colossians	1595	Colossians 1:1-29	☐
Letter to Philemon	1600	Philemon 1:1-25	☐
Letter to the Ephesians	1601	Ephesians 1:1-23	☐
Letter to the Philippians	1608	Philippians 1:1-27	☐

WEEK FIFTY-ONE

First Letter to Timothy	1613	1 Timothy 1:1-20	☐
Letter to Titus	1618	Titus 1:1-10	☐
Second Letter to Timothy	1620	2 Timothy 1:1-18	☐
Letter by James	1624	James 1:1-27	☐
Letter by Jude	1629	Jude 1-25	☐
First Letter by Peter	1631	1 Peter 1:1-25	☐
Second Letter by Peter	1636	2 Peter 1:1-21	☐

WEEK FIFTY-TWO

Letter to the Hebrews	1640	Hebrews 1:1-14	☐
First Letter by John	1656	1 John 1:1-10	☐
Second Letter by John	1661	2 John 1-13	☐
Third Letter by John	1662	3 John 1-14	☐
The Revelation to John	1663	Revelation 1:1-20	☐

CHAPTER 11

CHARACTER EVALUATION

ERECTING THE BUILDING

It may be difficult, at first, reexamining our beliefs and attitudes about education. It is essential that we compare our educational goals to God's Word. Education affects every area of human experience. The way we see our world, the values we hold important, the skills we feel are necessary, our opinions of the past, present, and future—all are clearly affected by our education and our educational philosophies. Education is a process of forming one for life.

We can teach a child self-control by using external force until the child ultimately learns his own self-control by using his internal force. We can also teach a child to yield himself to God by giving up fleshly desires.

I beseech you therefore, brethren, by the mercies of God, that ye present your bodies a living sacrifice, holy, acceptable unto God, which is your reasonable service. And be not conformed to this world: but be ye transformed by the renewing of your mind, that ye may prove what is that good, and acceptable, and perfect, will of God. (Romans 12:1-2).

All the virtues and holy tempers of Christianity are not ours unless they become the virtues and tempers of our ordinary life. In that Christianity is so far from leaving us to live in the common ways of life, conforming to the folly of customs, and gratifying the passions and tempers which the spirit of the world delights in, it is equally as far from indulging us in any of these things. Its virtues, which it makes necessary to salvation are only so many ways of living above and contrary to the world, in all the common actions of our life. If our common life is not a common course of humility, self-denial, renunciation of the world, poverty of spirit, and heavenly affection, we do not live the lives of Christians.

This story on the next page is an illustration that morals and values according to God's Word are far superior to the state's intellectual wisdom.

Hiring A Qualified Employee

You are the owner of a bakery store and you need to hire a manager. You have two people to choose from. Whom would you hire?

1. An expert baker with no morals and values.
2. An inexperienced person with godly morals and values.

Yes, it would be nice to hire an experienced baker with morals and values, but a number 3 is not available. Let's look at what could happen, over a period of time, if you hired number 1 as opposed to number 2.

Months 1-3

Hiring number 1 would give you a jump-start in business. The expert baker could already plan recipes, bake, keep records, take care of all ordering and deliveries, deliver products on time, and answer customers' questions. How wonderful for you. You are able to leave the store and attend to other business with the security of knowing your new manager can take care of any problem. You are thinking of opening a second bakery.

Hiring number 2 will require you to be present in the store to train your new employee. You will have to train him to follow all policies and procedures, to bake, keep records, take care of all ordering and deliveries, deliver products on time, and answer questions. Mistakes may be made and orders may be late. You may even encounter some angry customers who will not return. You cannot leave the store because the new employee may need you to handle a problem he has not encountered.

Month 4

Number 1 continues to produce good products, although he calls in sick frequently. You start questioning some of the record keeping. When you ask number 1 about any problem, the replies seem inconsistent with accounts he is recording. Number 1 wants to do things his way, and you are aggravated because you want business handled differently. Two customers have complained about receiving the wrong change. You start staying at the store more because things just seem strange. You start praying for wisdom to handle this situation.

Number 2 learns well. He is caring, has been very diligent, prompt, industrious, and hardworking in all areas. You can now leave the store and only call to check on things. Once in a while he makes a minor mistake but is willing to learn from mistakes and is very respectful.

Month 10

Your accountant calls to tell you that you are $xxxx in the red. You look over the records and realize number 1 has been fixing the records and probably skimming from the register. Number 1 has also been flirting with one of the female customers and she is suing your business for sexual harassment. You have lost all profits made for the entire year.

Number 2 is handling business just the way you like things done. You are able to leave the store and attend to other business with the security of knowing your new manager can take care of any problem. The food is great and word of mouth about your bakery spreads. Business prospers and expands. You are thinking of opening a second bakery.

That may be an exaggerated account, but it is very possible. The point is, if you hire someone you can trust you can always train him or her. If he or she is a Christian, striving to follow God's will, your employee should be diligent, honest, and respectful. Academic skills are secondary. There are thousands of workers like our number 1, but very few of the dependable kind of workers like the story's number 2.

Character Traits

TRAIT WORD	DEFINITION	SCRIPTURE REFERENCE
APPRECIATIVE:	Expressing in words, actions, and thoughts, value to the actions of God and others the ways they have served me.	1 Thessalonians 5:18—*In every thing give thanks: for this is the will of God in Christ Jesus concerning you.*
ATTENTIVE:	Being intent; observant; regarding a situation or person with care. When a person is attentive to the words, the manner and matter of a speaker at the same time. Demonstrating that the person is worthy by giving genuine attention and consideration to God's Word or a person's words.	Hebrews 2:1—*Therefore we ought to give the more earnest heed to the things which we have heard, lest at any time we should let them slip.*
AVAILABLE:	Being accessible for others. Scheduling priorities to serve others in need.	Matthew 9:9—*And as Jesus passed forth from thence, he saw a man, named Matthew, sitting at the receipt of custom: and he saith unto him, Follow me. And he arose, and followed him.*
COMMITTED:	To give in trust; to put into the hands or power of another.	2 Timothy 2—*The things thou hast heard of me, commit to faithful men.* Psalms 37:5 *Commit thy way unto the LORD; trust also in him; and he shall bring it to pass.*
COMPASSIONATE:	Giving of love and sorrow; at least some portion of love generally attends the pain or regret, to meet another's needs without experiencing anything in return.	Psalms 78—*He being full of compassion, forgave their iniquity.* Luke 15 *His father had compassion, and ran, and fell on his neck, and kissed him.* 1 Peter 3:8 *Finally, be ye all of one mind, having compassion one of another, love as brethren, be pitiful, be courteous:*
CONCERNED:	Regarding another with care. Bearing one another's burdens with tenderness and respect.	Galatians 6:2—*Bear ye one another's burdens, and so fulfill the law of Christ.*
CONFIDENT:	Having trust that whatever I say or do will benefit me and others.	Philippians 4:13—*I can do all things through Christ which strengtheneth me.*
CONSIDERATE:	Being thoughtful of others and their feelings.	Philippians 2:4—*Look not every man on his own things, but every man also on the things of others.*
CONSISTENT:	Being fixed or firm in mind, purpose, affection or principle; unshaken; unmoved. Being certain; steady; firm and adherent to God's principles. diligent to purpose, or to duties.	1 Corinthians 15:58—*Therefore, my beloved brethren, be ye steadfast, unmoveable, always abounding in the work of the Lord, forasmuch as ye know that your labour is not in vain in the Lord.*
CONTENT:	Having rest or quietness of mind in the present condition; satisfaction which holds the mind in peace. Not having opposition, or further desire. Implying a degree of happiness in all situations because God will provide all our needs.	Philippians 4:11—*Not that I speak in respect of want: for I have learned, in whatsoever state I am, therewith to be content.* 1 Timothy 6 *Having food and raiment, let us be therewith content.*

Character Traits

Trait Word	Definition	Scripture Reference
Cooperative:	Working with other Christians in harmony. Note: This is far different from what the state calls cooperation.	Psalms 33:1— *Behold, how good and how pleasant it is for brethren to dwell together in unity!*
Courageous:	Realizing God is giving us strength to endure any trial or danger. Being brave; having that quality of mind which enables men to encounter danger and difficulties with firmness, boldness; and resolution. Courage arises from a sense of duty, acts in a uniform manner.	Deuteronomy 31:6—*Be strong and of good courage, fear not, nor be afraid of them: for the LORD thy God, he it is that doth go with thee; he will not fail thee, nor forsake thee.*
Creative:	Being able to perform a necessity or task from a different point of view.	Romans 12:2—*And be not conformed to this world: but be ye transformed by the renewing of your mind, that ye may prove what is that good, and acceptable, and perfect, will of God.*
Decisive:	Having the quality of determining a subject of deliberation or putting an end to a controversy by relying on the perfect will of God.	Joshua 24:15—*And if it seem evil unto you to serve the LORD, choose you this day whom ye will serve; whether the gods which your fathers served that were on the other side of the flood, or the gods of the Amorites, in whose land ye dwell: but as for me and my house, we will serve the LORD.*
Dependable	Being worthy of trust, to the point someone can depend on you. Doing what I said I would do even if it means self-denial. We depend on God for existence; we depend on air for respiration; vegetation depends on heat and moisture; the peace of society depends on good laws and a faithful administration.	1 Timothy 6:20—*O Timothy, keep that which is committed to thy trust, avoiding profane and vain babblings, and oppositions of science falsely so called....*
Determined:	Having a firm or fixed purpose, as a determined man; or manifesting a firm resolution, to accomplish God's will.	1 Corinthians 2:2—*For I determined not to know any thing among you, save Jesus Christ, and him crucified.*
Diligent:	Not just a trait—a command from God. Steady in application to business; not careless; constant in effort or exertion to accomplish what is undertaken; industrious; not idle or negligent; applied to persons.	Deuteronomy 6:17—*Ye shall diligently keep the commandments of the Lord your God.* Proverbs 22:29–*Seest thou a man diligent in his business? He shall stand before kings.* Colossians 3:23—*And whatsoever ye do, do it heartily, as to the Lord, and not unto men;*
Discerning:	Having power to discern; capable of seeing, discriminating, knowing and judging a difficult situation and being able to make an accurate judgment.	Ezekiel 44:23—*And they shall teach my people the difference between the holy and profane, and cause them to discern between the unclean and the clean.*
Discreet	Prudent; wise in avoiding errors or evil, and in selecting the best means to accomplish a purpose; circumspect; cautious. It is the dis-	Genesis 41:33—*Let Pharaoh look out a man discreet and wise.* Psalms 112:5—*A good man showeth*

Character Traits

TRAIT WORD	DEFINITION	SCRIPTURE REFERENCE
	creet man, not the witty, nor the learned, nor the brave, who guides the conversation, and gives measures to society.	*favour, and lendeth: he will guide his affairs with discretion.*
EFFICIENT:	Causing effects or producing; The efficient cause is that which produces; the final cause is that for which it is produced. Preparing yourself to accomplish the greatest productiveness.	Ephesians 5:16—*Redeeming the time, because the days are evil.*
EQUITABLE:	Being equal in regard to the rights of others; distributing equal justice; giving each his due; being just and impartial according to God's law.	Proverbs 1:3—*To receive the instruction of wisdom, justice, and judgment, and equity.*
FAIR:	Honest; honorable; mild; opposed to insidious and compulsory actions. To be able to accomplish a thing by looking at everyone's side.	Matthew 7:12—*Therefore all things whatsoever ye would that men should do to you, do ye even so to them: for this is the law and the prophets.*
FAITHFUL:	Firmly adhering to duty; of true fidelity; loyal; true to allegiance; as a faithful subject. Being constant in the performance of duties or services and attending to commands of authority.	1 Corinthians 4:2—*Moreover it is required in stewards, that a man be found faithful.*
FEARLESS:	Facing danger boldly and with determination, for God gave us a spirit of power.	2 Timothy 1:7—*For God hath not given us the spirit of fear; but of power, and of love, and of a sound mind.*
FLEXIBLE:	Setting affections on things above, not on earthly things that can be changed by others.	Colossians 3:2—*Set your affection on things above, not on things on the earth.*
FORGIVING:	Overlooking one another's faults by means of expressing to them Christ's love (responding as if there were no faults)	Colossians 3:13—*Forbearing one another, and forgiving one another, if any man have a quarrel against any: even as Christ forgave you, so also do ye.*
FORTITUDE:	Having the strength or firmness of mind or soul which enables a person to encounter danger with coolness and courage, or to bear pain or adversity without murmuring, depression or despondency. Fortitude is the basis or source of genuine courage or intrepidity in danger, of patience in suffering, of forbearance under injuries, and of magnanimity in all conditions of life. Having patience to bear continued suffering.	Proverbs 18:24—*A man that hath friends must show himself friendly: and there is a friend that sticketh closer than a brother.*
FRIENDLY:	Having the temper and disposition of a friend; kind; favorable; disposed to promoting the good of another. Thou to mankind be good and friendly still, and oft return.	Acts 20:35—*I have showed you all things, how that so labouring ye ought to support the weak, and to remember the words of the Lord Jesus, how he said, It is more blessed to give than to receive.*

Character Traits

TRAIT WORD	DEFINITION	SCRIPTURE REFERENCE
GENTLE:	Liberal; bountiful; munificent; free to give; as a generous friend; a generous father.	2 Timothy 2:24—*And the servant of the Lord must not strive; but be gentle unto all men, apt to teach, patient,*
HONEST:	Mild; meek; soft; bland; not rough, harsh or severe; as a gentle nature, temper or disposition; a gentle manner; a gentle address; a gentle voice.	2 Corinthians 8:21—*Providing for honest things, not only in the sight of the Lord, but also in the sight of men.*
HUMBLE:	Upright; just; fair in dealing with others; free from trickiness and fraud; acting and having the disposition to act at all times according to justice or correct moral principles; applied to persons.	James 4—*God resisteth the proud, but giveth grace to the humble.* 1 Peter 5:5-6—*Likewise, ye younger, submit yourselves unto the elder. Yea, all of you be subject one to another, and be clothed with humility: for God resisteth the proud, and giveth grace to the humble. Humble yourselves therefore under the mighty hand of God, that he may exalt you in due time:*
JOYFUL:	Modest; meek; submissive; opposed to proud, haughty, arrogant or assuming. In an evangelical sense, having a low opinion of one's self, and a deep sense of unworthiness in the sight of God.	Ephesians 5:19—*Speaking to yourselves in psalms and hymns and spiritual songs, singing and making melody in your heart to the Lord;*
KIND:	Full of joy; very glad; exulting.	Ephesians 4:32—*And be ye kind one to another, tenderhearted, forgiving one another, even as God for Christ's sake hath forgiven you.*
LOYAL:	Disposed to do good to others, and to make them happy by granting their requests, supplying their wants or assisting them in distress; having tenderness or goodness of nature; benevolent; benignant.	John 15:13—*Greater love hath no man than this, that a man lay down his life for his friends.*
MEEK:	Faithful to a friend or superior; true to plighted faith, duty or love; not treacherous; used of subjects to their king, and of husband, wife, children.	Numbers 12:3—*Now the man Moses was very meek, above all men.* Matthew 11:29—Christ says, "*Learn of me, for I am meek and lowly in heart, and ye shall find rest to your souls.*" Matthew 5:5—*Blessed are the meek, for they shall inherit the earth…*
MERCIFUL:	Mild of temper; soft; gentle; not easily provoked or irritated; yielding; given to forbearance under injuries. Appropriately, humble, in an evangelical sense; submissive to the divine will; not proud, self-sufficient or refractory; not peevish and apt to complain.	Exodus 34:6—*The Lord passed before him and proclaimed, the Lord, the Lord God, merciful and gracious, long-suffering and abundant in goodness and truth.* Luke 6:36—*Be ye therefore merciful, as your Father also is merciful.*
OBSERVANT:	Compassionate; tender; disposed to pity offenders and to forgive their offenses; unwilling to punish for injuries; applied appropriately to the Supreme being.	Mark 14:38—*Watch ye and pray, lest ye enter into temptation. The spirit truly is ready, but the flesh is weak.*

Character Traits

TRAIT WORD	DEFINITION	SCRIPTURE REFERENCE
OPTIMISTIC:	Taking notice; attentively viewing or noticing; as an observant spectator or traveler. Obedient; adhering to in practice; with of. i.e. He is very observant of the rules of his order.	Romans 8:25—*But if we hope for that we see not, then do we with patience wait for it.*
PATIENT:	Concentrating on the best conditions of any situation.	Hebrews 12:1—*Wherefore seeing we also are compassed about with so great a cloud of witnesses, let us lay aside every weight, and the sin which doth so easily beset us, and let us run with patience the race that is set before us,*
PEACEFUL:	Having the quality of enduring evils without murmuring or fretfulness; sustaining afflictions of body or mind with fortitude, calmness or Christian submission to the divine will; as a patient person, or a person of patient temper.	John 16:33—*These things I have spoken unto you, that in me ye might have peace. In the world ye shall have tribulation: but be of good cheer; I have overcome the world.*
PERSEVERANT:	Quiet; undisturbed; not in a state of commotion; mild; calm; as peaceful words; a peaceful temper.	Galatians 6:9—*And let us not be weary in well doing: for in due season we shall reap, if we faint not.*
PLEASING:	Persistence in any thing undertaken; continued pursuit or prosecution of business or enterprise begun.	1 Corinthians 10:33—*Even as I please all men in all things, not seeking mine own profit, but the profit of many, that they may be saved.*
PRUDENT:	One that pleases or gratifies; one that courts favor by humoring or flattering compliance or a show of obedience.	Proverbs 14:15—*The simple believeth every word: but the prudent man looketh well to his going.*
PUNCTUAL:	Cautious; circumspect; practically wise; careful of the consequences of enterprises, measures or actions.	Ecclesiastes 3:1—*To every thing there is a season, and a time to every purpose under the heaven:*
PURPOSEFUL:	Having scrupulous regard to time, appointments, promises or rules; as, to attend a meeting punctually; to pay debts or rent punctually; to observe punctually one's engagements.	Psalms 119:2—*Blessed are they that keep his testimonies, and that seek him with the whole heart.*
RESOURCEFUL:	By design; intentionally; with predetermination.	1 Thessalonians 4:11—*And that ye study to be quiet, and to do your own business, and to work with your own hands, as we commanded you...*
RESPECTFUL:	Efficient and willing to take upon oneself projects that others may overlook.	1 Thessalonians 5:12-13—*And we beseech you, brethren, to know them which labour among you, and are over you in the Lord, and admonish you; And to esteem them very highly in love for their work's sake. And be at peace among yourselves.*
RESPONSIBLE:	To view or consider others with a degree of	Romans 14:12—*So then every one of us*

Character Traits

TRAIT WORD	DEFINITION	SCRIPTURE REFERENCE
	reverence; to esteem as possessed of worth.	*shall give account of himself to God.*
SECURE:	Governed by reason; being under the influence of reason; thinking, speaking or acting rationally or according to the dictates of reason.	Job 11:18—*And thou shalt be secure, because there is hope; yea, thou shalt dig about thee, and thou shalt take thy rest in safety.*
SELF-CONTROLLED:	Confident; not distrustful, having faith in God that He will work all things to His glory.	(Galatians 5:24-25) Proverbs 25:28—*He that hath no rule over his own spirit is like a city that is broken down, and without walls.*
SINCERE:	To check; to restrain; to govern ones tongue, deeds and actions. Having instant obedience to the Holy Spirit, developed through outward discipline.	Joshua 24:14—*Now therefore fear the LORD, and serve him in sincerity and in truth: and put away the gods which your fathers served on the other side of the flood, and in Egypt; and serve ye the LORD.*
SUBMISSIVE:	Honestly; with real purity of heart; without simulation or disguise.	Hebrews 13:17—*Obey them that have the rule over you, and submit yourselves: for they watch for your souls, as they that must give account, that they may do it with joy, and not with grief: for that is unprofitable for you.*
TACTFUL:	Cheerfully yielding to the will or power of another; obedient.	Colossians 4:6—*Let your speech be alway with grace, seasoned with salt, that ye may know how ye ought to answer every man.*
THRIFTY:	Saying and doing the right things with concern for other's feelings.	Proverbs 21:20 *There is treasure to be desired and oil in the dwelling of the wise; but a foolish man spendeth it up.*
TOLERANT:	Frugal; sparing; using economy and good management of property.	Romans 14:13—*Let us not therefore judge one another any more: but judge this rather, that no man put a stumbling block or an occasion to fall in his brother's way.*
TRUTHFUL:	Enduring; accepting others and willing to endure.	Ephesians 4:25—*Wherefore putting away lying, speak every man truth with his neighbor: for we are members one of another.*
VIRTUOUS:	Earned trust by reporting facts accurately. Morally good; abstaining from vice.	Philippians 4:8—*Finally, brethren, whatsoever things are true, whatsoever things are honest, whatsoever things are just, whatsoever things are pure, whatsoever things are lovely, whatsoever things are of good report; if there be any virtue, and if there be any praise, think on these things.*

Let no man despise thy youth; but be thou an example of the believers,
in the word, in conversation, in charity, in spirit, in faith, in purity.
Till I come, give attendance to reading, to exhortation, to doctrine.

1 TIMOTHY 4:12-13 (KJV)

LANGUAGE ARTS

Language Mechanics • Language Expression • Spelling • Study Skills • Reading

EVALUATION CHECK LIST FOR
KINDERGARTEN
LANGUAGE ARTS

Kindergarten students should be able to do the following:	CHILD'S NAME	CHILD'S NAME	CHILD'S NAME	CHILD'S NAME	CHILD'S NAME
Develop skill in gross motor functioning.	☐	☐	☐	☐	☐
Develop fine motor functioning.	☐	☐	☐	☐	☐
Develop hand-eye coordination.	☐	☐	☐	☐	☐
Recognize likenesses and differences of objects and pictures.	☐	☐	☐	☐	☐
Group objects and pictures into categories.	☐	☐	☐	☐	☐
Develop skill in auditory discrimination.	☐	☐	☐	☐	☐
Follow progression such as left-to-right, top-to-bottom and front-to-back.	☐	☐	☐	☐	☐
Position papers properly and hold a crayon or pencil correctly.	☐	☐	☐	☐	☐
Demonstrate basic handwriting strokes.	☐	☐	☐	☐	☐
Print own first name	☐	☐	☐	☐	☐
Recognize name when printed	☐	☐	☐	☐	☐
Recognize and name letters of the alphabet.	☐	☐	☐	☐	☐
Discriminate and identify upper-case and lower-case letters	☐	☐	☐	☐	☐
Speak in complete sentences, most of the time.	☐	☐	☐	☐	☐
Complete sentences using context clues.	☐	☐	☐	☐	☐
Verbalize own experiences, needs, and wants.	☐	☐	☐	☐	☐
Make and describe observations.	☐	☐	☐	☐	☐
Ask questions.	☐	☐	☐	☐	☐
Describe the contents of a picture.	☐	☐	☐	☐	☐
Listen to a five-to ten-minute story.	☐	☐	☐	☐	☐
Retell a story.	☐	☐	☐	☐	☐
Listen to answer questions, predict an event or outcome, find the main idea or identify sequence.	☐	☐	☐	☐	☐
Repeat verses from memory.	☐	☐	☐	☐	☐

EVALUATION CHECK LIST FOR

KINDERGARTEN

LANGUAGE ARTS

	CHILD'S NAME	CHILD'S NAME	CHILD'S NAME	CHILD'S NAME	CHILD'S NAME
Use vocabulary necessary to describe self.	☐	☐	☐	☐	☐
Recognize rhyme, rhythm, and repetition in spoken words or literature.	☐	☐	☐	☐	☐
Identify colors.	☐	☐	☐	☐	☐
Name common objects.	☐	☐	☐	☐	☐
Speak clearly, properly, and politely.	☐	☐	☐	☐	☐

Evaluation Check List for

First Grade

Language Arts

First-grade students should be able to do the following:

	Child's Name	Child's Name	Child's Name	Child's Name	Child's Name
Language Mechanics and Expression					
Alphabetize words through the first letter.	☐	☐	☐	☐	☐
Identify correct capitalization of the pronoun "I."	☐	☐	☐	☐	☐
Recognize letters of the alphabet and the sounds they represent.	☐	☐	☐	☐	☐
Hold a pencil correctly, position the paper appropriately for left-or right-handedness, and sit in the correct writing position.	☐	☐	☐	☐	☐
Form all letters in manuscript, both upper and lower case.	☐	☐	☐	☐	☐
Print own name correctly.	☐	☐	☐	☐	☐
Copy simple sentences and/or short paragraphs.	☐	☐	☐	☐	☐
Use proper spacing between letters of a word and words of a sentence.	☐	☐	☐	☐	☐
Identify correct capitalization of the first word of a sentence.	☐	☐	☐	☐	☐
Identify the correct use of periods.	☐	☐	☐	☐	☐
Identify the correct use of question marks.	☐	☐	☐	☐	☐
Identify complete telling sentences.	☐	☐	☐	☐	☐
Identify complete asking sentences.	☐	☐	☐	☐	☐
Spelling					
Spell words in isolation and in sentence dictation.	☐	☐	☐	☐	☐
Identify letter-sound associations for single initial consonants (excluding q and x).	☐	☐	☐	☐	☐

EVALUATION CHECK LIST FOR
FIRST GRADE
LANGUAGE ARTS

	CHILD'S NAME	CHILD'S NAME	CHILD'S NAME	CHILD'S NAME	CHILD'S NAME
Substitute initial consonants to form new words with the known word families (*-at, -ed, -it, -in, -ill, -ake, -ate, -an, -ax, -en, and -ing*).	☐	☐	☐	☐	☐
Identify letter-sound associations for single final consonants.	☐	☐	☐	☐	☐
Identify letter-sound associations for initial consonant digraphs (*ch*, *sh*, and "voiceless" *th*).	☐	☐	☐	☐	☐
Identify letter-sound associations for final consonant digraphs (*ch*, *sh*, *ck*).	☐	☐	☐	☐	☐
Identify letter-sound associations for initial consonant blends (consonant + *i* and consonant + *r* blends).	☐	☐	☐	☐	☐
Identify letter-sound associations for final consonant blends (*st*, *sk*).	☐	☐	☐	☐	☐
Identify plural noun endings.	☐	☐	☐	☐	☐
Identify letter-sound associations for short vowels.	☐	☐	☐	☐	☐
Identify letter-sound associations for long vowels.	☐	☐	☐	☐	☐
Blend sounds together to form simple words.	☐	☐	☐	☐	☐
Recognize sight words.	☐	☐	☐	☐	☐
STUDY SKILLS					
Demonstrate the ability to alphabetize words with different first letters	☐	☐	☐	☐	☐
LISTENING AND COMPREHENSION					
Listen and respond to directions	☐	☐	☐	☐	☐
Listen for the purpose of answering simple questions.	☐	☐	☐	☐	☐
Listen to identify words that rhyme.	☐	☐	☐	☐	☐

Evaluation Check List for
First Grade
Language Arts

	Child's Name	Child's Name	Child's Name	Child's Name	Child's Name
Listen for the purpose of distinguishing like and unlike sounds.	☐	☐	☐	☐	☐
Listen to simple stories and retell in sequence.	☐	☐	☐	☐	☐
Use correct pronunciation in oral reading (period, question mark, comma and exclamation point).	☐	☐	☐	☐	☐
Use correct phrasing in oral reading.	☐	☐	☐	☐	☐
Recall what has been read silently or aloud.	☐	☐	☐	☐	☐
Participate in dramatization projects.	☐	☐	☐	☐	☐
Use details to identify story elements.	☐	☐	☐	☐	☐
Sequence events from a selection.	☐	☐	☐	☐	☐
Draw conclusions from given facts.	☐	☐	☐	☐	☐
Recognize words or phrases that tell who, what, when, where, why, or how.	☐	☐	☐	☐	☐
Answer simple questions after listening to a reading selection.	☐	☐	☐	☐	☐
Participate in a discussion by making relevant contribution to a specific topic.	☐	☐	☐	☐	☐
Communicate thoughts and feelings orally.	☐	☐	☐	☐	☐
Pronounce the basic 220 Dolch sight words.	☐	☐	☐	☐	☐

Evaluation Check List for

Second Grade

Language Arts

Second-grade students should be able to do the following:	Child's Name	Child's Name	Child's Name	Child's Name	Child's Name
Language Mechanics and Expression					
Print legibly and neatly.	☐	☐	☐	☐	☐
Copy simple sentences using proper spacing between words within words and between sentences.	☐	☐	☐	☐	☐
Write simple sentences from dictation.	☐	☐	☐	☐	☐
Arrange words in logical order to form sentences.	☐	☐	☐	☐	☐
Identify correct capitalization of the first word of a sentence.	☐	☐	☐	☐	☐
Identify correct capitalization of the pronoun "I."	☐	☐	☐	☐	☐
Identify correct capitalization of proper nouns.	☐	☐	☐	☐	☐
Identify correct use of periods.	☐	☐	☐	☐	☐
Identify correct use of question marks.	☐	☐	☐	☐	☐
Identify complete telling sentences.	☐	☐	☐	☐	☐
Identify complete asking sentences.	☐	☐	☐	☐	☐
Identify common and proper nouns.	☐	☐	☐	☐	☐
Identify the two parts of a simple sentence.	☐	☐	☐	☐	☐
Verbalize own experiences, needs, and wants.	☐	☐	☐	☐	☐
Speak in complete and connected sentences.	☐	☐	☐	☐	☐
Use appropriate manner of speaking and control of voice in a given situation.	☐	☐	☐	☐	☐
Participate in conversation and discussion.	☐	☐	☐	☐	☐
Spelling					
Spell words in isolation and from sentence dictation.	☐	☐	☐	☐	☐
Identify and complete rhymes.	☐	☐	☐	☐	☐

Evaluation Check List for

Second Grade

Language Arts

	Child's Name	Child's Name	Child's Name	Child's Name	Child's Name
Identify correctly spelled words.	☐	☐	☐	☐	☐
Identify and form compound words.	☐	☐	☐	☐	☐
Identify the base words in those formed with the following endings: *-s, -es, -d, -ed, -ing, -ly, -er, -est.*	☐	☐	☐	☐	☐
Divide words into syllables using the *VC/CV* rule.	☐	☐	☐	☐	☐
Recognize sight words.	☐	☐	☐	☐	☐
Identify contractions.	☐	☐	☐	☐	☐
Identify letter-sound associations for consonants in the medial position.	☐	☐	☐	☐	☐
Identify letter-sound associations for initial consonant blends.	☐	☐	☐	☐	☐
Identify letter-sound associations for final consonant blends.	☐	☐	☐	☐	☐
Recognize letter-sound associations for consonant digraphs (*ch, sh, wh, th, ck, ng, nk*).	☐	☐	☐	☐	☐
Recognize letter-sound associations for long vowels.	☐	☐	☐	☐	☐
Recognize letter-sound associations for vowel digraphs.	☐	☐	☐	☐	☐
Identify letter-sound associations for short vowels.	☐	☐	☐	☐	☐
Use spelling patterns as clues to vowel sounds associated with the following rules.	☐	☐	☐	☐	☐
A word with a single vowel is usually short (*cap, hop, cup*).	☐	☐	☐	☐	☐
An *e* at the end of a one-syllable word usually makes the preceding vowel long (like, hope, make). If two vowels are together in a one-syllable word, the first is usually long and the second is silent (*goat, keep, pie*).	☐	☐	☐	☐	☐

EVALUATION CHECK LIST FOR

SECOND GRADE

LANGUAGE ARTS

	CHILD'S NAME	CHILD'S NAME	CHILD'S NAME	CHILD'S NAME	CHILD'S NAME
Vowels followed by an *r* in one-syllable words are pronounced as *ar* and *er* (*her*, *first*, *fur*, *car* and *horn*).	☐	☐	☐	☐	☐
Identify word pairs that are synonyms, antonyms, and homonyms.	☐	☐	☐	☐	☐
STUDY SKILLS					
Perform a task by following simple, oral directions.	☐	☐	☐	☐	☐
Alphabetize words through the second letter.	☐	☐	☐	☐	☐
Use a primary picture dictionary.	☐	☐	☐	☐	☐
Group words and objects into categories.	☐	☐	☐	☐	☐
LISTENING AND COMPREHENSION					
Select a title for a selection.	☐	☐	☐	☐	☐
Read to find the answer to a specific question.	☐	☐	☐	☐	☐
Read to verify a statement.	☐	☐	☐	☐	☐
Read silently to answer specific questions and/or gain information.	☐	☐	☐	☐	☐
Read selected material to:					
predict outcomes.	☐	☐	☐	☐	☐
draw conclusions.	☐	☐	☐	☐	☐
sequence events.	☐	☐	☐	☐	☐
distinguish between fact and fiction (reality and fantasy).	☐	☐	☐	☐	☐
identify cause and effect.	☐	☐	☐	☐	☐
identify the main idea (stated).	☐	☐	☐	☐	☐
identify story details.	☐	☐	☐	☐	☐
Select a title.	☐	☐	☐	☐	☐
Compose a thank-you note.	☐	☐	☐	☐	☐

EVALUATION CHECK LIST FOR
THIRD GRADE
LANGUAGE ARTS

Third-grade students should be able to do the following:

	CHILD'S NAME	CHILD'S NAME	CHILD'S NAME	CHILD'S NAME	CHILD'S NAME
LANGUAGE MECHANICS AND EXPRESSION					
Improve use of manuscript in the first six weeks.	☐	☐	☐	☐	☐
Use basic strokes of cursive style to form letters and words legibly and neatly.	☐	☐	☐	☐	☐
Identify complete sentences.	☐	☐	☐	☐	☐
Arrange words in logical order to form sentences.	☐	☐	☐	☐	☐
Identify correct use of periods.	☐	☐	☐	☐	☐
Identify correct use of question marks.	☐	☐	☐	☐	☐
Identify correct use of exclamation marks.	☐	☐	☐	☐	☐
Identify correct use of commas in dates, cities, and states.	☐	☐	☐	☐	☐
Use the apostrophe to form contractions and possessives.	☐	☐	☐	☐	☐
Identify correct use of singular and plural nouns.	☐	☐	☐	☐	☐
Identify correct capitalization of proper nouns, the first word of a sentence, the pronoun "I," addresses and dates.	☐	☐	☐	☐	☐
Recognize the simple subject of a sentence.	☐	☐	☐	☐	☐
Recognize the simple predicate of a sentence.	☐	☐	☐	☐	☐
Recognize and use correct forms of regular verbs (present and past tense).	☐	☐	☐	☐	☐
Select words that add detail to sentences.	☐	☐	☐	☐	☐
Compose a simple, original paragraph.	☐	☐	☐	☐	☐
Recognize parts of a friendly letter.	☐	☐	☐	☐	☐
Write abbreviations of commonly used words.	☐	☐	☐	☐	☐
Write creatively about selected subjects.	☐	☐	☐	☐	☐

EVALUATION CHECK LIST FOR

THIRD GRADE

LANGUAGE ARTS

	CHILD'S NAME	CHILD'S NAME	CHILD'S NAME	CHILD'S NAME	CHILD'S NAME
SPELLING					
Spell words in isolation and in sentence dictation.	☐	☐	☐	☐	☐
Spell the basic Dolch sight words.	☐	☐	☐	☐	☐
Use the following basic study steps to master spelling words:					
look at the word.	☐	☐	☐	☐	☐
sound the word.	☐	☐	☐	☐	☐
spell the word.	☐	☐	☐	☐	☐
write the word.	☐	☐	☐	☐	☐
Recognize correctly spelled words using sound or symbol relationships (consonant blends, long and short vowels, vowel diphthongs)...	☐	☐	☐	☐	☐
Recognize sight words.	☐	☐	☐	☐	☐
Identify unknown records through context clues.	☐	☐	☐	☐	☐
Know and use antonyms, synonyms, homonyms, and words that rhyme.	☐	☐	☐	☐	☐
Identify the base word from words containing the following prefixes and suffixes: *a, al, be, un, in, ful, less*.	☐	☐	☐	☐	☐
Identify correctly spelled affixes including prefixes *re* and *un* and suffixes s and *ed* and base words.	☐	☐	☐	☐	☐
Form new words using prefixes and suffixes.	☐	☐	☐	☐	☐
Identify correctly spelled contractions.	☐	☐	☐	☐	☐
Recognize letter-sound relationships for long vowels.	☐	☐	☐	☐	☐
Recognize letter-sound relationships for two-letter consonant blends in the initial and final position (*sc, sp, sk, sm, sn, st*).	☐	☐	☐	☐	☐

EVALUATION CHECK LIST FOR

THIRD GRADE

LANGUAGE ARTS

	CHILD'S NAME	CHILD'S NAME	CHILD'S NAME	CHILD'S NAME	CHILD'S NAME
Recognize letter-sound relationship for three-letter consonant blends in the initial position (*spl, str, spr, scr*).	☐	☐	☐	☐	☐
Recognize letter-sound associations for consonant digraphs (*ng, nk, wh, th, ph*).	☐	☐	☐	☐	☐
Recognize letter-sound associations for vowel digraphs (*ai, ay, ee, ea*).	☐	☐	☐	☐	☐
Recognize letter-sound associations for vowel diphthongs (*oi, oy, oo*).	☐	☐	☐	☐	☐
Use spelling patterns as clues to vowel sounds in words.	☐	☐	☐	☐	☐
Differentiate between hard and soft sounds of *c* and *g*.	☐	☐	☐	☐	☐
Divide two-syllable words into syllables using the *VC / CV* rule.	☐	☐	☐	☐	☐
STUDY SKILLS					
Use guide words to find words and entries in a dictionary.	☐	☐	☐	☐	☐
Locate the page on which a story begins by using the table of contents.	☐	☐	☐	☐	☐
Arrange words in alphabetical order to the second letter.	☐	☐	☐	☐	☐
Use a glossary.	☐	☐	☐	☐	☐
Classify and categorize words.	☐	☐	☐	☐	☐
Locate the title, author and illustrator on the title page.	☐	☐	☐	☐	☐
LISTENING AND COMPREHENSION					
Read for the following specific purposes:					
to gain pleasure.	☐	☐	☐	☐	☐

EVALUATION CHECK LIST FOR
THIRD GRADE
LANGUAGE ARTS

	CHILD'S NAME	CHILD'S NAME	CHILD'S NAME	CHILD'S NAME	CHILD'S NAME
to answer questions.	☐	☐	☐	☐	☐
to predict outcomes.	☐	☐	☐	☐	☐
Recall story details of material read.	☐	☐	☐	☐	☐
Respond to questions on who, what, when, where, or why after reading a selection.	☐	☐	☐	☐	☐
Identify and describe the characters of stories.	☐	☐	☐	☐	☐
Predict events in a story.	☐	☐	☐	☐	☐
Identify relevant and irrelevant information in a paragraph.	☐	☐	☐	☐	☐
Differentiate between possible and impossible situations.	☐	☐	☐	☐	☐
Compare or contrast items.	☐	☐	☐	☐	☐
Read selected material to:					
use context to select from given predictions.	☐	☐	☐	☐	☐
use context to select from possible conclusions.	☐	☐	☐	☐	☐
distinguish between fact and fiction.	☐	☐	☐	☐	☐
identify cause and effect.	☐	☐	☐	☐	☐
sequence events.	☐	☐	☐	☐	☐
identify the main idea (stated).	☐	☐	☐	☐	☐

EVALUATION CHECK LIST FOR

FOURTH GRADE

LANGUAGE ARTS

Fourth-grade students should be able to do the following:

LANGUAGE MECHANICS AND EXPRESSION

	CHILD'S NAME	CHILD'S NAME	CHILD'S NAME	CHILD'S NAME	CHILD'S NAME
Write legibly in cursive style.	☐	☐	☐	☐	☐
Identify complete sentences.	☐	☐	☐	☐	☐
Classify sentences according to type.	☐	☐	☐	☐	☐
Identify subject and predicate (simple).	☐	☐	☐	☐	☐
Identify correct use of subject-predicate agreement (natural order).	☐	☐	☐	☐	☐
Identify correct use of nouns (common/proper, singular/plural).	☐	☐	☐	☐	☐
Form plurals and possessives of nouns.	☐	☐	☐	☐	☐
Identify use of regular verbs (present and past tense).	☐	☐	☐	☐	☐
Identify correct use of adjectives.	☐	☐	☐	☐	☐
Identify correct use of adverbs.	☐	☐	☐	☐	☐
Identify correct capitalization of the first word of sentences, addresses, titles, dates, the pronoun *I,* and proper nouns.	☐	☐	☐	☐	☐
Write abbreviations of commonly used words.	☐	☐	☐	☐	☐
Identify correct capitalization and periods in abbreviations, including titles and initials.	☐	☐	☐	☐	☐
Identify correct use of ending punctuation marks, including: periods, question marks, and exclamation points.	☐	☐	☐	☐	☐
Identify correct use of commas in friendly letters, words in a series, dates, and addresses.	☐	☐	☐	☐	☐
Identify correct use of subject pronouns.	☐	☐	☐	☐	☐
Identify parts of a paragraph (topic sentence, indented first line and supporting detail					

	CHILD'S NAME	CHILD'S NAME	CHILD'S NAME	CHILD'S NAME	CHILD'S NAME
sentences).	☐	☐	☐	☐	☐
Identify relevant and irrelevant information in a paragraph.	☐	☐	☐	☐	☐
Identify parts of friendly letters and envelopes.	☐	☐	☐	☐	☐
Compose an invitation.	☐	☐	☐	☐	☐
SPELLING					
Recognize sight words (including the complete Dolch word list).	☐	☐	☐	☐	☐
Spell words in isolation and in sentence dictation.	☐	☐	☐	☐	☐
Recognize letter-sound associations for vowel digraphs (*ea, ee ei*).	☐	☐	☐	☐	☐
Recognize letter-sound associations for vowel diphthongs (*ou, aw, au*).	☐	☐	☐	☐	☐
Recognize correctly spelled words using sound/symbol relationships (consonant blends, long vowels, vowel diphthong and digraphs).	☐	☐	☐	☐	☐
Identify silent consonants in words.	☐	☐	☐	☐	☐
Apply letter-sound association for the two sounds of *c* and *g*.	☐	☐	☐	☐	☐
Identify correctly spelled words containing affixes (prefixes *in*, *un*, *dis*, and *re*, and suffixes *s*, *ed*, *er*, *est* and *ilu*).	☐	☐	☐	☐	☐
Identify contractions and their meanings.	☐	☐	☐	☐	☐
Proofread for errors (letter sequence, letter omission).	☐	☐	☐	☐	☐
Recognize syllable patterns (*VC/CV*, *V/CV*, *VC/V*).	☐	☐	☐	☐	☐
Divide polysyllabic words using syllabication rules.	☐	☐	☐	☐	☐

Evaluation Check List for
Fourth Grade

Language Arts

	Child's Name	Child's Name	Child's Name	Child's Name	Child's Name
Speak in a manner appropriate to the occasion.	☐	☐	☐	☐	☐
Pronounce words clearly and correctly.	☐	☐	☐	☐	☐
Demonstrate following directions (oral and written).	☐	☐	☐	☐	☐
Listening and Comprehension					
Give oral directions.	☐	☐	☐	☐	☐
Listen to answer specific questions.	☐	☐	☐	☐	☐
Listen to restate main ideas.	☐	☐	☐	☐	☐
Read for specific purpose:					
to gain pleasure.	☐	☐	☐	☐	☐
to answer questions.	☐	☐	☐	☐	☐
to predict outcomes.	☐	☐	☐	☐	☐
Study Skills					
Select the appropriate reference material (encyclopedia, dictionary, etc.).	☐	☐	☐	☐	☐
Arrange library cards in alphabetical order.	☐	☐	☐	☐	☐
Identify and use parts of books (glossary, table of contents, chapter headings, and index).	☐	☐	☐	☐	☐
Use context to identify new words, determine the meaning of known words,verify predictions and verify conclusions.	☐	☐	☐	☐	☐
Read selected material to:					
identify story details.	☐	☐	☐	☐	☐
sequence events.	☐	☐	☐	☐	☐
identify main idea (stated).	☐	☐	☐	☐	☐
identify central message.	☐	☐	☐	☐	☐
recognize author's purpose.	☐	☐	☐	☐	☐
recognize first- and third-person narratives (point of view).	☐	☐	☐	☐	☐

EVALUATION CHECK LIST FOR

FOURTH GRADE

LANGUAGE ARTS

	CHILD'S NAME	CHILD'S NAME	CHILD'S NAME	CHILD'S NAME	CHILD'S NAME
identify basic conflicts and solutions.	☐	☐	☐	☐	☐
classify statements of evidence.	☐	☐	☐	☐	☐
distinguish between fact and opinion.	☐	☐	☐	☐	☐
distinguish reality and fantasy.	☐	☐	☐	☐	☐
distinguish fiction from nonfiction.	☐	☐	☐	☐	☐
identify idioms.	☐	☐	☐	☐	☐
identify cause and effect relationships.	☐	☐	☐	☐	☐
make comparisons from given information.	☐	☐	☐	☐	☐
interpret the feeling and behavior of characters.	☐	☐	☐	☐	☐
select from possible conclusions.	☐	☐	☐	☐	☐
select from given predictions.	☐	☐	☐	☐	☐

EVALUATION CHECK LIST FOR

FIFTH GRADE

LANGUAGE ARTS

Fifth-grade students should be able to do the following:

	CHILD'S NAME	CHILD'S NAME	CHILD'S NAME	CHILD'S NAME	CHILD'S NAME
LANGUAGE MECHANICS AND EXPRESSION					
Write legibly in cursive style.	☐	☐	☐	☐	☐
Use manuscript skills for labeling, graphing, and identification.	☐	☐	☐	☐	☐
Recognize complete sentences in spoken and written language.	☐	☐	☐	☐	☐
Write complete sentences using correct capitalization and punctuation.	☐	☐	☐	☐	☐
Identify correct capitalization of words in titles, addresses, and dates.	☐	☐	☐	☐	☐
Identify correct capitalization and use of periods in abbreviations, including initials and titles.	☐	☐	☐	☐	☐
Identify correct use of ending punctuation.	☐	☐	☐	☐	☐
Identify correct use of commas in friendly letters, words in a series, dates, addresses, and between the quoted words of a speaker and the rest of the sentence.	☐	☐	☐	☐	☐
Use commas in introductory expressions and direct address.	☐	☐	☐	☐	☐
Classify sentences according to type.	☐	☐	☐	☐	☐
Distinguish between complete and incomplete sentences.	☐	☐	☐	☐	☐
Identify subject and predicate (simple and compound).	☐	☐	☐	☐	☐
Form compound sentences.	☐	☐	☐	☐	☐
Within the context of phrase(s), sentence(s) or a short paragraph, identify correct use of					

	CHILD'S NAME	CHILD'S NAME	CHILD'S NAME	CHILD'S NAME	CHILD'S NAME
the following:					
nouns (common/proper, singular/plural).	☐	☐	☐	☐	☐
principal parts of regular verbs....................	☐	☐	☐	☐	☐
verb tense (present, past, and future).	☐	☐	☐	☐	☐
linking and auxiliary verbs.	☐	☐	☐	☐	☐
pronouns (case usage).	☐	☐	☐	☐	☐
possessive pronouns.	☐	☐	☐	☐	☐
adjectives.	☐	☐	☐	☐	☐
adverbs.	☐	☐	☐	☐	☐
articles.	☐	☐	☐	☐	☐
subject-predicate agreement (natural order).	☐	☐	☐	☐	☐
SPELLING					
Spell words in isolation or in sentence dictation.	☐	☐	☐	☐	☐
Recognize sight words..................................	☐	☐	☐	☐	☐
Identify and form compound words.	☐	☐	☐	☐	☐
Recognize correctly spelled words using sound/symbol relationships (controlled vowels, schwa sound).	☐	☐	☐	☐	☐
Use base words with suffixes and prefixes.	☐	☐	☐	☐	☐
Proofread for errors (letter sequence, letter omission).	☐	☐	☐	☐	☐
Recognize syllable patterns (*V/C, V/CV, VC/V*).	☐	☐	☐	☐	☐
Recognize correct spelling of contractions.	☐	☐	☐	☐	☐
Recognize correct spelling of possessives (nouns/pronouns).	☐	☐	☐	☐	☐
Identify correct spelling of plural nouns...........	☐	☐	☐	☐	☐
Identify stressed and unstressed syllables.	☐	☐	☐	☐	☐
Identify synonyms, given the context of sen-					

	CHILD'S NAME	CHILD'S NAME	CHILD'S NAME	CHILD'S NAME	CHILD'S NAME
tence(s) or a short paragraph.	☐	☐	☐	☐	☐
Identify antonyms, given the context of sentence(s) or a short paragraph.	☐	☐	☐	☐	☐
Decode words by applying rules for syllabication.	☐	☐	☐	☐	☐
Unlock the meanings of words through use of the following:					
base words, prefixes and suffixes.	☐	☐	☐	☐	☐
contextual clues.	☐	☐	☐	☐	☐
homonyms and heteronyms.	☐	☐	☐	☐	☐
Apply basic word attack skills.	☐	☐	☐	☐	☐
Utilize a written and oral vocabulary appropriate to the grade level.	☐	☐	☐	☐	☐
Arrange sentences in logical order to form a paragraph.	☐	☐	☐	☐	☐
Develop simple, original paragraphs.	☐	☐	☐	☐	☐
Identify parts of friendly letters and envelopes.	☐	☐	☐	☐	☐
STUDY SKILLS					
Use the dictionary as a guide for alphabetizing, finding definitions, spelling, syllabication and pronunciation.	☐	☐	☐	☐	☐
Interpret diacritical marks.	☐	☐	☐	☐	☐
Determine the appropriate meaning of a word using the dictionary.	☐	☐	☐	☐	☐
Select and use the appropriate reference mate-	☐	☐	☐	☐	☐
rial (dictionary, encyclopedia, etc).	☐	☐	☐	☐	☐
Identify and use parts of books.	☐	☐	☐	☐	☐
Be able to find the following parts of books:					
table of contents.	☐	☐	☐	☐	☐
index.	☐	☐	☐	☐	☐

EVALUATION CHECK LIST FOR
FIFTH GRADE
LANGUAGE ARTS

	CHILD'S NAME	CHILD'S NAME	CHILD'S NAME	CHILD'S NAME	CHILD'S NAME
glossary.	☐	☐	☐	☐	☐
title page.	☐	☐	☐	☐	☐
Use the table of contents and index to find on what page certain information can be found.	☐	☐	☐	☐	☐
Be able to identify what is in a chapter from the table of contents.	☐	☐	☐	☐	☐
Identify the following information on cards by using the card catalog:					
author.	☐	☐	☐	☐	☐
title.	☐	☐	☐	☐	☐
subject.	☐	☐	☐	☐	☐
publisher.	☐	☐	☐	☐	☐
call number.	☐	☐	☐	☐	☐
Be able to look up a specific person's telephone number and address in the telephone directory.	☐	☐	☐	☐	☐
Be able to organize topic words in an outline form.	☐	☐	☐	☐	☐
Understand main heading and subheadings.	☐	☐	☐	☐	☐
LISTENING AND COMPREHENSION					
Demonstrate following directions in emergency situations.	☐	☐	☐	☐	☐
Interpret graphs, charts, tables, maps and diagrams.	☐	☐	☐	☐	☐
Follow oral and written directions.	☐	☐	☐	☐	☐
Use recall, sequence, and order in expressing written and oral ideas.	☐	☐	☐	☐	☐
Speak with inflections, pauses, and the necessary intonations to express punctuation and give meaning to sentences.	☐	☐	☐	☐	☐

EVALUATION CHECK LIST FOR

FIFTH GRADE

LANGUAGE ARTS

	CHILD'S NAME	CHILD'S NAME	CHILD'S NAME	CHILD'S NAME	CHILD'S NAME
Form accurate oral descriptions in discussion.	☐	☐	☐	☐	☐
Write brief reports using notes and pertinent data.	☐	☐	☐	☐	☐
Read selected material to:					
select from given predictions.	☐	☐	☐	☐	☐
select from possible conclusions.	☐	☐	☐	☐	☐
identify cause and effect relationships.	☐	☐	☐	☐	☐
recognize author's purpose.	☐	☐	☐	☐	☐
identify the main idea (stated).	☐	☐	☐	☐	☐
identify story details.	☐	☐	☐	☐	☐
sequence events from a selection.	☐	☐	☐	☐	☐
distinguish fact from opinion.	☐	☐	☐	☐	☐
classify statements of evidence.	☐	☐	☐	☐	☐
recognize conflicts and their solutions.	☐	☐	☐	☐	☐
Identify the theme or central message of a selection.	☐	☐	☐	☐	☐
Identify figurative language.	☐	☐	☐	☐	☐
Recognize time and place relationships (setting).	☐	☐	☐	☐	☐
Recognize the following types of literature:					
autobiography.	☐	☐	☐	☐	☐
biography.	☐	☐	☐	☐	☐
folk and fairy tales.	☐	☐	☐	☐	☐
historical fiction.	☐	☐	☐	☐	☐
informative articles.	☐	☐	☐	☐	☐
myths and legends.	☐	☐	☐	☐	☐
Use context clues to formulate ideas.	☐	☐	☐	☐	☐

Evaluation Check List for

Sixth Grade

Language Arts

CHILD'S NAME | CHILD'S NAME | CHILD'S NAME | CHILD'S NAME | CHILD'S NAME

Sixth-grade students should be able to do the following:

Language Mechanics and Expression

Improve speed while maintaining accuracy and legibility in handwriting. ☐ ☐ ☐ ☐ ☐

Identify correct capitalization of words in titles of books, songs, magazines, newspapers, appropriate words in outlines, and of proper nouns and adjectives. ☐ ☐ ☐ ☐ ☐

Identify correct use of ending punctuation including periods, question marks and exclamation marks. ☐ ☐ ☐ ☐ ☐

Identify correct use of capitalization and periods in abbreviations, including initials and titles. ☐ ☐ ☐ ☐ ☐

Identify correct use of capitalization in the name of a historical period. ☐ ☐ ☐ ☐ ☐

Identify correct use of commas:

- in dates. ☐ ☐ ☐ ☐ ☐
- in addresses. ☐ ☐ ☐ ☐ ☐
- in words in a series. ☐ ☐ ☐ ☐ ☐
- in letters. ☐ ☐ ☐ ☐ ☐
- between the quoted words of a speaker and the rest of the sentence. ☐ ☐ ☐ ☐ ☐
- to set off an introductory phrase. ☐ ☐ ☐ ☐ ☐
- to set off an appositive phrase. ☐ ☐ ☐ ☐ ☐
- after closing of a friendly letter. ☐ ☐ ☐ ☐ ☐
- to set off a name in direct address. ☐ ☐ ☐ ☐ ☐

Distinguish between simple and compound sentences. ☐ ☐ ☐ ☐ ☐

EVALUATION CHECK LIST FOR
SIXTH GRADE
LANGUAGE ARTS

	CHILD'S NAME	CHILD'S NAME	CHILD'S NAME	CHILD'S NAME	CHILD'S NAME
Distinguish between simple and complete subjects and predicates.	☐	☐	☐	☐	☐
Identify simple and compound subjects and predicates (natural order).	☐	☐	☐	☐	☐
Within the context of phrase(s), sentence(s) or a short paragraph, identify correct use of the following:					
nouns (common/proper, singular/plural, and possessive).	☐	☐	☐	☐	☐
subject-predicate agreement.	☐	☐	☐	☐	☐
case usage of pronouns (nominative, objective, possessive).	☐	☐	☐	☐	☐
principal parts of regular verbs.	☐	☐	☐	☐	☐
demonstrative adjectives.	☐	☐	☐	☐	☐
comparative and superlative forms of adjectives.	☐	☐	☐	☐	☐
verb tense (present, past, and future).	☐	☐	☐	☐	☐
conjunctions.	☐	☐	☐	☐	☐
prepositions.	☐	☐	☐	☐	☐
negative words.	☐	☐	☐	☐	☐
"good" and "well."	☐	☐	☐	☐	☐

SPELLING

Spell words in isolation and in sentence dictation.	☐	☐	☐	☐	☐
Recognize sight words.	☐	☐	☐	☐	☐
Identify base words and correct spelling of affixed words.	☐	☐	☐	☐	☐
Recognize correct spelling of possessives (nouns/pronouns)	☐	☐	☐	☐	☐
Identify correct spelling of homophones.	☐	☐	☐	☐	☐
Recognize correct spelling of plurals of nouns.	☐	☐	☐	☐	☐

Evaluation Check List for

Sixth Grade

Language Arts

	Child's Name	Child's Name	Child's Name	Child's Name	Child's Name
Distinguish compound words from polysyllabic words in sentences, paragraphs or standing alone.	☐	☐	☐	☐	☐
Divide polysyllabic words into syllables.	☐	☐	☐	☐	☐
Use context as a clue to the meanings of unfamiliar words (synonyms, antonyms, definition, restatement, example).	☐	☐	☐	☐	☐
Apply basic word attack skills.	☐	☐	☐	☐	☐
Study Skills					
Use the dictionary.	☐	☐	☐	☐	☐
Choose the appropriate reference book to find specific information (telephone directory, encyclopedia, dictionary).	☐	☐	☐	☐	☐
Demonstrate following written or graphic (map) directions.	☐	☐	☐	☐	☐
Write directions.	☐	☐	☐	☐	☐
Identify and use parts of a book.	☐	☐	☐	☐	☐
Identify the following information on cards by:					
using the card catalog.	☐	☐	☐	☐	☐
author.	☐	☐	☐	☐	☐
title.	☐	☐	☐	☐	☐
subject.	☐	☐	☐	☐	☐
publisher.	☐	☐	☐	☐	☐
call number.	☐	☐	☐	☐	☐
year of publication.	☐	☐	☐	☐	☐
Use the encyclopedia.	☐	☐	☐	☐	☐
Use an atlas.	☐	☐	☐	☐	☐
Use radio and television schedules.	☐	☐	☐	☐	☐
Use a telephone directory.	☐	☐	☐	☐	☐
Use a newspaper to find certain information.	☐	☐	☐	☐	☐

EVALUATION CHECK LIST FOR
SIXTH GRADE
LANGUAGE ARTS

	CHILD'S NAME	CHILD'S NAME	CHILD'S NAME	CHILD'S NAME	CHILD'S NAME
Calculate the number of sections in a news-	☐	☐	☐	☐	☐
paper.	☐	☐	☐	☐	☐
Interpret graphs, maps, charts, tables, and diagrams.	☐	☐	☐	☐	☐
Sequence sentences correctly in a paragraph.	☐	☐	☐	☐	☐
Construct a paragraph with appropriate title, indentation, margins, punctuation, and spelling.	☐	☐	☐	☐	☐
Identify parts of letters and envelopes.	☐	☐	☐	☐	☐
Compose a business letter and address appropriate envelope.	☐	☐	☐	☐	☐
Develop simple outlines.	☐	☐	☐	☐	☐
Understand main heading and subheadings.					
Present an oral report.	☐	☐	☐	☐	☐
Make formal and informal introductions.	☐	☐	☐	☐	☐
Participate in a discussion by making relevant contributions to a specific topic.	☐	☐	☐	☐	☐
Make oral and written summaries of any material read.	☐	☐	☐	☐	☐
Given the organizing principle of a list, determine the order in which the topics should appear.	☐	☐	☐	☐	☐

LISTENING AND COMPREHENSION

Locate facts to support the main idea.	☐	☐	☐	☐	☐
Use simple outline skills to demonstrate comprehension.	☐	☐	☐	☐	☐
Skim for specific information.	☐	☐	☐	☐	☐
Identify the central message of a selection.	☐	☐	☐	☐	☐
Read selected material to identify the main idea (stated):					

SIXTH GRADE

LANGUAGE ARTS

	CHILD'S NAME	CHILD'S NAME	CHILD'S NAME	CHILD'S NAME	CHILD'S NAME
identify story details.	☐	☐	☐	☐	☐
sequence events from a selection.	☐	☐	☐	☐	☐
select from possible inferences and conclusions.	☐	☐	☐	☐	☐
make inferences based on statements of evidence.	☐	☐	☐	☐	☐
select from given predictions.	☐	☐	☐	☐	☐
identify cause and effect relationship.	☐	☐	☐	☐	☐
distinguish fact from opinion.	☐	☐	☐	☐	☐
distinguish fiction from nonfiction.	☐	☐	☐	☐	☐
Identify the various forms of fiction and nonfiction.	☐	☐	☐	☐	☐
Distinguish literal from figurative language (idioms, hyperboles, similes, and metaphors).	☐	☐	☐	☐	☐
Recognize sound devices (alliteration).	☐	☐	☐	☐	☐

Evaluation Check List for
Seventh Grade
Language Arts

Seventh-grade students should be able to do the following:

	Child's Name	Child's Name	Child's Name	Child's Name	Child's Name
Language Mechanics and Expression					
Assess cursive writing for legibility.	☐	☐	☐	☐	☐
Identify correct capitalization of proper nouns, the first word in a direct quotation, greetings and closing of letters and appropriate words in outlines.	☐	☐	☐	☐	☐
Understand correct capitalization of a direction used as the name of a region and use lower case when used as a direction (South Carolina, he went south).	☐	☐	☐	☐	☐
Identify correct use of commas in dates, addresses, words in a series, in letters, between quoted words of a speaker and the rest of the sentence, in compound sentences, and after introductory phrases.	☐	☐	☐	☐	☐
Use an apostrophe to form the possessive of a singular noun or to form the possessive of a plural noun.	☐	☐	☐	☐	☐
Use semicolon and colon correctly.	☐	☐	☐	☐	☐
Differentiate between complete and incomplete sentences.	☐	☐	☐	☐	☐
Identify simple and compound sentences.	☐	☐	☐	☐	☐
Recognize complex sentences.	☐	☐	☐	☐	☐
Identify simple and compound subjects and predicates.	☐	☐	☐	☐	☐
Within the context of phrase(s), sentence(s) or a short paragraph, identify correct use of the following:					

Evaluation Check List for
Seventh Grade
Language Arts

	Child's Name	Child's Name	Child's Name	Child's Name	Child's Name
subject-predicate agreement.	☐	☐	☐	☐	☐
agreement of pronoun and antecedent.	☐	☐	☐	☐	☐
comparative and superlative forms of adjectives and adverbs.	☐	☐	☐	☐	☐
case usage of pronouns.	☐	☐	☐	☐	☐
types of pronouns (possessive, reflexive, interrogative, relative, demonstrative, and indefinite).	☐	☐	☐	☐	☐
principal parts of regular and irregular verbs.	☐	☐	☐	☐	☐
verb tense (present, past, and future).	☐	☐	☐	☐	☐
conjunctions.	☐	☐	☐	☐	☐
prepositions and prepositional phrases.	☐	☐	☐	☐	☐
negative words.	☐	☐	☐	☐	☐
Distinguish between common/proper nouns, concrete/abstract nouns, and collective nouns.	☐	☐	☐	☐	☐
Use possessive forms of nouns.	☐	☐	☐	☐	☐
Use apostrophes correctly.	☐	☐	☐	☐	☐
Distinguish between transitive and intransitive verbs.	☐	☐	☐	☐	☐
Recognize and use direct and indirect objects.	☐	☐	☐	☐	☐
Recognize and use predicate nominatives and predicate adjectives.	☐	☐	☐	☐	☐
Combine sentences using adjectives, adverbs, and conjunctions.	☐	☐	☐	☐	☐
Identify run-on sentences.	☐	☐	☐	☐	☐
Distinguish between relevant and irrelevant information in a paragraph.	☐	☐	☐	☐	☐
Sequence sentences in a paragraph.	☐	☐	☐	☐	☐

EVALUATION CHECK LIST FOR

SEVENTH GRADE

LANGUAGE ARTS

	CHILD'S NAME	CHILD'S NAME	CHILD'S NAME	CHILD'S NAME	CHILD'S NAME
SPELLING					
Use sound/symbol relationships to spell words.	☐	☐	☐	☐	☐
Recognize correctly spelled affixed and base words.	☐	☐	☐	☐	☐
Recognize correct spelling of contractions.	☐	☐	☐	☐	☐
Recognize correct spelling of possessives (nouns/pronouns).	☐	☐	☐	☐	☐
Identify correctly spelled homophones within the context of sentences or phrases.	☐	☐	☐	☐	☐
Recognize correct spelling of plurals of nouns.	☐	☐	☐	☐	☐
Recognize sight words.	☐	☐	☐	☐	☐
Distinguish compound words from polysyllabic words.	☐	☐	☐	☐	☐
Divide polysyllabic words into syllables.	☐	☐	☐	☐	☐
Use context as a clue to the meaning of unfamiliar words.	☐	☐	☐	☐	☐
STUDY SKILLS					
Use the dictionary as a spelling aid.	☐	☐	☐	☐	☐
Apply dictionary skills by:					
using guide words.	☐	☐	☐	☐	☐
identifying parts of speech.	☐	☐	☐	☐	☐
identifying accented syllable.	☐	☐	☐	☐	☐
interpreting diacritical marks.	☐	☐	☐	☐	☐
interpreting the derivation of a word.	☐	☐	☐	☐	☐
determining meaning.	☐	☐	☐	☐	☐
Identify the following information on cards by using the card catalog:					
author.	☐	☐	☐	☐	☐
title.	☐	☐	☐	☐	☐
subject.	☐	☐	☐	☐	☐

Evaluation Check List for
Seventh Grade
Language Arts

	Child's Name	Child's Name	Child's Name	Child's Name	Child's Name
publisher	☐	☐	☐	☐	☐
call number.	☐	☐	☐	☐	☐
year of publication	☐	☐	☐	☐	☐
illustrator	☐	☐	☐	☐	☐
Locate information in an encyclopedia.	☐	☐	☐	☐	☐
Use various reference materials:					
atlas	☐	☐	☐	☐	☐
thesaurus.	☐	☐	☐	☐	☐
Use parts of a book to find:					
copyright	☐	☐	☐	☐	☐
information in a specific chapter.	☐	☐	☐	☐	☐
meaning of a word	☐	☐	☐	☐	☐
category of the book.	☐	☐	☐	☐	☐
Locate information in telephone directories.	☐	☐	☐	☐	☐
Use radio and television schedules.	☐	☐	☐	☐	☐
Demonstrate following written or graphic (map) directions.	☐	☐	☐	☐	☐
Identify parts of business letters and envelopes.	☐	☐	☐	☐	☐
Use note-taking skills.	☐	☐	☐	☐	☐
Identify correct outline form.	☐	☐	☐	☐	☐
Write reports.	☐	☐	☐	☐	☐
Proofread and revise writing.	☐	☐	☐	☐	☐

Listening and Comprehension

	Child's Name	Child's Name	Child's Name	Child's Name	Child's Name
Use expanded vocabulary to enhance oral communication	☐	☐	☐	☐	☐
Make comparisons and contrasts.	☐	☐	☐	☐	☐
Identify inconsistencies in logic.	☐	☐	☐	☐	☐
Use analogies to describe relationships.	☐	☐	☐	☐	☐
Prepare and give an oral presentation.	☐	☐	☐	☐	☐

EVALUATION CHECK LIST FOR

SEVENTH GRADE

LANGUAGE ARTS

	CHILD'S NAME	CHILD'S NAME	CHILD'S NAME	CHILD'S NAME	CHILD'S NAME
Read selected material to:					
identify the main idea (stated).	☐	☐	☐	☐	☐
identify story details.	☐	☐	☐	☐	☐
sequence events from a selection.	☐	☐	☐	☐	☐
select from possible conclusions.	☐	☐	☐	☐	☐
make inferences based on statements of evidence.	☐	☐	☐	☐	☐
select from given predictions.	☐	☐	☐	☐	☐
identify cause and effect relationships.	☐	☐	☐	☐	☐
distinguish fact from opinion.	☐	☐	☐	☐	☐
identify author's choice of form or purpose.	☐	☐	☐	☐	☐
identify foreshadowing.	☐	☐	☐	☐	☐
recognize first-and third-person narratives (point of view).	☐	☐	☐	☐	☐
Distinguish and interpret figurative language.	☐	☐	☐	☐	☐
Distinguish types of sensory language.	☐	☐	☐	☐	☐
Identify the theme or central message.	☐	☐	☐	☐	☐
Identify forms of literature such as fables, tall tales, novels, short stories, essays, drama and poetry.	☐	☐	☐	☐	☐
Describe plot development in a literary selection.	☐	☐	☐	☐	☐
Make critical evaluations.	☐	☐	☐	☐	☐

Evaluation Check List for
Eighth Grade
Language Arts

CHILD'S NAME | CHILD'S NAME | CHILD'S NAME | CHILD'S NAME | CHILD'S NAME

Eighth-grade students should be able to do the following:

Language Mechanics and Expression

Produce legible cursive handwriting. ☐ ☐ ☐ ☐ ☐

Identify correct capitalization in:

dates. ☐ ☐ ☐ ☐ ☐

addresses. ☐ ☐ ☐ ☐ ☐

letter parts. ☐ ☐ ☐ ☐ ☐

proper nouns. ☐ ☐ ☐ ☐ ☐

proper adjectives. ☐ ☐ ☐ ☐ ☐

titles. ☐ ☐ ☐ ☐ ☐

outlines. ☐ ☐ ☐ ☐ ☐

quotations. ☐ ☐ ☐ ☐ ☐

Identify correct use of standard punctuation. ☐ ☐ ☐ ☐ ☐

Recognize errors in sentence structure (fragment, run-on, etc.). ☐ ☐ ☐ ☐ ☐

Combine sentences, avoiding run-ons and comma splices, to form a correctly structured new sentence. ☐ ☐ ☐ ☐ ☐

Analyze sentence structure (simple, compound, complex). ☐ ☐ ☐ ☐ ☐

Identify simple and compound subjects and predicates (natural and inverted order, interrogative, intervening phrases). ☐ ☐ ☐ ☐ ☐

Within the context of phrase(s), sentence(s), or a short paragraph, identify correct use of the following:

agreement (between subject/verb and pronoun/antecedent). ☐ ☐ ☐ ☐ ☐

comparative and superlative forms of adjec-

	CHILD'S NAME	CHILD'S NAME	CHILD'S NAME	CHILD'S NAME	CHILD'S NAME
tives and adverbs.	☐	☐	☐	☐	☐
case usage of pronouns.	☐	☐	☐	☐	☐
types of pronouns (possessive, reflexive, interrogative, demonstrative and indefinite).	☐	☐	☐	☐	☐
noun forms (singular, plural, possessive).	☐	☐	☐	☐	☐
principal parts of verbs (regular, irregular, troublesome).	☐	☐	☐	☐	☐
verb tense.	☐	☐	☐	☐	☐
prepositional phrases as modifiers.	☐	☐	☐	☐	☐
negative words.	☐	☐	☐	☐	☐
conjunctions.	☐	☐	☐	☐	☐
interjections.	☐	☐	☐	☐	☐
Identify and use participles and participial phrases.	☐	☐	☐	☐	☐
Identify and use gerunds and gerund phrases.	☐	☐	☐	☐	☐
Identify and use infinitives and infinitive phrases.	☐	☐	☐	☐	☐
SPELLING					
Use sound/symbol relationships to spell words.	☐	☐	☐	☐	☐
Recognize correctly spelled affixed and base words.	☐	☐	☐	☐	☐
Recognize correct spelling of contractions.	☐	☐	☐	☐	☐
Identify correct forms of possessives (nouns/pronouns).	☐	☐	☐	☐	☐
Identify correctly spelled homophones within the context of sentences or phrases.	☐	☐	☐	☐	☐
Recognize correct spelling of plurals of nouns.	☐	☐	☐	☐	☐
Define and spell compound words.	☐	☐	☐	☐	☐
Recognize multiple meanings of words.	☐	☐	☐	☐	☐
Recognize sight words.	☐	☐	☐	☐	☐

EVALUATION CHECK LIST FOR

EIGHTH GRADE

LANGUAGE ARTS

CHILD'S NAME | CHILD'S NAME | CHILD'S NAME | CHILD'S NAME | CHILD'S NAME

Divide polysyllabic words into syllables. ☐ ☐ ☐ ☐ ☐

Use context as a clue to determine word meanings. ☐ ☐ ☐ ☐ ☐

STUDY SKILLS

Locate information from various sources. ☐ ☐ ☐ ☐ ☐

Use parts of a book to find: ☐ ☐ ☐ ☐ ☐

- copyright ☐ ☐ ☐ ☐ ☐
- information in a specific chapter. ☐ ☐ ☐ ☐ ☐
- meaning of a word.
- category of the book. ☐ ☐ ☐ ☐ ☐

Demonstrate following written or graphic (map) directions. ☐ ☐ ☐ ☐ ☐

Identify parts of friendly or business letters and envelopes. ☐ ☐ ☐ ☐ ☐

LISTENING AND COMPREHENSION

Demonstrate effective oral communication skills. ☐ ☐ ☐ ☐ ☐

Elaborate on an idea. ☐ ☐ ☐ ☐ ☐

Recognize logical fallacies (faulty reasoning, generalization, rationalization, etc.). ☐ ☐ ☐ ☐ ☐

Recognize and define propaganda techniques. ☐ ☐ ☐ ☐ ☐

Write and evaluate paragraphs with respect to unity, arrangement of details and effective use of language. ☐ ☐ ☐ ☐ ☐

Proofread and revise writing. ☐ ☐ ☐ ☐ ☐

Identify correct outline form. ☐ ☐ ☐ ☐ ☐

Write a report. ☐ ☐ ☐ ☐ ☐

Read selected material to:

- identify the main idea or theme (stated or implied). ☐ ☐ ☐ ☐ ☐

	CHILD'S NAME	CHILD'S NAME	CHILD'S NAME	CHILD'S NAME	CHILD'S NAME
identify story details.	☐	☐	☐	☐	☐
sequence events from a selection.	☐	☐	☐	☐	☐
select from possible conclusions based on inferences or statements of evidence.	☐	☐	☐	☐	☐
make inferences based on statements of evidence.	☐	☐	☐	☐	☐
identify cause and effect relationships.	☐	☐	☐	☐	☐
distinguish fact from opinion.	☐	☐	☐	☐	☐
identify author's purpose.	☐	☐	☐	☐	☐
make critical evaluations (point of view).	☐	☐	☐	☐	☐
identify first-and third-person narrative.	☐	☐	☐	☐	☐
identify foreshadowing.	☐	☐	☐	☐	☐
Distinguish and interpret examples of figurative language.	☐	☐	☐	☐	☐
Identify forms of literature such as fables, tall tales, novels, short stories, essays, drama and poetry.	☐	☐	☐	☐	☐
Recognize sensory language.	☐	☐	☐	☐	☐
Describe plot development in a selection.	☐	☐	☐	☐	☐
Summarize a selection.	☐	☐	☐	☐	☐

Who hath measured the waters in the hollow of his hand,
and meted out heaven with the span, and
comprehended the dust of the earth in a measure, and
weighed the mountains in scales, and the hills in a balance?

ISAIAH 40:12 (KJV)

MATHEMATICS

Concepts of Numbers • Computation of Whole Numbers • Geometry • Measurement • Fractions • Decimals • Integers • Percents • Charts, Graphs, and Tables • Problem Solving

KINDERGARTEN

FIRST-GRADE

SECOND GRADE

THIRD GRADE

FOURTH GRADE

FIFTH GRADE

SIXTH GRADE

SEVENTH GRADE

EIGHTH GRADE

Evaluation Check List for KINDERGARTEN

Mathematics

Kindergarten students should be able to do the following:

	CHILD'S NAME	CHILD'S NAME	CHILD'S NAME	CHILD'S NAME	CHILD'S NAME
CONCEPTS OF NUMBERS					
Determine which is larger/smaller, longer/shorter, taller/shorter, etc., when given two similar objects.	☐	☐	☐	☐	☐
Demonstrate terms of relative position (above, under, right, behind, etc.).	☐	☐	☐	☐	☐
Identify, match, and reproduce shapes with given shapes (circle, square, triangle, and rectangle).	☐	☐	☐	☐	☐
Match terms with given shapes.	☐	☐	☐	☐	☐
Identify equivalent sets (1-10) by one to one correspondence.	☐	☐	☐	☐	☐
Identify sets of 1-5 on sight	☐	☐	☐	☐	☐
Show and state that when objects are taken from a set, the set becomes smaller.	☐	☐	☐	☐	☐
Show and state that when objects are added to a set, the set becomes larger.	☐	☐	☐	☐	☐
Count to 10; identify numerals 0-10.	☐	☐	☐	☐	☐
Tell which of two numbers is less or which is greater up to 10.	☐	☐	☐	☐	☐
MEASUREMENT					
Identify a penny and a nickel.	☐	☐	☐	☐	☐
Recognize clocks and watches as instruments for measuring time.	☐	☐	☐	☐	☐
Recognize the thermometer as a device to measure temperatures.	☐	☐	☐	☐	☐

EVALUATION CHECK LIST FOR

FIRST GRADE

MATHEMATICS

First-grade students should be able to do the following:	CHILD'S NAME	CHILD'S NAME	CHILD'S NAME	CHILD'S NAME	CHILD'S NAME
RECOGNIZE NAMES OF NUMBERS					
Identify word names of numbers 0-20	☐	☐	☐	☐	☐
Identify word names by tens from 10 to 96	☐	☐	☐	☐	☐
Identify word names 0-10.	☐	☐	☐	☐	☐
Identify ordinal numbers through 12th.	☐	☐	☐	☐	☐
COUNTING					
Count and write by ones, fives, and tens to 100	☐	☐	☐	☐	☐
Sequence or order numbers, 0-99; identify which comes before, between, or after.	☐	☐	☐	☐	☐
Show which of two numbers, 0-50, is less or greater	☐	☐	☐	☐	☐
OPERATIONS					
Recognize and use symbols: Plus (+), minus (-), equals (=).	☐	☐	☐	☐	☐
Recognize the following mathematical terms: add, subtract, longer, shorter, more than, less than, equal, largest, smallest, before, between, after, addend, and sum.	☐	☐	☐	☐	☐
PLACE VALUE					
Identify the place value and total value of each digit for numbers 0-99.	☐	☐	☐	☐	☐
Recognize place value for ones, tens, and hundreds.	☐	☐	☐	☐	☐
Compare whole numbers through 99.	☐	☐	☐	☐	☐

EVALUATION CHECK LIST FOR
FIRST GRADE
MATHEMATICS

	CHILD'S NAME	CHILD'S NAME	CHILD'S NAME	CHILD'S NAME	CHILD'S NAME
ADDITION AND SUBTRACTION					
Recall basic addition and subtraction facts with sums and differences of ten or less.	☐	☐	☐	☐	☐
Add two one-digit numbers, horizontally or vertically, with no regrouping (facts to 10).	☐	☐	☐	☐	☐
Add three one-digit numbers, horizontally or vertically, with no regrouping.	☐	☐	☐	☐	☐
Add two two-digit numbers without regrouping.	☐	☐	☐	☐	☐
Subtract two one-digit numbers, horizontally or vertically, with no renaming (facts to 10, minuend from 1-9, and subtrahend from 0-9).	☐	☐	☐	☐	☐
Subtract a one-digit number from a two-digit number without regrouping.	☐	☐	☐	☐	☐
Demonstrate an understanding of the commutative property of addition (3 + 4 = 4 + 3, etc.).					
Find the missing addend (facts to 10).	☐	☐	☐	☐	☐
Demonstrate the understanding that when zero is added to or subtracted from any number, the sum or remainder is always the beginning number.	☐	☐	☐	☐	☐
Identify number sentences, involving addition or subtraction with a sum from 1 thru 9, by using illustrations and word problems.	☐	☐	☐	☐	☐
GEOMETRY					
Recognize the triangle, square, rectangle, and circle.	☐	☐	☐	☐	☐
Match terms with given shapes.	☐	☐	☐	☐	☐
Identify the longer and the shorter of two objects.	☐	☐	☐	☐	☐
Identify equivalent and nonequivalent sets					

	CHILD'S NAME	CHILD'S NAME	CHILD'S NAME	CHILD'S NAME	CHILD'S NAME
by using illustrations.	☐	☐	☐	☐	☐
MEASUREMENT					
Estimate the amount a container will hold.	☐	☐	☐	☐	☐
Identify the following coins: penny, nickel, dime, quarter, in terms of pennies (cents).	☐	☐	☐	☐	☐
Tell time to the nearest half-hour, using a standard clock.	☐	☐	☐	☐	☐
Identify the hotter/colder temperature on a thermometer by selecting the higher/lower column of two thermometers	☐	☐	☐	☐	☐
Name periods of time in sequence.	☐	☐	☐	☐	☐
Mark specified days and dates on a calendar.	☐	☐	☐	☐	☐
Compare liquid capacities using customary (cup, pint, and quart) or metric (liter) measures	☐	☐	☐	☐	☐
Use a ruler to measure a line segment to the nearest whole unit [customary (inch) or metric (centimeter)].	☐	☐	☐	☐	☐
FRACTIONS					
Identify a shape divided into equal parts.	☐	☐	☐	☐	☐
Distinguish shapes divided into halves.	☐	☐	☐	☐	☐
Determine when one-fourth of an object is shaded	☐	☐	☐	☐	☐
CHARTS, GRAPHS AND TABLES					
Interpret a simple bar graph of pictured objects in vertical format.	☐	☐	☐	☐	☐
Identify how much more one frequency is than another pertaining to a simple graph.	☐	☐	☐	☐	☐

EVALUATION CHECK LIST FOR

SECOND GRADE

MATHEMATICS

	CHILD'S NAME	CHILD'S NAME	CHILD'S NAME	CHILD'S NAME	CHILD'S NAME
Second-grade students should be able to do the following:					
Recognizing Names of Numbers	☐	☐	☐	☐	☐
Identify word names of numbers 0-20	☐	☐	☐	☐	☐
Identify word names by 10s from 10 to 90.	☐	☐	☐	☐	☐
Identify word names 0-10.	☐	☐	☐	☐	☐
Identify odd or even numbers randomly selected from 1-20.	☐	☐	☐	☐	☐
COUNTING					
Count, recognize and write to 100 by twos, fives or tens from any point.	☐	☐	☐	☐	☐
Count by threes to 99.	☐	☐	☐	☐	☐
Count and write to 200 by ones from any point.	☐	☐	☐	☐	☐
Count and write to 900 by hundreds.	☐	☐	☐	☐	☐
Compare and determine sequence of numbers to 999; identify which comes before, between, or after.	☐	☐	☐	☐	☐
OPERATIONS					
Determine the appropriate sign to be used in a number sentence.	☐	☐	☐	☐	☐
Estimate the sum of two two-digit numbers given in horizontal form. Demonstrate knowledge that multiplication is repeated addition (for example, 2 + 2 + 2 + 2 = 8).	☐	☐	☐	☐	☐
PLACE VALUE					
Identify place value and total value for numbers 0-999.	☐	☐	☐	☐	☐

EVALUATION CHECK LIST FOR SECOND GRADE

MATHEMATICS

	CHILD'S NAME	CHILD'S NAME	CHILD'S NAME	CHILD'S NAME	CHILD'S NAME
Match cardinals to corresponding ordinal numbers through 20.	☐	☐	☐	☐	☐
Demonstrate an understanding of math terms and symbols: plus (+), minus (-), equals (=), greater than (>), less than (<), minuend, subtrahend, and difference	☐	☐	☐	☐	☐
Demonstrate knowledge and understanding of place value of three-digit numerals using concrete objects or pictures (ones, tens, hundreds).	☐	☐	☐	☐	☐
ADDITION AND SUBTRACTION					
Demonstrate recall of basic addition and subtraction facts up to the sum of 18	☐	☐	☐	☐	☐
Demonstrate a knowledge of the commutative property of addition	☐	☐	☐	☐	☐
Add three one-digit numbers with a sum of 0-18.	☐	☐	☐	☐	☐
Add up to two two-digit numbers, horizontally and vertically, with or without regrouping.	☐	☐	☐	☐	☐
Add three two-digit numbers, vertically, without regrouping	☐	☐	☐	☐	☐
Subtract up to two two-digit numbers, horizontally and vertical, with or without regrouping.	☐	☐	☐	☐	☐
Subtract a two-digit number from a three-digit number without regrouping	☐	☐	☐	☐	☐
MULTIPLICATION AND DIVISION					
Identify "x" for multiplication	☐	☐	☐	☐	☐
Name the products for multiplication facts with products less than 25	☐	☐	☐	☐	☐

Evaluation Check List for

Second Grade

Mathematics

	Child's Name	Child's Name	Child's Name	Child's Name	Child's Name
Name the product for a basic multiplication problem presented in horizontal form.	☐	☐	☐	☐	☐
Name the product for a basic multiplication problem presented in vertical form.	☐	☐	☐	☐	☐
Be able to name the quotient for basic division facts with dividends less than 25.	☐	☐	☐	☐	☐
Geometry					
Identify, name, and match triangle, square, rectangle, and circle.	☐	☐	☐	☐	☐
Identify specified plane figures.	☐	☐	☐	☐	☐
Determine the perimeter of a rectangle given all four sides.	☐	☐	☐	☐	☐
Measurements					
Indicate time up to the quarter hour.	☐	☐	☐	☐	☐
Be able to distinguish the time difference given two different clocks.	☐	☐	☐	☐	☐
Determine the value of a collection of coins, including pennies (cents), nickels, dimes, quarters, and half-dollars in terms of pennies (cents).	☐	☐	☐	☐	☐
Determine money value from a collection of coins and bills to $1.00.	☐	☐	☐	☐	☐
Identify day of month and day of week on a calendar.	☐	☐	☐	☐	☐
Measure lengths using a nonstandard measure of ten units.	☐	☐	☐	☐	☐
Identify the hotter/colder temperature by selecting the higher/lower column of two thermometers.	☐	☐	☐	☐	☐

EVALUATION CHECK LIST FOR

SECOND GRADE

MATHEMATICS

	CHILD'S NAME	CHILD'S NAME	CHILD'S NAME	CHILD'S NAME	CHILD'S NAME
FRACTIONS					
Identify fractional parts of a region ½, ¼, ⅒.	☐	☐	☐	☐	☐
Match word names to fractions (halves, fourths, thirds, and tenths) and match fractions to word names.	☐	☐	☐	☐	☐
CHARTS, GRAPHS, AND TABLES					
Interpret and solve problems with bar graphs. Use a table to determine how much more one frequency is than another.	☐	☐	☐	☐	☐
PROBLEM SOLVING					
Interpret pictographs and solve problems with pictographs (exclude partial figures).	☐	☐	☐	☐	☐
Complete number sentences with a missing addend, sums 10-18.	☐	☐	☐	☐	☐
Solve one-step word problems involving addition and subtraction up to two-digit numbers, with or without regrouping.	☐	☐	☐	☐	☐
Solve one-step word problems involving money up to $1.00.	☐	☐	☐	☐	☐

EVALUATION CHECK LIST FOR

THIRD GRADE

MATHEMATICS

Third-grade students should be able to do the following:

	CHILD'S NAME	CHILD'S NAME	CHILD'S NAME	CHILD'S NAME	CHILD'S NAME
RECOGNIZE NAMES FOR NUMBERS					
Identify the name of a three-digit number.	☐	☐	☐	☐	☐
Identify the name of a four-digit number.	☐	☐	☐	☐	☐
Identify the name of a five-digit number.	☐	☐	☐	☐	☐
Identify word names for numbers through 9,999.	☐	☐	☐	☐	☐
Identify ordinals to twentieth.	☐	☐	☐	☐	☐
Identify any even and odd numbers to 99.	☐	☐	☐	☐	☐
COUNTING					
Order numbers through 9,999 in short sequence.	☐	☐	☐	☐	☐
Count by twos, threes, fives, and tens to 100, starting at any point	☐	☐	☐	☐	☐
Identify a number greater than a given number in the thousands.	☐	☐	☐	☐	☐
OPERATIONS					
Estimate the sum of two two-digit numbers.	☐	☐	☐	☐	☐
Identify and use the symbols: >, <, =.	☐	☐	☐	☐	☐
PLACE VALUE					
Round two-digit numerals to the nearest ten.	☐	☐	☐	☐	☐
Identify place value up to four digits and expanded form up to three digits.	☐	☐	☐	☐	☐
Compare whole numbers up to four digits.	☐	☐	☐	☐	☐
Express a number as a number of tens and ones when the number of ones is greater than nine.	☐	☐	☐	☐	☐

EVALUATION CHECK LIST FOR
THIRD GRADE
MATHEMATICS

	CHILD'S NAME	CHILD'S NAME	CHILD'S NAME	CHILD'S NAME	CHILD'S NAME
Round a number in hundredths to the nearest ten.	☐	☐	☐	☐	☐
ADDITION AND SUBTRACTION					
Add multi-digit numbers (up to three-digits).	☐	☐	☐	☐	☐
Add a four-digit number and a three-digit number.	☐	☐	☐	☐	☐
Subtract up to two three-digit numbers.	☐	☐	☐	☐	☐
Subtract a one-digit number from a two-digit number, renaming tens to ones.	☐	☐	☐	☐	☐
Subtract a two-digit number from a three-digit number, renaming hundreds to tens.	☐	☐	☐	☐	☐
Subtract a three-digit number from a three-digit number.	☐	☐	☐	☐	☐
MULTIPLICATION AND DIVISION					
Name the product for a multiplication fact given in horizontal form.	☐	☐	☐	☐	☐
Name the product for a multiplication fact given in vertical form.	☐	☐	☐	☐	☐
Demonstrate an understanding of the terms multiplicand, multiplier, and product.	☐	☐	☐	☐	☐
Complete a function table using multiplication facts.	☐	☐	☐	☐	☐
Recall multiplication tables through fives.	☐	☐	☐	☐	☐
Multiply one-digit numbers.	☐	☐	☐	☐	☐
Multiply a two-digit number by a one-digit number.	☐	☐	☐	☐	☐
Use division facts (1-5) out of sequence.	☐	☐	☐	☐	☐

Evaluation Check List for

Third Grade

Mathematics

	CHILD'S NAME	CHILD'S NAME	CHILD'S NAME	CHILD'S NAME	CHILD'S NAME
Geometry					
Identify points, lines, and line segments.	☐	☐	☐	☐	☐
Relate spatial relationships to symmetry.	☐	☐	☐	☐	☐
Find area of a square counting square units.	☐	☐	☐	☐	☐
Understand a triangle has three equal sides.	☐	☐	☐	☐	☐
Measurement					
Read and write money amounts using dollar symbols, decimal notation, and cent symbols.	☐	☐	☐	☐	☐
Indicate time up to the nearest five-minute interval.	☐	☐	☐	☐	☐
Read temperature on a weather thermometer to the nearest 10 degrees.	☐	☐	☐	☐	☐
Make change for a dollar.	☐	☐	☐	☐	☐
Determine money value for a collection of coins and bills to $10.00.	☐	☐	☐	☐	☐
Select the most appropriate unit of length, mass, and capacity.	☐	☐	☐	☐	☐
Measure to nearest inch or centimeter.	☐	☐	☐	☐	☐
Fractions					
Identify fractional parts of a region (denominators through 10) using >, <, =.	☐	☐	☐	☐	☐
Compare two fractions representing shaded regions or sets.	☐	☐	☐	☐	☐
Identify fractions such as $\frac{3}{3}$, $\frac{4}{4}$, and $\frac{10}{10}$ as equal to 1.	☐	☐	☐	☐	☐
Decimals					
Match decimal numbers from 0.1 to 0.9 to shaded regions.	☐	☐	☐	☐	☐

Evaluation Check List for

Third Grade

Mathematics

	CHILD'S NAME	CHILD'S NAME	CHILD'S NAME	CHILD'S NAME	CHILD'S NAME
PROBLEM SOLVING					
Find the missing subtrahend or factor.	☐	☐	☐	☐	☐
Identify information not needed to solve a problem.	☐	☐	☐	☐	☐
Solve one-step word problems involving addition and subtraction of numbers up to three digits.	☐	☐	☐	☐	☐
Solve one-step word problems involving multiplication of a one- or two-digit number by a one-digit number.	☐	☐	☐	☐	☐
GRAPHS, CHARTS, AND TABLES					
Construct a bar graph or picture graph.	☐	☐	☐	☐	☐
Interpret picture and bar graphs	☐	☐	☐	☐	☐
Solve problems with graphs (picture, bar, or table-partial pictures should only be in -½ figures).	☐	☐	☐	☐	☐

EVALUATION CHECK LIST FOR

FOURTH GRADE

MATHEMATICS

	CHILD'S NAME	CHILD'S NAME	CHILD'S NAME	CHILD'S NAME	CHILD'S NAME

Fourth-grade students should be able to do the following:

RECOGNIZE NAMES FOR NUMBERS

Read and write numbers through 999,999....... ☐ ☐ ☐ ☐ ☐

Identify word names for numbers through 999,999. .... ☐ ☐ ☐ ☐ ☐

COMPARE AND ORDER NUMBERS

Order or compare numbers to 99,999. .... ☐ ☐ ☐ ☐ ☐

Recognize and continue number patterns. ...... ☐ ☐ ☐ ☐ ☐

Write ordinals to twentieth.............................. ☐ ☐ ☐ ☐ ☐

Recognize and indicate the value of the following Roman numeral symbols: I, V, X, L, C. .... ☐ ☐ ☐ ☐ ☐

Identify even and odd numbers through 999. .. ☐ ☐ ☐ ☐ ☐

Identify the least of four numbers in the ten thousands. .... ☐ ☐ ☐ ☐ ☐

Order five numbers in the hundreds................ ☐ ☐ ☐ ☐ ☐

PLACE VALUE

Identify place value and numbers in expanded form through 99,999. .... ☐ ☐ ☐ ☐ ☐

Round two-, three-, and four-digit numbers to the nearest ten and hundred. .... ☐ ☐ ☐ ☐ ☐

Identify a number expressed in expanded form, numbered in the thousands................ ☐ ☐ ☐ ☐ ☐

Name the number for a number of thousands, hundredths, tens, and ones. .... ☐ ☐ ☐ ☐ ☐

ADDITION AND SUBTRACTION

Add numbers up to four digits (column should

	CHILD'S NAME	CHILD'S NAME	CHILD'S NAME	CHILD'S NAME	CHILD'S NAME
be only up to three addends).	☐	☐	☐	☐	☐
Add two five-digit numbers.	☐	☐	☐	☐	☐
Subtract numbers up to four digits.	☐	☐	☐	☐	☐
Add a column of three- and four-digit numbers.	☐	☐	☐	☐	☐
Name the missing addend in an addition sentence.	☐	☐	☐	☐	☐
MULTIPLICATION AND DIVISION					
Recall from memory, in and out of sequence multiplication and division facts through 9.	☐	☐	☐	☐	☐
Multiply up to a four-digit number by a one-digit number.	☐	☐	☐	☐	☐
Divide one- and two-digit numbers by a one-digit number with and without a remainder.	☐	☐	☐	☐	☐
Demonstrate an understanding of the terms *divisor, dividend, quotient,* and *remainder.*	☐	☐	☐	☐	☐
GEOMETRY					
Identify points, lines, rays, and line segments.	☐	☐	☐	☐	☐
Locate points on a grid by counting to right and up.	☐	☐	☐	☐	☐
Identify right angles.	☐	☐	☐	☐	☐
Find the perimeter of a polygon with four sides or less. Measure the area of a figure by counting square units.	☐	☐	☐	☐	☐
MEASUREMENT					
Indicate time to the nearest minute on a standard clock.	☐	☐	☐	☐	☐
Identify time relationships (minute/hour, hour/day, a.m./p.m., day/week).	☐	☐	☐	☐	☐

EVALUATION CHECK LIST FOR

FOURTH GRADE

MATHEMATICS

	CHILD'S NAME	CHILD'S NAME	CHILD'S NAME	CHILD'S NAME	CHILD'S NAME
Indicate temperature to the nearest degree on a Celsius or Fahrenheit thermometer.	☐	☐	☐	☐	☐
Measure length, weight (mass), and liquid capacity in customary or metric units.	☐	☐	☐	☐	☐
Determine money value from a collection of coins and bills to \$100.00.	☐	☐	☐	☐	☐
FRACTIONS					
Identify the numerator and denominator of a fraction.	☐	☐	☐	☐	☐
Identify and compare fractions with like denominators.	☐	☐	☐	☐	☐
Add fractions having like denominators without regrouping, using denominators through 10.	☐	☐	☐	☐	☐
Subtract fractions having like denominators without regrouping, using denominators through 10.	☐	☐	☐	☐	☐
Add a whole number and a mixed fractional number.	☐	☐	☐	☐	☐
Subtract a whole number from a mixed fractional number.	☐	☐	☐	☐	☐
DECIMALS					
Identify the place value and total value of a digit in a decimal numeral up to hundredths place.	☐	☐	☐	☐	☐
Identify the place value and total value of a mixed decimal (to hundredths).	☐	☐	☐	☐	☐
Determine the decimal equivalent of a fraction with a denominator of 10 or 100.	☐	☐	☐	☐	☐
Identify information needed to solve a word problem.	☐	☐	☐	☐	☐

Evaluation Check List for

Fourth Grade

Mathematics

Problem Solving

	Child's Name	Child's Name	Child's Name	Child's Name	Child's Name
Solve one-step word problems involving addition, subtractions, multiplication, and basic division facts.	☐	☐	☐	☐	☐
Solve money problems using addition and subtractions up to $99.	☐	☐	☐	☐	☐
Solve a rate problem.	☐	☐	☐	☐	☐
Determine probability given the proper facts.	☐	☐	☐	☐	☐

Charts, Graphs, and Tables

	Child's Name	Child's Name	Child's Name	Child's Name	Child's Name
Interpret simple charts, graphs, and tables.	☐	☐	☐	☐	☐
Use information from tables, charts, and graphs to solve problems involving the four basic operations on whole numbers.	☐	☐	☐	☐	☐
Identify categories with most or least frequency using tables, charts, or graphs.	☐	☐	☐	☐	☐

EVALUATION CHECK LIST FOR

FIFTH GRADE

MATHEMATICS

Fifth-grade students should be able to do the following:

	CHILD'S NAME	CHILD'S NAME	CHILD'S NAME	CHILD'S NAME	CHILD'S NAME
RECOGNIZE NAMES OF NUMBERS					
Read and write numerals through 9,999,999.	☐	☐	☐	☐	☐
Identify word names for numbers through 9,999,999.	☐	☐	☐	☐	☐
Identify numbers in expanded form through 999,999.	☐	☐	☐	☐	☐
Recognize, read and write Roman numerals to 1,000.	☐	☐	☐	☐	☐
Recognize prime numbers less than 20.	☐	☐	☐	☐	☐
PLACE VALUE					
Identify place value for up to seven-digit numerals.	☐	☐	☐	☐	☐
Round four- and five-digit numerals to the nearest thousand, hundredth or tenth.	☐	☐	☐	☐	☐
ADDITION AND SUBTRACTION					
Add multi-digit numbers (up to five addends).					
Subtract multi-digit numbers.	☐	☐	☐	☐	☐
Identify the common factors of two whole numbers, each of which is less than 100.	☐	☐	☐	☐	☐
Identify the greatest common factor of two whole numbers, each of which is less than 100.	☐	☐	☐	☐	☐
MULTIPLICATION AND DIVISION					
Identify common multiples of two whole numbers.	☐	☐	☐	☐	☐
Identify the least common multiple of two whole numbers.	☐	☐	☐	☐	☐

EVALUATION CHECK LIST FOR

FIFTH GRADE

MATHEMATICS

	CHILD'S NAME	CHILD'S NAME	CHILD'S NAME	CHILD'S NAME	CHILD'S NAME
Multiply two- and three-digit numbers with and without a zero.	☐	☐	☐	☐	☐
Divide a two-digit number by a two-digit number with or without a remainder.	☐	☐	☐	☐	☐
Divide a three-digit number by a one-digit number with or without a remainder.	☐	☐	☐	☐	☐
Determine the mean of five one- or two-digit numbers without a remainder.	☐	☐	☐	☐	☐
GEOMETRY					
Determine the area of a square, rectangle, and triangle using a formula.	☐	☐	☐	☐	☐
Draw circles and label diameter, circumference, radius, and center.	☐	☐	☐	☐	☐
Identify acute, right, obtuse, and straight angles.	☐	☐	☐	☐	☐
Recognize and name congruent triangles from a set of triangles and congruent rectangles from a set of rectangles.	☐	☐	☐	☐	☐
MEASUREMENT					
Identify standard temperatures on a thermometer.	☐	☐	☐	☐	☐
Identify time relationships (minutes in an hour, hours in a day, a.m., or p.m.,	☐	☐	☐	☐	☐
days in a week, etc) and perform conversions between units of time.	☐	☐	☐	☐	☐
Identify metric and customary relationships (m./cm., kg./g, km./m, lb./oz., ft./in., yd./ft., and yd./in.).	☐	☐	☐	☐	☐
Measure to the nearest millimeter or quarter inch.	☐	☐	☐	☐	☐

Evaluation Check List for
Fifth Grade
Mathematics

	Child's Name	Child's Name	Child's Name	Child's Name	Child's Name
Solve addition, subtraction, multiplication and division problems involving monetary units.	☐	☐	☐	☐	☐
Identify the change due in bills and coins when bills are used for payment.	☐	☐	☐	☐	☐
Fractions					
Read simple word problems, including those with whole numbers, fractions, or decimals, and use the appropriate operation to calculate the answer.	☐	☐	☐	☐	☐
Identify fractions in lowest terms using the greatest common factor.	☐	☐	☐	☐	☐
Compare fractions having unlike denominators by finding the common denominator.	☐	☐	☐	☐	☐
Identify a mixed number as an improper fraction and vice versa.	☐	☐	☐	☐	☐
Change improper fractions to mixed numbers and vice versa, reducing fractions to lowest terms.	☐	☐	☐	☐	☐
Add fraction having like denominators with regrouping.	☐	☐	☐	☐	☐
Subtract fractions having like denominators with regrouping.	☐	☐	☐	☐	☐
Add fractions having unlike denominators without regrouping.	☐	☐	☐	☐	☐
Rename mixed fractional numbers.	☐	☐	☐	☐	☐
Add and subtract mixed numbers.	☐	☐	☐	☐	☐
Decimals					
Identify decimal numbers to thousandths.	☐	☐	☐	☐	☐
Identify decimal place value to thousandths.	☐	☐	☐	☐	☐

EVALUATION CHECK LIST FOR

FIFTH GRADE

MATHEMATICS

	CHILD'S NAME	CHILD'S NAME	CHILD'S NAME	CHILD'S NAME	CHILD'S NAME
Write the word name for a decimal number to thousandths. Identify the greater or lesser of two decimal numbers to thousandths.	☐	☐	☐	☐	☐
Add decimal numbers (including mixed number) to thousandths.	☐	☐	☐	☐	☐
Subtract decimal numbers (including mixed numbers) to thousandths.	☐	☐	☐	☐	☐
Round decimal numbers to the nearest whole number or tenth.	☐	☐	☐	☐	☐
Add and subtract using decimals, money, and cent symbols correctly.	☐	☐	☐	☐	☐
CHARTS, GRAPHS, AND TABLES					
Read and interpret a picture graph with partial figures.	☐	☐	☐	☐	☐
Read and interpret simple circle graphs.	☐	☐	☐	☐	☐
Read and interpret bar graphs using estimation.	☐	☐	☐	☐	☐
PROBLEM SOLVING					
Solve word problems involving perimeter of three- and four-sided figures.	☐	☐	☐	☐	☐
Perform operations based on the use of parentheses, (distributive property).	☐	☐	☐	☐	☐
Solve one- and two-step word problems involving any combination of basic operation on whole numbers.	☐	☐	☐	☐	☐
Complete a number sentence with a missing number using one of the four basic operations on whole numbers.	☐	☐	☐	☐	☐
Solve problems using whole number data from charts, tables, graphs, and maps.	☐	☐	☐	☐	☐

Evaluation Check List for

Sixth Grade

Mathematics

Sixth-grade students should be able to do the following:	Child's Name	Child's Name	Child's Name	Child's Name	Child's Name
Whole Numbers					
Recall and write numerals through 999,999,999,999.	☐	☐	☐	☐	☐
Identify word names through 999,999,999.	☐	☐	☐	☐	☐
Round off numbers to the nearest ten-thousand, thousand, hundred, or ten.	☐	☐	☐	☐	☐
Identify prime numbers and composite numbers less than 100.	☐	☐	☐	☐	☐
Recognize the base and the exponent of an expression and calculate its value.	☐	☐	☐	☐	☐
Recognize the Roman numeral symbols I, V, X, L, C, D, and M, indicate their value and Roman numerals up to 2,000.	☐	☐	☐	☐	☐
Measurement					
Determine temperature changes on both Celsius and Fahrenheit thermometers without negative numbers.	☐	☐	☐	☐	☐
Identify the change in bills and coins due when bills and coins are used in payment.	☐	☐	☐	☐	☐
Perform conversions between linear units with the metric and customary systems.	☐	☐	☐	☐	☐
Perform conversions within the metric or customary system of measuring mass or weight.	☐	☐	☐	☐	☐
Add and subtract linear units of measurement using renaming (metric or customary).	☐	☐	☐	☐	☐
Perform conversions between units of time.	☐	☐	☐	☐	☐

EVALUATION CHECK LIST FOR

SIXTH GRADE

MATHEMATICS

	CHILD'S NAME	CHILD'S NAME	CHILD'S NAME	CHILD'S NAME	CHILD'S NAME
Perform conversions between units of capacity within the metric and customary systems...	☐	☐	☐	☐	☐
Recognize and identify perpendicular lines, polygons by name, and chord, center, diameter, radius, and arc of a circle.	☐	☐	☐	☐	☐
GEOMETRY					
Measure simple angles to the nearest degree. Determine the area of a triangle and a parallelogram using the formula.	☐	☐	☐	☐	☐
Determine the volume of a rectangular solid..	☐	☐	☐	☐	☐
MULTIPLICATION AND DIVISION					
Identify the greatest common factor of two whole numbers.	☐	☐	☐	☐	☐
Multiply two four-digit numbers.	☐	☐	☐	☐	☐
Divide a four-digit number by a two- or three-digit number.	☐	☐	☐	☐	☐
Divide two two-digit numbers with remainder.	☐	☐	☐	☐	☐
Identify the least common multiple of two whole numbers.	☐	☐	☐	☐	☐
Add fractions having unlike denominators with regrouping.	☐	☐	☐	☐	☐
FRACTIONS					
Subtract fractions having unlike denominators with regrouping.	☐	☐	☐	☐	☐
Add mixed numbers having like denominators with and without regrouping	☐	☐	☐	☐	☐
Add mixed numbers having unlike denominators with regrouping.	☐	☐	☐	☐	☐

EVALUATION CHECK LIST FOR

SIXTH GRADE

MATHEMATICS

	CHILD'S NAME	CHILD'S NAME	CHILD'S NAME	CHILD'S NAME	CHILD'S NAME
Subtract mixed numbers having like denominators with and without regrouping.	☐	☐	☐	☐	☐
Subtract mixed numbers having unlike denominators with regrouping.	☐	☐	☐	☐	☐
Add or subtract whole numbers and mixed numbers.	☐	☐	☐	☐	☐
Multiply a proper fraction by a proper fraction, using denominators through 10.	☐	☐	☐	☐	☐
Divide a fraction by a fraction.	☐	☐	☐	☐	☐
Write the reciprocal of a rational number.	☐	☐	☐	☐	☐
Multiply or divide a whole number by a fraction.	☐	☐	☐	☐	☐
DECIMALS					
Order decimal numbers to ten-thousandths.	☐	☐	☐	☐	☐
Write the decimal word name to the ten-thousandths.	☐	☐	☐	☐	☐
Round decimal numbers to the nearest whole number, tenth hundredth, or thousandth.	☐	☐	☐	☐	☐
Add or subtract two decimal numbers through ten-thousandths.	☐	☐	☐	☐	☐
Multiply two mixed decimal numbers with factors to thousandths.	☐	☐	☐	☐	☐
Divide a decimal by a whole number and vice versa.	☐	☐	☐	☐	☐
Divide two decimals without repeating decimals in the quotients.	☐	☐	☐	☐	☐
Change proper fractions to decimals, then to percents.	☐	☐	☐	☐	☐
Compute a given percent of a whole number.	☐	☐	☐	☐	☐

EVALUATION CHECK LIST FOR

SIXTH GRADE

MATHEMATICS

	CHILD'S NAME	CHILD'S NAME	CHILD'S NAME	CHILD'S NAME	CHILD'S NAME
Determine the mean of ten one- or two-digit numbers with a remainder.	☐	☐	☐	☐	☐
PROBLEM SOLVING					
Solve practical problems involving the mean.	☐	☐	☐	☐	☐
Write a mathematical expression using variables.	☐	☐	☐	☐	☐
Evaluate one-step mathematical expressions.	☐	☐	☐	☐	☐
Solve one-step word problems involving any combination of basic operations on whole numbers, decimals, or fractions.	☐	☐	☐	☐	☐
Solve two-step word problems involving any combination of basic operations on whole numbers, decimals, or fractions.	☐	☐	☐	☐	☐
CHARTS, TABLES, GRAPHS					
Read and interpret bar, line, and partial pictographs.	☐	☐	☐	☐	☐
Read and interpret charts and schedules.	☐	☐	☐	☐	☐
Interpret data in percent form from a circle graph.	☐	☐	☐	☐	☐
Determine the range of data in a frequency table.	☐	☐	☐	☐	☐
Determine the probability of an event occurring.	☐	☐	☐	☐	☐
Write and solve a proportion, given a word problem.	☐	☐	☐	☐	☐
Identify a ratio comparing the number of objects in two sets using three forms.	☐	☐	☐	☐	☐
Identify equivalent ratios for a given ratio.	☐	☐	☐	☐	☐
Determine the missing number in a proportion.	☐	☐	☐	☐	☐

Evaluation Check List for
Sixth Grade
Mathematics

	Child's Name	Child's Name	Child's Name	Child's Name	Child's Name
Convert fractions with denominators of 100 to percent and vice versa.	☐	☐	☐	☐	☐
Convert a decimal (no more than two significant digits) to a percent and vice versa.	☐	☐	☐	☐	☐
Recognize a negative integer on a number line.	☐	☐	☐	☐	☐
Multiply and divide using dollar and cent symbols correctly.	☐	☐	☐	☐	☐

EVALUATION CHECK LIST FOR

SEVENTH GRADE

MATHEMATICS

Seventh-grade students should be able to do the following:

	CHILD'S NAME	CHILD'S NAME	CHILD'S NAME	CHILD'S NAME	CHILD'S NAME
WHOLE NUMBERS					
Round numbers to the nearest ten-thousand, thousand, hundred, or ten.	☐	☐	☐	☐	☐
Identify numbers divisible by 2, 3, 4, 5, 6, 9 and 10 using divisibility rules.	☐	☐	☐	☐	☐
Determine the square of any number less than 100	☐	☐	☐	☐	☐
Identify the positive square root of a perfect square less than 150.	☐	☐	☐	☐	☐
Identify the base and the exponent of an expression and calculate its value	☐	☐	☐	☐	☐
Identify numbers and their expanded form through 10 to the third power.	☐	☐	☐	☐	☐
Identify the prime factors of any number through 100.	☐	☐	☐	☐	☐
INTEGERS					
Compare integers.	☐	☐	☐	☐	☐
Order integers on a number line from least to greatest.	☐	☐	☐	☐	☐
Identify the greater and lesser of two integers.	☐	☐	☐	☐	☐
Determine the absolute value of an integer.	☐	☐	☐	☐	☐
Add integers having like signs.	☐	☐	☐	☐	☐
Add integers having unlike signs.	☐	☐	☐	☐	☐
Subtract integers having like signs.	☐	☐	☐	☐	☐
Subtract integers having unlike signs.	☐	☐	☐	☐	☐

EVALUATION CHECK LIST FOR
SEVENTH GRADE
MATHEMATICS

	CHILD'S NAME	CHILD'S NAME	CHILD'S NAME	CHILD'S NAME	CHILD'S NAME
MEASUREMENT					
Determine the time in one time zone when given time in another zone (contiguous United States time zones).	☐	☐	☐	☐	☐
GEOMETRY					
Bisect a line segment using a compass and straight edge.	☐	☐	☐	☐	☐
Draw an angle with a given measure.	☐	☐	☐	☐	☐
Bisect an angle using a compass and a straightedge.	☐	☐	☐	☐	☐
Determine the circumference of a circle using the formula.	☐	☐	☐	☐	☐
Classify triangles according to angle size.	☐	☐	☐	☐	☐
Classify triangles by the lengths of sides.	☐	☐	☐	☐	☐
MULTIPLICATION AND DIVISION					
Divide a three- or four-digit number by a two- or three-digit number with a remainder.	☐	☐	☐	☐	☐
Multiply a four-digit number by three- or four-digit numbers.	☐	☐	☐	☐	☐
FRACTIONS					
Add three mixed numbers having unlike denominators with regrouping.	☐	☐	☐	☐	☐
Subtract mixed numbers having unlike denominators with regrouping.	☐	☐	☐	☐	☐
Subtract a fraction or a mixed number from a whole number.	☐	☐	☐	☐	☐
Multiply three factors in any combination of fractions, mixed fractional numbers and					

	CHILD'S NAME	CHILD'S NAME	CHILD'S NAME	CHILD'S NAME	CHILD'S NAME
whole numbers.	☐	☐	☐	☐	☐
Write the reciprocal of a mixed fractional number.	☐	☐	☐	☐	☐
Determine, using division, the decimal number equivalent of a fraction or a mixed number.	☐	☐	☐	☐	☐
Divide a whole number, fraction, or mixed number by a mixed number.	☐	☐	☐	☐	☐
Determine if a fraction converts to a terminating or repeating decimal.	☐	☐	☐	☐	☐
DECIMALS					
Read and write decimal numbers to the millionths place.	☐	☐	☐	☐	☐
Write decimal numbers in expanded form to millionths place.	☐	☐	☐	☐	☐
Divide a whole number or decimal by a decimal with a repeating decimal in tile quotient.	☐	☐	☐	☐	☐
Divide a whole number or a decimal by a decimal and round the quotient to tile hundredths place.	☐	☐	☐	☐	☐
Calculate the decimal number that is the equivalent of a fraction or a mixed number.	☐	☐	☐	☐	☐
Read and interpret dual bar graphs and dual broken-line graphs.	☐	☐	☐	☐	☐
Identify the quadrants and signs of a coordinate plane.	☐	☐	☐	☐	☐
Locate a point using ordered pairs of integers on the coordinate plane.	☐	☐	☐	☐	☐
Evaluate mathematical expressions with two operations (whole numbers).	☐	☐	☐	☐	☐

EVALUATION CHECK LIST FOR

SEVENTH GRADE

MATHEMATICS

	CHILD'S NAME	CHILD'S NAME	CHILD'S NAME	CHILD'S NAME	CHILD'S NAME
PROBLEM SOLVING					
Solve one-step equations with one variable using addition and subtraction of whole numbers.	☐	☐	☐	☐	☐
Solve word problems with metric and customary measurements.	☐	☐	☐	☐	☐
Solve word problems using multiplication and division of monetary amounts.	☐	☐	☐	☐	☐
Given a word problem identify and solve a proportion.	☐	☐	☐	☐	☐
Define a probability of 1 and a probability of 0.	☐	☐	☐	☐	☐
Determine the possible outcomes in a situation with two variables.	☐	☐	☐	☐	☐
Determine the missing number in a proportion.	☐	☐	☐	☐	☐
PERCENT					
Find the percent of a number.	☐	☐	☐	☐	☐
Identify the percent equivalent of a fraction.	☐	☐	☐	☐	☐
Identify the fractional equivalent of a percent.	☐	☐	☐	☐	☐
Solve percentage statements in proportional form.	☐	☐	☐	☐	☐

EVALUATION CHECK LIST FOR

EIGHTH GRADE

MATHEMATICS

CHILD'S NAME | CHILD'S NAME | CHILD'S NAME | CHILD'S NAME | CHILD'S NAME

Eighth-grade students should be able to do the following:

WHOLE NUMBERS

Recognize numbers in expanded form using exponents through 10 to the 10th power (10_{10}). ☐ ☐ ☐ ☐ ☐

Evaluate expressions using the order of operations. ☐ ☐ ☐ ☐ ☐

Evaluate expressions which include exponents. ☐ ☐ ☐ ☐ ☐

GEOMETRY

Find the perimeter and area of polygons. ☐ ☐ ☐ ☐ ☐

Determine the area of a circle using the formula. ☐ ☐ ☐ ☐ ☐

Determine the circumference of a circle using the formula. ☐ ☐ ☐ ☐ ☐

Determine the area of a trapezoid using the formula. ☐ ☐ ☐ ☐ ☐

Determine the volume of a rectangular solid and a cylinder. ☐ ☐ ☐ ☐ ☐

Calculate the volume of a sphere. ☐ ☐ ☐ ☐ ☐

Use the Pythagorean Theorem. ☐ ☐ ☐ ☐ ☐

Identify central and inscribed angles of a circle. ☐ ☐ ☐ ☐ ☐

Identify the properties of congruent triangles. ☐ ☐ ☐ ☐ ☐

Identify the properties of similar triangles. ☐ ☐ ☐ ☐ ☐

Identify corresponding angles. ☐ ☐ ☐ ☐ ☐

Identify vertical angles. ☐ ☐ ☐ ☐ ☐

Evaluation Check List for

Eighth Grade

Mathematics

	Child's Name	Child's Name	Child's Name	Child's Name	Child's Name
Operations					
Perform basic operations with whole numbers, decimals, and integers (with like and unlike signs).	☐	☐	☐	☐	☐
Perform basic operations with fractions, whole numbers and mixed numbers.	☐	☐	☐	☐	☐
Identify rational numbers using the number line.	☐	☐	☐	☐	☐
Use the commutative and associative properties of addition with rational numbers.	☐	☐	☐	☐	☐
Identify examples of the commutative and associative properties of multiplication with rational numbers.	☐	☐	☐	☐	☐
Demonstrate application of the distributive property over a number.	☐	☐	☐	☐	☐
Fractions					
Write the fractional equivalent of a repeating decimal.	☐	☐	☐	☐	☐
Convert a number in standard form to scientific notation and vice versa.	☐	☐	☐	☐	☐
Identify the simplified form of a complex fraction.	☐	☐	☐	☐	☐
Problem Solving					
Solve one- and two-step equations using whole numbers.	☐	☐	☐	☐	☐
Solve one-step equations using fractions.	☐	☐	☐	☐	☐
Solve distance problems using the formula.	☐	☐	☐	☐	☐
Solve word problems using metric and customary measurements.	☐	☐	☐	☐	☐

EVALUATION CHECK LIST FOR

EIGHTH GRADE

MATHEMATICS

	CHILD'S NAME	CHILD'S NAME	CHILD'S NAME	CHILD'S NAME	CHILD'S NAME
Solve one- and two-step word problems using whole numbers, decimals, or fractions.	☐	☐	☐	☐	☐
Determine the missing value in a simple interest formula.	☐	☐	☐	☐	☐
Determine possible outcomes in a situation with two variables.	☐	☐	☐	☐	☐
Identify the mean.	☐	☐	☐	☐	☐
Identify the mode.	☐	☐	☐	☐	☐
Identify the median of a series of two-digit numbers.	☐	☐	☐	☐	☐
Calculate fraction, decimal, and percent equivalence.	☐	☐	☐	☐	☐
Determine the percent of increase and/or decrease.	☐	☐	☐	☐	☐
Determine the unit cost of items to compare prices.	☐	☐	☐	☐	☐

PERCENT

Determine simple interest for one year.	☐	☐	☐	☐	☐
Determine the discount on a sale item.	☐	☐	☐	☐	☐
Determine the commission on a sale.	☐	☐	☐	☐	☐
Locate a point using ordered pairs of integers on the coordinate plane.	☐	☐	☐	☐	☐
Locate the quadrant in which an ordered pair of integers is located.	☐	☐	☐	☐	☐

CHARTS, GRAPHS, AND TABLES

Interpret graphs, tables, scales, and charts by making identification, comparisons and calculations.	☐	☐	☐	☐	☐

When he made a decree for the rain, and a way for the lighting of the the thunder:
Then did he see it, yea, and searched it out. And unto man he said, Behold, the fear of the Lord,
that is wisdom; and to depart from evil is understanding.

JOB 28:25-28 (KJV)

SCIENCE

Earth and Space • Biological Sciences: Animals/Plants • Physical Science • Science Processing Skills

KINDERGARTEN

FIRST GRADE

SECOND GRADE

THIRD GRADE

FOURTH GRADE

FIFTH GRADE

SIXTH GRADE

SEVENTH GRADE

EIGHTH GRADE

EVALUATION CHECK LIST FOR
KINDERGARTEN
SCIENCE

Kindergarten students should be able to do the following:

	CHILD'S NAME	CHILD'S NAME	CHILD'S NAME	CHILD'S NAME	CHILD'S NAME
EARTH AND SPACE					
Realize weather conditions change from day to day.	☐	☐	☐	☐	☐
Realize rocks are part of the earth's composition.	☐	☐	☐	☐	☐
Develop an appreciation for the earth's environment and the necessity for keeping it clean.	☐	☐	☐	☐	☐
BIOLOGICAL SCIENCE					
Understand animals reproduce by having young.	☐	☐	☐	☐	☐
Recognize animals live in a variety of habitats and change with the different seasons.	☐	☐	☐	☐	☐
Understand plants as living things that grow and change.	☐	☐	☐	☐	☐
Recognize human beings have similarities and differences.	☐	☐	☐	☐	☐
Understand human beings experience their world through the use of the senses.	☐	☐	☐	☐	☐
PHYSICAL SCIENCE					
Understand electricity is not only useful but can be dangerous.	☐	☐	☐	☐	☐
Learn the importance of observing safety rules when using electricity.	☐	☐	☐	☐	☐
Learn magnets can both attract and repel.	☐	☐	☐	☐	☐
Recognize there are different kinds and sources of sound.	☐	☐	☐	☐	☐

Evaluation Check List for First Grade

Science

First-grade students should be able to do the following:

	Child's Name	Child's Name	Child's Name	Child's Name	Child's Name
Earth and Space					
Understand earth is our home planet.	☐	☐	☐	☐	☐
Know the common astronomical bodies (clouds, sun, stars, etc.).	☐	☐	☐	☐	☐
Understand the planets rotate.	☐	☐	☐	☐	☐
Understand fossils provide information about the past.	☐	☐	☐	☐	☐
Understand water evaporates.	☐	☐	☐	☐	☐
Biological Science					
Understand the general functions of the:					
heart.	☐	☐	☐	☐	☐
lungs.	☐	☐	☐	☐	☐
brain.	☐	☐	☐	☐	☐
stomach.	☐	☐	☐	☐	☐
Understand proper nutrition and caring for the body.	☐	☐	☐	☐	☐
Be able to tell which food group a food item fits into.	☐	☐	☐	☐	☐
Understand food processing makes a difference in nutrition.	☐	☐	☐	☐	☐
Biological Science: Animals					
Understand the difference between living and non-living things.	☐	☐	☐	☐	☐
Understand animals are living things with specific needs and characteristics.	☐	☐	☐	☐	☐
Understand reproductive differences in animals.	☐	☐	☐	☐	☐

EVALUATION CHECK LIST FOR

FIRST GRADE

SCIENCE

	CHILD'S NAME	CHILD'S NAME	CHILD'S NAME	CHILD'S NAME	CHILD'S NAME
Identify an animal that sleeps through the winter.	☐	☐	☐	☐	☐
BIOLOGICAL SCIENCE: PLANTS					
Understand plants are living things with specific needs and characteristics.	☐	☐	☐	☐	☐
Realize all living things grow and develop.	☐	☐	☐	☐	☐
Identify a living thing can grow from a seed.	☐	☐	☐	☐	☐
Understand plants are living things with specific needs and characteristics.	☐	☐	☐	☐	☐
Understand how parts of a plant function.	☐	☐	☐	☐	☐
PHYSICAL SCIENCE					
Understand different states of matter (solid, liquid, gas).	☐	☐	☐	☐	☐
Understand heat, light, and energy come from the sun.	☐	☐	☐	☐	☐
Recognize scientists work by using experiments.	☐	☐	☐	☐	☐
Recognize machines are not only useful to man but can be dangerous to use.	☐	☐	☐	☐	☐
Understand the concept of weight.	☐	☐	☐	☐	☐
Understand the use for common household appliances.	☐	☐	☐	☐	☐
Understand matter exists in various states and has identifiable properties.	☐	☐	☐	☐	☐
SCIENCE PROCESSING SKILLS					
Analyze a simple bar graph.	☐	☐	☐	☐	☐
Predict results of water evaporation.	☐	☐	☐	☐	☐
Determine the sequence of events in space.	☐	☐	☐	☐	☐

Evaluation Check List for

Second Grade

Science

Second-grade students should be able to do the following:	Child's Name	Child's Name	Child's Name	Child's Name	Child's Name
Earth and Space					
Understand different bodies of water provide important resources.	☐	☐	☐	☐	☐
Understand the effects of gravity.	☐	☐	☐	☐	☐
Recognize weather is the result of changing atmospheric conditions.	☐	☐	☐	☐	☐
Understand man's environment is affected by the activities of the earth's inhabitants.	☐	☐	☐	☐	☐
Understand the effects of the following:					
earthquake.	☐	☐	☐	☐	☐
hurricane.	☐	☐	☐	☐	☐
tornado.	☐	☐	☐	☐	☐
flood.	☐	☐	☐	☐	☐
Be able to recognize the names of planets.	☐	☐	☐	☐	☐
Biological Science: Animals					
Realize animals differ in various ways and all living things experience life cycles.	☐	☐	☐	☐	☐
Understand animals have like offspring.	☐	☐	☐	☐	☐
Realize animals live in different environments.	☐	☐	☐	☐	☐
Be able to classify common animals (reptile, bird, mammal, etc.)	☐	☐	☐	☐	☐
Understand the growth and development of different animal stages.	☐	☐	☐	☐	☐
Biological Science: Plants					
Determine what is required for seed development...	☐	☐	☐	☐	☐
Understand plants are living things with spe-					

	CHILD'S NAME	CHILD'S NAME	CHILD'S NAME	CHILD'S NAME	CHILD'S NAME
cific needs and characteristics.	☐	☐	☐	☐	☐
Understand how parts of plants function.	☐	☐	☐	☐	☐
PHYSICAL SCIENCE					
Understand sound is produced by vibrations and is transmitted through matter in all directions.	☐	☐	☐	☐	☐
Compare energy sources with energy uses (sun, heat, etc.)	☐	☐	☐	☐	☐
Understand different states of matter (solid, liquid, gas).	☐	☐	☐	☐	☐
Recognize heat and light as related forms of energy that come from various sources.	☐	☐	☐	☐	☐
Understand heat energy affects matter in various ways.	☐	☐	☐	☐	☐
Recognize energy exists in many types and must be conserved.	☐	☐	☐	☐	☐
Understand electricity is not only useful, but can be dangerous.	☐	☐	☐	☐	☐
Learn the importance of observing safety rules when using electricity.	☐	☐	☐	☐	☐
SCIENCE PROCESSING SKILLS					
Analyze data charts, graphs, and tables.	☐	☐	☐	☐	☐
Given a dangerous situation, predict the proper action.	☐	☐	☐	☐	☐
Be able to classify into which food group a food item fits.	☐	☐	☐	☐	☐
Use observation skills to classify an object.	☐	☐	☐	☐	☐
Use observation skills to estimate measurement.	☐	☐	☐	☐	☐

EVALUATION CHECK LIST FOR

THIRD GRADE

SCIENCE

	CHILD'S NAME	CHILD'S NAME	CHILD'S NAME	CHILD'S NAME	CHILD'S NAME
Third-grade students should be able to do the following:					
EARTH AND SPACE					
Realize the solar system is composed of many objects which revolve around a star.	☐	☐	☐	☐	☐
Understand rocks and soil move through a continuous cycle.	☐	☐	☐	☐	☐
Understand day and night result from the rotation of the earth.	☐	☐	☐	☐	☐
Understand earth's temperature differs with sun ray angle.	☐	☐	☐	☐	☐
Understand fossils.	☐	☐	☐	☐	☐
Recognize living things are affected by changes in the environment.	☐	☐	☐	☐	☐
Understand the evaporation process.	☐	☐	☐	☐	☐
Understand precipitation.	☐	☐	☐	☐	☐
Predict the effects of pollution.	☐	☐	☐	☐	☐
BIOLOGICAL SCIENCE					
Be able to match skeletal parts to body sections.	☐	☐	☐	☐	☐
Understand body organs and their functions.	☐	☐	☐	☐	☐
Understand the four food groups.	☐	☐	☐	☐	☐
Recognize the various body systems that support and protect the human body.	☐	☐	☐	☐	☐
Understand the habitat is the environment in which particular organisms live.	☐	☐	☐	☐	☐
BIOLOGICAL SCIENCE: ANIMALS					
Identify common features of animals to determine class.	☐	☐	☐	☐	☐

Evaluation Check List for

Third Grade

Science

	Child's Name	Child's Name	Child's Name	Child's Name	Child's Name
Understand basic animal needs for adult and baby animals.	☐	☐	☐	☐	☐
Classify common animals (bird, mammal, reptile, etc.).	☐	☐	☐	☐	☐
Biological Science: Plants					
Realize plants reproduce and grow in various ways.	☐	☐	☐	☐	☐
Identify common plant forms.	☐	☐	☐	☐	☐
Understand composition of plants.	☐	☐	☐	☐	☐
Physical Science					
Understand classifying.	☐	☐	☐	☐	☐
Understand the force of gravity.	☐	☐	☐	☐	☐
Be able to classify a simple machine.	☐	☐	☐	☐	☐
Be able to measure the length of an object in centimeters.	☐	☐	☐	☐	☐
Understand uses of machines to make work	☐	☐	☐	☐	☐
easier.	☐	☐	☐	☐	☐
Realize all matter is made up of atoms in constant motion.	☐	☐	☐	☐	☐
Understand different states of matter.	☐	☐	☐	☐	☐
Science Processing Skills					
Be able to interpret charts and graphs.	☐	☐	☐	☐	☐
Be able to explain a food chain sequence.	☐	☐	☐	☐	☐
Be able to classify objects into their proper groups.	☐	☐	☐	☐	☐
Use observation skills to predict outcomes of experiments.	☐	☐	☐	☐	☐
Be able to classify forms of energy.	☐	☐	☐	☐	☐

Evaluation Check List for

Fourth Grade

Science

Fourth-grade students should be able to do the following:	CHILD'S NAME	CHILD'S NAME	CHILD'S NAME	CHILD'S NAME	CHILD'S NAME
Earth and Space					
Understand the human body is composed of sensory organs which detect heat, light, and sound.	☐	☐	☐	☐	☐
Understand a solar eclipse.	☐	☐	☐	☐	☐
Realize proper growth and development are dependent on many factors working together.	☐	☐	☐	☐	☐
Realize differing atmospheric conditions.	☐	☐	☐	☐	☐
Realize the importance of oceans to life on earth.	☐	☐	☐	☐	☐
Realize chemicals may be harmful to the environment.	☐	☐	☐	☐	☐
Understand environmental problems may vary from one community to another.	☐	☐	☐	☐	☐
Realize each individual impacts the environment.	☐	☐	☐	☐	☐
Determine past environment based on specific information.	☐	☐	☐	☐	☐
Understand why we have four seasons on earth.	☐	☐	☐	☐	☐
Forecast the form of precipitation at certain temperatures.	☐	☐	☐	☐	☐
Know what scientists study to learn about the past.	☐	☐	☐	☐	☐
Biological Science					
Identify the effect of the sun on humans.	☐	☐	☐	☐	☐
Identify major food groups.	☐	☐	☐	☐	☐

Evaluation Check List for

Fourth Grade

Science

	Child's Name	Child's Name	Child's Name	Child's Name	Child's Name
Identify the major organs in the human body.	☐	☐	☐	☐	☐
Biological Science: Animals					
Understand major animal groups.	☐	☐	☐	☐	☐
Recognize the differences among animals.	☐	☐	☐	☐	☐
Predict the habitation of a given animal.	☐	☐	☐	☐	☐
Understand the food chain.	☐	☐	☐	☐	☐
Know how a given animal gives birth (live or eggs).	☐	☐	☐	☐	☐
Understand how animals move (fly, crawl, walk).	☐	☐	☐	☐	☐
Understand how an animal adapts to its environment.	☐	☐	☐	☐	☐
Use observation skills to classify an animal.	☐	☐	☐	☐	☐
Biological Science: Plants					
Understand the functioning of a plant.	☐	☐	☐	☐	☐
Understand the functions of plant parts.	☐	☐	☐	☐	☐
Understand the importance of plant reproduction.	☐	☐	☐	☐	☐
Physical Science					
Classify different forms of energy.	☐	☐	☐	☐	☐
Interpret measurements of mass.	☐	☐	☐	☐	☐
Recognize magnets are fundamental parts of generators and are required to produce current electricity.	☐	☐	☐	☐	☐
Realize current electricity may travel along one or more paths.	☐	☐	☐	☐	☐
Realize all matter conducts electricity.	☐	☐	☐	☐	☐
Understand sound travels by molecular motion.	☐	☐	☐	☐	☐

EVALUATION CHECK LIST FOR
FOURTH GRADE
SCIENCE

	CHILD'S NAME	CHILD'S NAME	CHILD'S NAME	CHILD'S NAME	CHILD'S NAME
Realize heat and light are obtained from various sources.	☐	☐	☐	☐	☐
SCIENCE PROCESSING SKILLS					
Use research skills to explain why certain shapes have different shadows.	☐	☐	☐	☐	☐
Interpret graphs, tables, and charts.	☐	☐	☐	☐	☐
Analyze an experiment and predict the outcome.	☐	☐	☐	☐	☐
Evaluate the suitability of an environment for certain animals.	☐	☐	☐	☐	☐
Analyze a simple circuit.	☐	☐	☐	☐	☐

EVALUATION CHECK LIST FOR
FIFTH GRADE
SCIENCE

Fifth-grade students should be able to do the following:

	CHILD'S NAME	CHILD'S NAME	CHILD'S NAME	CHILD'S NAME	CHILD'S NAME
EARTH AND SPACE					
Be able to explain what plant lives well in a certain environment.	☐	☐	☐	☐	☐
Identify an egg-laying animal.	☐	☐	☐	☐	☐
Explain the effect sun has on humans.	☐	☐	☐	☐	☐
Understand common forms of major animal groups.	☐	☐	☐	☐	☐
Understand the four food groups and their nutritional values.	☐	☐	☐	☐	☐
Identify major body organs and their functions.	☐	☐	☐	☐	☐
Realize plants have complex structures with specialized functions.	☐	☐	☐	☐	☐
Recognize there are two basic types of seed plants.	☐	☐	☐	☐	☐
Realize humans have specialized systems responsible for body functioning.	☐	☐	☐	☐	☐
Realize each body system is subject to disease.	☐	☐	☐	☐	☐
Realize microscopic organisms are essential to life.	☐	☐	☐	☐	☐
Explain how the earth rotates.	☐	☐	☐	☐	☐
Understand how fossils form.	☐	☐	☐	☐	☐
Understand the effect of gravity.	☐	☐	☐	☐	☐
Understand the cause of seasonal change.	☐	☐	☐	☐	☐
Predict the form of precipitation at different temperatures.	☐	☐	☐	☐	☐
Understand the functions of plant parts.	☐	☐	☐	☐	☐
Classify animals into major groups.	☐	☐	☐	☐	☐
Understand seed germination.	☐	☐	☐	☐	☐

EVALUATION CHECK LIST FOR

FIFTH GRADE

SCIENCE

	CHILD'S NAME	CHILD'S NAME	CHILD'S NAME	CHILD'S NAME	CHILD'S NAME
Understand the topography of the ocean floor is in constant change.	☐	☐	☐	☐	☐
Realize energy consumption impacts the environment.	☐	☐	☐	☐	☐
Realize each local community has important plants and animals.	☐	☐	☐	☐	☐
PHYSICAL SCIENCE					
Realize use of machines increases productivity...	☐	☐	☐	☐	☐
Realize machines can be used to alter a force...	☐	☐	☐	☐	☐
Tell temperature on a thermometer.	☐	☐	☐	☐	☐
Be able to classify different forms of energy.	☐	☐	☐	☐	☐
Understand a simple electrical unit.	☐	☐	☐	☐	☐
Understand matter consists of atoms.	☐	☐	☐	☐	☐
Understand energy exists in many forms.	☐	☐	☐	☐	☐
Understand the properties of matter can be identified and measured.	☐	☐	☐	☐	☐
Classify a simple machine.	☐	☐	☐	☐	☐
Realize motion of objects is affected by friction.	☐	☐	☐	☐	☐
SCIENCE PROCESSING SKILLS					
Interpret graphs and charts.	☐	☐	☐	☐	☐
Predict the outcome of an experiment	☐	☐	☐	☐	☐

EVALUATION CHECK LIST FOR

SIXTH GRADE

SCIENCE

Sixth-grade students should be able to do the following:

	CHILD'S NAME	CHILD'S NAME	CHILD'S NAME	CHILD'S NAME	CHILD'S NAME
EARTH AND SPACE					
Realize the universe has various components.	☐	☐	☐	☐	☐
Recognize changes are constantly occurring in and on the earth.	☐	☐	☐	☐	☐
Understand communities address their energy needs in differing ways.	☐	☐	☐	☐	☐
Recognize factors influencing the stability of ecosystems.	☐	☐	☐	☐	☐
BIOLOGICAL SCIENCE					
Recognize traits are passed from parents to offspring.	☐	☐	☐	☐	☐
Understand why we have safety rules.	☐	☐	☐	☐	☐
Identify the source of a disease.	☐	☐	☐	☐	☐
Identify the function of major body organs.	☐	☐	☐	☐	☐
Understand energy used in muscles.	☐	☐	☐	☐	☐
BIOLOGICAL SCIENCE: ANIMALS					
Understand animal adaptation to the environment.	☐	☐	☐	☐	☐
Identify characteristics of animals.	☐	☐	☐	☐	☐
Understand the food chain.	☐	☐	☐	☐	☐
Use observation skills to determine if an animal is suited to an environment.	☐	☐	☐	☐	☐
BIOLOGICAL SCIENCE: PLANTS					
Understand photosynthesis and cellular respiration are life-sustaining plant processes.	☐	☐	☐	☐	☐

EVALUATION CHECK LIST FOR

SIXTH GRADE

SCIENCE

	CHILD'S NAME	CHILD'S NAME	CHILD'S NAME	CHILD'S NAME	CHILD'S NAME
Understand the life cycle of plants.	☐	☐	☐	☐	☐
Using observation methods, evaluate plant growth in different environments.	☐	☐	☐	☐	☐
Identify plant parts.	☐	☐	☐	☐	☐
PHYSICAL SCIENCE					
Recognize magnets as either natural or man-made.	☐	☐	☐	☐	☐
Identify various sources of energy that can be utilized in the production of electricity.	☐	☐	☐	☐	☐
Understand electricity involves the movement of electrons.	☐	☐	☐	☐	☐
Understand electricity can be harmful.	☐	☐	☐	☐	☐
Understand sound is produced by vibrating matter and is transmitted in all directions.	☐	☐	☐	☐	☐
SCIENCE PROCESSING SKILLS					
Read charts, graphs, and tables to gather information.	☐	☐	☐	☐	☐
Use a model of the food chain to predict the results of the chain.	☐	☐	☐	☐	☐
Analyze an experiment and predict the results.	☐	☐	☐	☐	☐

EVALUATION CHECK LIST FOR
SEVENTH GRADE
SCIENCE

Seventh-grade students should be able to do the following:

	CHILD'S NAME	CHILD'S NAME	CHILD'S NAME	CHILD'S NAME	CHILD'S NAME
EARTH AND SPACE					
Realize the earth's weather is an interaction of many parts of the environment.	☐	☐	☐	☐	☐
Recognize the force of gravity.	☐	☐	☐	☐	☐
Anticipate the findings of a change in gravitational pull.	☐	☐	☐	☐	☐
Know the importance of the ocean, its life forms, its physical features and resources.	☐	☐	☐	☐	☐
Understand ecosystems are dependent on interrelationships within the environment.	☐	☐	☐	☐	☐
Recognize a property of a common rock type.	☐	☐	☐	☐	☐
Predict the forecast of a solar eclipse.	☐	☐	☐	☐	☐
Determine causes of air pollution.	☐	☐	☐	☐	☐
Understand the rotation of the earth.	☐	☐	☐	☐	☐
BIOLOGICAL SCIENCE					
Know the human body is composed of different biological systems that are interrelated.	☐	☐	☐	☐	☐
Know the human body is dependent upon good nutrition.	☐	☐	☐	☐	☐
Know the cell is the basic unit of living things.	☐	☐	☐	☐	☐
Know the importance of body organs based on their functions.	☐	☐	☐	☐	☐
Classify foods based on nutritional value.	☐	☐	☐	☐	☐
Using observation skills, match a group of skeleton bones to the body section.	☐	☐	☐	☐	☐
Identify major body systems.	☐	☐	☐	☐	☐
Associate structure and function of cells.	☐	☐	☐	☐	☐

Evaluation Check List for

Seventh Grade

Science

	Child's Name	Child's Name	Child's Name	Child's Name	Child's Name
Biological Science: Animals					
Sequence food chains.	☐	☐	☐	☐	☐
Understand a model of a food web.	☐	☐	☐	☐	☐
Compare and classify common animals.	☐	☐	☐	☐	☐
Realize animals and plants are classified according to various structures.	☐	☐	☐	☐	☐
Given an animal, evaluate the proper ability to adapt to an environment.	☐	☐	☐	☐	☐
Biological Science: Plants					
Understand the coloring pigment in a plant.	☐	☐	☐	☐	☐
Identify plant parts and functions.	☐	☐	☐	☐	☐
Physical Science	☐	☐	☐	☐	☐
Understand simple and compound machines make work easier.	☐	☐	☐	☐	☐
Understand matter and energy in the universe are governed by physical laws.	☐	☐	☐	☐	☐
Science Processing Skills					
Be able to interpret charts, graphs and tables.					
Be able to identify a compound.	☐	☐	☐	☐	☐
Draw conclusions when given an experiment.					
Understand simple machines.	☐	☐	☐	☐	☐
Show an understanding of a chemical formula					
Estimate the measurement of an item.	☐	☐	☐	☐	☐

EVALUATION CHECK LIST FOR

EIGHTH GRADE

SCIENCE

Eighth-grade students should be able to do the following:

	CHILD'S NAME	CHILD'S NAME	CHILD'S NAME	CHILD'S NAME	CHILD'S NAME
EARTH AND SPACE					
Realize the knowledge of the universe is expanding.	☐	☐	☐	☐	☐
Realize the earth is constantly changing.	☐	☐	☐	☐	☐
Know civilization is dependent upon both renewable and non-renewable resources.	☐	☐	☐	☐	☐
Realize people influence the quality of the environment.	☐	☐	☐	☐	☐
Determine the differences in climates (tropical, polar, marine, desert, etc.).	☐	☐	☐	☐	☐
Understand the earth's motions.	☐	☐	☐	☐	☐
Recognize the effect of different layers of our atmosphere.	☐	☐	☐	☐	☐
BIOLOGICAL SCIENCE					
Realize the continuation of a species is maintained through heredity.	☐	☐	☐	☐	☐
BIOLOGICAL SCIENCE: ANIMALS					
Understand the different roles in the ecosystem.	☐	☐	☐	☐	☐
Formulate a conclusion based on the understanding of reproduction and mutation rates.	☐	☐	☐	☐	☐
BIOLOGICAL SCIENCE: PLANTS					
Understand the functions of plant parts.	☐	☐	☐	☐	☐
Formulate a consequence based on the understanding of plant structure.	☐	☐	☐	☐	☐

EVALUATION CHECK LIST FOR

EIGHTH GRADE

SCIENCE

	CHILD'S NAME	CHILD'S NAME	CHILD'S NAME	CHILD'S NAME	CHILD'S NAME
PHYSICAL SCIENCE					
Realize electricity and magnetism are related forms of energy.	☐	☐	☐	☐	☐
Understand sound, heat, and light are integral parts of the environment.	☐	☐	☐	☐	☐
Understand observation and experimentation are the bases of scientific reasoning.	☐	☐	☐	☐	☐
Understand all matter has a definite structure which determines physical and chemical properties.	☐	☐	☐	☐	☐
Understand what produces a chemical change.	☐	☐	☐	☐	☐
SCIENCE PROCESSING SKILLS					
Use observation skills to determine the use of a simple machine.	☐	☐	☐	☐	☐
Be able to interpret charts, graphs, and tables.	☐	☐	☐	☐	☐
Be able to identify a compound.	☐	☐	☐	☐	☐
Draw conclusions when given an experiment.	☐	☐	☐	☐	☐
Show an understanding of a chemical formula.	☐	☐	☐	☐	☐
Estimate the measurement of an item.	☐	☐	☐	☐	☐

Go ye therefore, and teach all nations, baptizing them in the name of the Father, and of the Son, and of the Holy Ghost: Teaching them to observe all things whatsoever I have commanded you: and, lo, I am with you alway, even unto the end of the world. Amen.

MATTHEW 28:19-20 (KJV)

SOCIAL SCIENCES

Geography • History • Political Science • Economics • Psychology/Sociology

EVALUATION CHECK LIST FOR

KINDERGARTEN

SOCIAL SCIENCE

Kindergarten students should be able to do the following:

	CHILD'S NAME	CHILD'S NAME	CHILD'S NAME	CHILD'S NAME	CHILD'S NAME
GEOGRAPHY					
Recognize a map.	☐	☐	☐	☐	☐
Recognize a globe.	☐	☐	☐	☐	☐
HISTORY					
Understand different forms of transportation through history.	☐	☐	☐	☐	☐
Understand individuals have a personal history (family tree).	☐	☐	☐	☐	☐
Understand things change over time.	☐	☐	☐	☐	☐
POLITICAL SCIENCE					
Recognize the need for rules at home and school.	☐	☐	☐	☐	☐
Understand the need for cultural rules and laws.	☐	☐	☐	☐	☐
Know rules of safety.	☐	☐	☐	☐	☐
Understand the need for environmental rules.	☐	☐	☐	☐	☐
Develop an understanding of space and spatial relationships.	☐	☐	☐	☐	☐
Understand environments and recognize their differences.	☐	☐	☐	☐	☐
Recognize the need for guidance from others.	☐	☐	☐	☐	☐
Understand the concept of being a citizen.	☐	☐	☐	☐	☐
Recognize different methods of meeting needs and wants.	☐	☐	☐	☐	☐
Understand the importance of jobs.	☐	☐	☐	☐	☐
PSYCHOLOGY/SOCIOLOGY					
Understand the worth of each individual and self.	☐	☐	☐	☐	☐

Evaluation Check List for

Kindergarten

Social Science

	Child's Name	Child's Name	Child's Name	Child's Name	Child's Name
Understand the similarities and differences among individuals.	☐	☐	☐	☐	☐
Know the roles of family members.	☐	☐	☐	☐	☐
Understand the behavior of individuals is changed by relationships with others.	☐	☐	☐	☐	☐
Understand the concept of culture and its effect on individuals.	☐	☐	☐	☐	☐
Know the contributions of different cultures.	☐	☐	☐	☐	☐
Understand many jobs require people working together.	☐	☐	☐	☐	☐
Understand the position of an individual to his family and the world.	☐	☐	☐	☐	☐

Evaluation Check List for

First Grade

Social Science

First-grade students should be able to do the following:

	Child's Name	Child's Name	Child's Name	Child's Name	Child's Name
Geography					
Recognize how geography affected early settlements.	☐	☐	☐	☐	☐
Know the location of land masses and bodies of water.	☐	☐	☐	☐	☐
Know the geographic location of the United States and your state on a globe or a map.	☐	☐	☐	☐	☐
Know directions on a globe or a map.	☐	☐	☐	☐	☐
Understand the difference between land and water on a map and globe.	☐	☐	☐	☐	☐
Realize there are seven main bodies of land on earth.	☐	☐	☐	☐	☐
Recognize map symbols and graph symbols.	☐	☐	☐	☐	☐
Be able to recognize major characteristics of each continent.	☐	☐	☐	☐	☐
History					
Know about the pilgrims.	☐	☐	☐	☐	☐
Grasp the concept that people were here on earth long ago.	☐	☐	☐	☐	☐
Recognize people have different religious beliefs	☐	☐	☐	☐	☐
Understand how communication has developed and improved through history.	☐	☐	☐	☐	☐
Understand American history as it relates to the holidays; why we celebrate the Fourth of July, etc.	☐	☐	☐	☐	☐

EVALUATION CHECK LIST FOR
FIRST GRADE

SOCIAL SCIENCE

	CHILD'S NAME	CHILD'S NAME	CHILD'S NAME	CHILD'S NAME	CHILD'S NAME
Be able to sequence historical periods by clothing of different time periods or means of transportation.	☐	☐	☐	☐	☐
Recognize the transformation countries have made from first settlement to the present.	☐	☐	☐	☐	☐
Develop a respect for and appreciation of other cultures in relation to families, homes and schools.	☐	☐	☐	☐	☐
Have an understanding of the development of the American flag.	☐	☐	☐	☐	☐

POLITICAL SCIENCE

Understand the development of neighborhoods and how they differ.	☐	☐	☐	☐	☐
Determine that individuals have rights.	☐	☐	☐	☐	☐
Understand neighborhood responsibilities and needs.	☐	☐	☐	☐	☐
Identify occupation in the community.	☐	☐	☐	☐	☐
Recognize the importance of both the individual and families as parts of neighborhoods.	☐	☐	☐	☐	☐
Understand environmental effects on homes.	☐	☐	☐	☐	☐
Understand the role of culture to a neighborhood.	☐	☐	☐	☐	☐
Understand the effect of environment upon jobs.	☐	☐	☐	☐	☐
Recognize the services provided by workers.	☐	☐	☐	☐	☐

PSYCHOLOGY/SOCIOLOGY

Understand the individual's responsibilities to a group as a citizen.	☐	☐	☐	☐	☐

Evaluation Check List for
First Grade
Social Science

	CHILD'S NAME	CHILD'S NAME	CHILD'S NAME	CHILD'S NAME	CHILD'S NAME
Understand why groups are formed.	☐	☐	☐	☐	☐
Understand the rules of communication.	☐	☐	☐	☐	☐
Recognize the uses of communication.	☐	☐	☐	☐	☐
Understand the role of language in communication.	☐	☐	☐	☐	☐
Recognize the importance of communication to people all over the world.	☐	☐	☐	☐	☐

EVALUATION CHECK LIST FOR

SECOND GRADE

SOCIAL SCIENCE

Second-grade students should be able to do the following:

	CHILD'S NAME	CHILD'S NAME	CHILD'S NAME	CHILD'S NAME	CHILD'S NAME
GEOGRAPHY					
Understand the concept of physical location.	☐	☐	☐	☐	☐
Know the need for certain geographical laws.	☐	☐	☐	☐	☐
Know the location of specific areas on maps.	☐	☐	☐	☐	☐
HISTORY					
Know the major exports of the country.	☐	☐	☐	☐	☐
Understand the necessity of imports.	☐	☐	☐	☐	☐
Identify national holidays.	☐	☐	☐	☐	☐
Sequence historical events by identifying communication, transportation, or clothing.	☐	☐	☐	☐	☐
Identify major events in American history.	☐	☐	☐	☐	☐
POLITICAL SCIENCE					
Understand the voting process.	☐	☐	☐	☐	☐
Understand how communities change with time.	☐	☐	☐	☐	☐
Understand community interdependence.	☐	☐	☐	☐	☐
Understand how communities form and adapt to their environment.	☐	☐	☐	☐	☐
Grasp the concept of cultural loyalty.	☐	☐	☐	☐	☐
Recognize the need for community government.	☐	☐	☐	☐	☐
Recognize different roles of community members in different cultures.	☐	☐	☐	☐	☐
Understand the role of culture in community rights and responsibilities.	☐	☐	☐	☐	☐

Evaluation Check List for

Second Grade

Social Science

	Child's Name	Child's Name	Child's Name	Child's Name	Child's Name
Know that communities produce goods and services.	☐	☐	☐	☐	☐
Understand jobs that provide community services.	☐	☐	☐	☐	☐
Recognize available careers and their dependent factors.	☐	☐	☐	☐	☐
Psychology/Sociology					
Understand the rights and responsibilities of individuals and community members.	☐	☐	☐	☐	☐
Understand the position of an individual in his community.	☐	☐	☐	☐	☐
Recognize the influence of other cultures in our lives.	☐	☐	☐	☐	☐

EVALUATION CHECK LIST FOR
THIRD GRADE
SOCIAL SCIENCE

Third-grade students should be able to do the following:	CHILD'S NAME	CHILD'S NAME	CHILD'S NAME	CHILD'S NAME	CHILD'S NAME
GEOGRAPHY					
Know specific places within the local community.	☐	☐	☐	☐	☐
Recognize the influence of land forms, climate, and natural resources in community location and growth.	☐	☐	☐	☐	☐
Recognize geographical and agricultural regions of the United States.	☐	☐	☐	☐	☐
Understand changes made by technological advances.	☐	☐	☐	☐	☐
Identify a continent on a map or globe.	☐	☐	☐	☐	☐
Identify the capitol of the United States.	☐	☐	☐	☐	☐
Identify main bodies of water.	☐	☐	☐	☐	☐
Apply map skills to determine a specific	☐	☐	☐	☐	☐
location.	☐	☐	☐	☐	☐
Use physical and political maps.	☐	☐	☐	☐	☐
Understand technological effects upon environment.	☐	☐	☐	☐	☐
Recognize the supply limits of natural resources.	☐	☐	☐	☐	☐
Understand the need for conservation.	☐	☐	☐	☐	☐
Recognize the family's cultural contribution to a community.	☐	☐	☐	☐	☐
HISTORY					
Identify activities of the pioneers.	☐	☐	☐	☐	☐
Understand how and why communities have developed and changed.	☐	☐	☐	☐	☐

EVALUATION CHECK LIST FOR

THIRD GRADE

SOCIAL SCIENCE

	CHILD'S NAME	CHILD'S NAME	CHILD'S NAME	CHILD'S NAME	CHILD'S NAME
Recognize the effects of mechanization and industrialization upon agricultural and urban communities.	☐	☐	☐	☐	☐
Identify a president of the United States.	☐	☐	☐	☐	☐
Associate a holiday with the event or season.	☐	☐	☐	☐	☐
Recognize the need for environmental protection.	☐	☐	☐	☐	☐
Recognize the factors leading to economic growth.	☐	☐	☐	☐	☐
Understand the role of culture in behavior, growth, and change in a community.	☐	☐	☐	☐	☐
Recognize the elements leading to future community changes.	☐	☐	☐	☐	☐
Understand the interdependence of the world's people.	☐	☐	☐	☐	☐
Understand the effects of technological changes upon the world's people.	☐	☐	☐	☐	☐

POLITICAL SCIENCE

Understand the laws, values, issues and concerns of communities.	☐	☐	☐	☐	☐
Understand the effect of population upon a community.	☐	☐	☐	☐	☐
Understand the relationship of local governments to the state and nation.	☐	☐	☐	☐	☐
Understand the need for international laws.	☐	☐	☐	☐	☐
Understand the Pledge of Allegiance.	☐	☐	☐	☐	☐
Understand the voting process.	☐	☐	☐	☐	☐
Know the length of term for the President.	☐	☐	☐	☐	☐
Be able to tell whether a service is provided by public or private domain.	☐	☐	☐	☐	☐

Evaluation Check List for
Third Grade
Social Science

	Child's Name	Child's Name	Child's Name	Child's Name	Child's Name
Economics					
Understand supply and demand.	☐	☐	☐	☐	☐
Identify different occupations.	☐	☐	☐	☐	☐
Understand how one buys on credit.	☐	☐	☐	☐	☐
Understand manufacturing.	☐	☐	☐	☐	☐
Psychology/Sociology					
Understand different forms of communication.	☐	☐	☐	☐	☐
Understand why and how individuals obtain values.	☐	☐	☐	☐	☐
Understand individuals' basic needs.	☐	☐	☐	☐	☐

Evaluation Check List for

Fourth Grade

Social Science

Fourth-grade students should be able to do the following:

	Child's Name	Child's Name	Child's Name	Child's Name	Child's Name
Geography					
Know the characteristics of natural land forms and how they are represented on different maps.	☐	☐	☐	☐	☐
Recognize regions, land forms, climate, vegetation, and natural resources of your state.	☐	☐	☐	☐	☐
Use longitudinal and latitudinal lines to locate natural regions on maps.	☐	☐	☐	☐	☐
Know the relationship between the characteristics of a natural region and its history.	☐	☐	☐	☐	☐
Name the capitol of the United States.	☐	☐	☐	☐	☐
Determine factors that influence certain crops.	☐	☐	☐	☐	☐
Distinguish between natural and political boundaries.	☐	☐	☐	☐	☐
Recognize differences in natural regions with respect to production, career opportunities, and technical opportunities.	☐	☐	☐	☐	☐
Recognize the importance of natural regions in development of cultural diversities, and regional growth.	☐	☐	☐	☐	☐
Know directional map lines (North, South, East, West).	☐	☐	☐	☐	☐
History					
Relate holidays with seasons.	☐	☐	☐	☐	☐
Recognize the importance of cultural values and priorities in shaping the future.	☐	☐	☐	☐	☐

EVALUATION CHECK LIST FOR

FOURTH GRADE

SOCIAL SCIENCE

	CHILD'S NAME	CHILD'S NAME	CHILD'S NAME	CHILD'S NAME	CHILD'S NAME
Know the important events in the history of your state and important factors which have affected this history.	☐	☐	☐	☐	☐
Know the individuals and groups who have had a major impact on your state.	☐	☐	☐	☐	☐
Identify a President of the United States.	☐	☐	☐	☐	☐
Understand the way pioneers lived.	☐	☐	☐	☐	☐
Understand the changes in transportation.	☐	☐	☐	☐	☐
Know individuals who have had a major impact on other societies.	☐	☐	☐	☐	☐
POLITICAL SCIENCE					
Understand the Pledge of Allegiance.	☐	☐	☐	☐	☐
Know the causes of pollution.	☐	☐	☐	☐	☐
Know the length of a presidential term.	☐	☐	☐	☐	☐
Recognize the similarities and differences among cultures.	☐	☐	☐	☐	☐
Understand how migration affects cultural diversity.	☐	☐	☐	☐	☐
Understand the population distribution of your state and the cultural diversity represented.	☐	☐	☐	☐	☐
Understand your state has a constitution.	☐	☐	☐	☐	☐
Understand the three branches of your state government.	☐	☐	☐	☐	☐
Know the major industrial and agricultural products of the state.	☐	☐	☐	☐	☐
Understand the role of taxation.	☐	☐	☐	☐	☐
Recognize different job opportunities in your state.	☐	☐	☐	☐	☐
Understand how your state interacts with					

	Child's Name	Child's Name	Child's Name	Child's Name	Child's Name
other states, our national government, and other nations.	☐	☐	☐	☐	☐
Understand differences in roles within groups.	☐	☐	☐	☐	☐
Know the importance of major social and political organizations.	☐	☐	☐	☐	☐
Understand the role of technology in your state's future.	☐	☐	☐	☐	☐
Psychology/Sociology					
Recognize the importance of physical location to a person's role in society.	☐	☐	☐	☐	☐
Recognize the individual's role in the cultural group.	☐	☐	☐	☐	☐
Recognize the individual's role at the local, state, national, and international levels.	☐	☐	☐	☐	☐
Recognize the importance of culture to one's individual identity.	☐	☐	☐	☐	☐
Identify different modes of communication.	☐	☐	☐	☐	☐

EVALUATION CHECK LIST FOR

FIFTH GRADE

SOCIAL SCIENCE

Fifth-grade students should be able to do the following:

	CHILD'S NAME	CHILD'S NAME	CHILD'S NAME	CHILD'S NAME	CHILD'S NAME
GEOGRAPHY					
Locate the United States using a global grid. ..	☐	☐	☐	☐	☐
Know the size, shape, and boundaries of the United States.	☐	☐	☐	☐	☐
Know land forms, climate, and natural resources of the United States.	☐	☐	☐	☐	☐
Apply map skills to determine various information.	☐	☐	☐	☐	☐
Relate an area with a given climate.	☐	☐	☐	☐	☐
Recognize names of major countries.	☐	☐	☐	☐	☐
Identify major bodies of water.	☐	☐	☐	☐	☐
Understand how land form characteristics influenced cultures in colonization.	☐	☐	☐	☐	☐
HISTORY					
Know the symbolic meaning of the American flag.	☐	☐	☐	☐	☐
Know the reasons for exploration of the United States.	☐	☐	☐	☐	☐
Understand the relationship of the British with the United States.	☐	☐	☐	☐	☐
Understand the changes in the government during the nation's development.	☐	☐	☐	☐	☐
Understand the people who lived in the United States prior to exploration and colonization.	☐	☐	☐	☐	☐
Understand the importance of migration and immigration upon the culture of the					

	CHILD'S NAME	CHILD'S NAME	CHILD'S NAME	CHILD'S NAME	CHILD'S NAME
United States.	☐	☐	☐	☐	☐
Arrange major historical events in historical order.	☐	☐	☐	☐	☐
Understand how the thirteen colonies developed.	☐	☐	☐	☐	☐
Know how the pilgrims lived.	☐	☐	☐	☐	☐
Analyze a time line.	☐	☐	☐	☐	☐
Know the major events in the nation's history which brought diverse cultures to the United States.	☐	☐	☐	☐	☐
ECONOMICS					
Understand the importance of the nation's economy to the world.	☐	☐	☐	☐	☐
Understand the effect of industrialization and urbanization upon careers.	☐	☐	☐	☐	☐
Understand the meaning of import and export.	☐	☐	☐	☐	☐
Realize why advertising is used.	☐	☐	☐	☐	☐
Recognize the need for changes to meet the future needs of society.	☐	☐	☐	☐	☐
Understand the economic development of the United States.	☐	☐	☐	☐	☐
Understand supply and demand.	☐	☐	☐	☐	☐
POLITICAL SCIENCE					
Understand the evolution of democracy and the legal system in the United States.	☐	☐	☐	☐	☐
Understand the individual's role in government.	☐	☐	☐	☐	☐
Know how the American government was					

	CHILD'S NAME	CHILD'S NAME	CHILD'S NAME	CHILD'S NAME	CHILD'S NAME
formed and its function according to the constitution.	☐	☐	☐	☐	☐
Understand the system of checks and balances.	☐	☐	☐	☐	☐
Understand how the constitution can be changed.	☐	☐	☐	☐	☐
Have an understanding of most laws in the United States.	☐	☐	☐	☐	☐
Recognize the importance of the American constitution to other nations.	☐	☐	☐	☐	☐
Understand being a citizen of a democracy.	☐	☐	☐	☐	☐
Know the rights and responsibilities provided in the Bill of Rights.	☐	☐	☐	☐	☐
Understand how career choices influence the economy.	☐	☐	☐	☐	☐
Recognize cultural contributions to American society.	☐	☐	☐	☐	☐
Recognize the contributions made by Blacks in American history.	☐	☐	☐	☐	☐
Understand the role of minority groups as they are incorporated into society.	☐	☐	☐	☐	☐
Understand the right of a person accused of a crime in the United States.	☐	☐	☐	☐	☐
Recognize the influence of other cultures upon our political system.	☐	☐	☐	☐	☐
Understand the principles of a constitutional government.	☐	☐	☐	☐	☐
Understand the major differences in the various cultural groups.	☐	☐	☐	☐	☐
Recognize the contribution of new cultures to the nation.	☐	☐	☐	☐	☐

EVALUATION CHECK LIST FOR
FIFTH GRADE
SOCIAL SCIENCE

	CHILD'S NAME	CHILD'S NAME	CHILD'S NAME	CHILD'S NAME	CHILD'S NAME
Understand the interrelationship and interdependency of cultural groups in the nation.	☐	☐	☐	☐	☐
PSYCHOLOGY/SOCIOLOGY					
Understand the individual's role and responsibility as a member of American society.	☐	☐	☐	☐	☐
Understand basic human needs.	☐	☐	☐	☐	☐
Determine how two people from different countries differ.	☐	☐	☐	☐	☐
Understand different means of communication.	☐	☐	☐	☐	☐

Evaluation Check List for
Sixth Grade
Social Science

Sixth-grade students should be able to do the following:	Child's Name	Child's Name	Child's Name	Child's Name	Child's Name
Geography					
Locate geographic centers of early civilization.	☐	☐	☐	☐	☐
Understand the importance of land forms, climate, resources, and heritage upon early civilizations.	☐	☐	☐	☐	☐
Name and find the different continents.	☐	☐	☐	☐	☐
Identify physical features of a continent.	☐	☐	☐	☐	☐
Locate the United States using a global grid.	☐	☐	☐	☐	☐
Know the size, shape, and boundaries of the United States.	☐	☐	☐	☐	☐
Know land forms, climate, and natural resources of the United States.	☐	☐	☐	☐	☐
Apply maps skills to determine various information.	☐	☐	☐	☐	☐
Find the equator.	☐	☐	☐	☐	☐
Relate an area with a given climate.	☐	☐	☐	☐	☐
Recognize names of major countries.	☐	☐	☐	☐	☐
Identify major bodies of water.	☐	☐	☐	☐	☐
Understand how land form characteristics influenced cultures in colonization.	☐	☐	☐	☐	☐
History					
Understand the factors which influenced the development of early civilizations.	☐	☐	☐	☐	☐
Recognize important leaders and events in the growth of ancient Greece and Rome.	☐	☐	☐	☐	☐
Understand the rise and decline of ancient civilizations.	☐	☐	☐	☐	☐

EVALUATION CHECK LIST FOR

SIXTH GRADE

SOCIAL SCIENCE

	CHILD'S NAME	CHILD'S NAME	CHILD'S NAME	CHILD'S NAME	CHILD'S NAME
Know major explorers and explorations of the world.	☐	☐	☐	☐	☐
Understand the causes of the Civil War.	☐	☐	☐	☐	☐
Understand the purpose of the Declaration of Independence.	☐	☐	☐	☐	☐
Know a country that helped America gain its independence.	☐	☐	☐	☐	☐
Identify a President during the Civil War.	☐	☐	☐	☐	☐
Understand the sequence of technological advancements in history.	☐	☐	☐	☐	☐
POLITICAL SCIENCE					
Recognize ideas concerning citizenship, government, and cultural groups in ancient civilizations.	☐	☐	☐	☐	☐
Understand the importance of trade, food production, weapons, and tools to early civilization.	☐	☐	☐	☐	☐
Recognize sources of conflict among cultural groups.	☐	☐	☐	☐	☐
Understand the influence of geographic factors upon world cultures.	☐	☐	☐	☐	☐
Understand the increasing complexity of societies.	☐	☐	☐	☐	☐
Understand the historical development of social and political organizations.	☐	☐	☐	☐	☐
Understand the historical impact of various forms of government.	☐	☐	☐	☐	☐
Know how tribal groups and caste systems affect cultures.	☐	☐	☐	☐	☐

EVALUATION CHECK LIST FOR

SIXTH GRADE

SOCIAL SCIENCE

	CHILD'S NAME	CHILD'S NAME	CHILD'S NAME	CHILD'S NAME	CHILD'S NAME
ECONOMICS					
Recognize the influence of capitalism upon economic growth.	☐	☐	☐	☐	☐
Understand the role of the natural environment in limiting, protecting, providing political power, and meeting needs.	☐	☐	☐	☐	☐
Know the impact of technological changes in societies.	☐	☐	☐	☐	☐
Know the effects of colonization, technology, and urbanization upon the economy of the nation.	☐	☐	☐	☐	☐
Know the effects of pollution for industrialized nations.	☐	☐	☐	☐	☐
Understand the effects of the types of government upon the citizens.	☐	☐	☐	☐	☐
Recognize the factors leading to a standard of living.	☐	☐	☐	☐	☐
Understand the Common Market.	☐	☐	☐	☐	☐
Understand the impact of global concerns.	☐	☐	☐	☐	☐
PSYCHOLOGY/SOCIOLOGY					
Recognize the importance of heritage to citizens.	☐	☐	☐	☐	☐
Recognize the increased interest in human rights.	☐	☐	☐	☐	☐
Understand roles and rights of citizens.	☐	☐	☐	☐	☐
Understand the basic needs of a human.	☐	☐	☐	☐	☐

EVALUATION CHECK LIST FOR

SEVENTH GRADE

SOCIAL SCIENCE

CHILD'S NAME | CHILD'S NAME | CHILD'S NAME | CHILD'S NAME | CHILD'S NAME

Seventh-grade students should be able to do the following:

(See the State History at the end of this section)

GEOGRAPHY

Understand the definition, purpose, and tools of geography. ☐ ☐ ☐ ☐ ☐

Understand the earth, its structure, and elements. ☐ ☐ ☐ ☐ ☐

Know the different characteristics and influences of physical features, natural resources, and climates on the peoples of:

North America ☐ ☐ ☐ ☐ ☐

Latin America ☐ ☐ ☐ ☐ ☐

Africa ☐ ☐ ☐ ☐ ☐

Asia ☐ ☐ ☐ ☐ ☐

Europe and Russia ☐ ☐ ☐ ☐ ☐

Know the different characteristics of oceans, and understand what natural resources can be found there. ☐ ☐ ☐ ☐ ☐

Compare different regions with different topography. ☐ ☐ ☐ ☐ ☐

HISTORY

Identify a ruler of a given country. ☐ ☐ ☐ ☐ ☐

Recognize the sequence of technology developments. ☐ ☐ ☐ ☐ ☐

Recognize the sequence of events in space exploration. ☐ ☐ ☐ ☐ ☐

Detect the purpose of the Boston Tea Party. ☐ ☐ ☐ ☐ ☐

EVALUATION CHECK LIST FOR
SEVENTH GRADE
SOCIAL SCIENCE

	CHILD'S NAME	CHILD'S NAME	CHILD'S NAME	CHILD'S NAME	CHILD'S NAME
Understand the industrial revolution.	☐	☐	☐	☐	☐
Identify accomplishments of famous Americans.	☐	☐	☐	☐	☐
Explain the reasoning for the stars on the U. S. Flag.	☐	☐	☐	☐	☐
Identify the location of the Renaissance.	☐	☐	☐	☐	☐
POLITICAL SCIENCE *(People as a Group).*					
Understand the term *Freedom of Press.*	☐	☐	☐	☐	☐
Understand the basic principles of the Bill of Rights.	☐	☐	☐	☐	☐
Explain the voting process.	☐	☐	☐	☐	☐
Understand the American political system.	☐	☐	☐	☐	☐
Explain the responsibility of local government.	☐	☐	☐	☐	☐
ECONOMICS					
Understand inflation.	☐	☐	☐	☐	☐
Define supply and demand.	☐	☐	☐	☐	☐
Determine what increases production in different industries.	☐	☐	☐	☐	☐
Identify communism.	☐	☐	☐	☐	☐
PSYCHOLOGY/SOCIOLOGY					
Understand individuals' rights.	☐	☐	☐	☐	☐
Explain learned behavior.	☐	☐	☐	☐	☐
Define sociology.	☐	☐	☐	☐	☐
Predict behavior in different situations.	☐	☐	☐	☐	☐
Understand different forms of communication.	☐	☐	☐	☐	☐

EVALUATION CHECK LIST FOR

EIGHTH GRADE

SOCIAL SCIENCE

Eighth-grade students should be able to do the following: *(See the State History Section at the end of this chapter)*	CHILD'S NAME	CHILD'S NAME	CHILD'S NAME	CHILD'S NAME	CHILD'S NAME
GEOGRAPHY					
Recognize the geographic regions, climate patterns and natural resources of North America.	☐	☐	☐	☐	☐
Understand how factors affect a country's climate.	☐	☐	☐	☐	☐
Understand and read map symbols and legends.	☐	☐	☐	☐	☐
HISTORY					
Understand the major social, economic, and political reasons for European exploration and colonization of the New World.	☐	☐	☐	☐	☐
Know the events that led to English domination of North America.	☐	☐	☐	☐	☐
Understand the governments, economies, and different lifestyles of the thirteen American colonies.	☐	☐	☐	☐	☐
Know the causes, major events, and personalities of the American Revolution.	☐	☐	☐	☐	☐
Know the weakness of the Articles of Confederation and that the United States Constitution created a stronger central government while protecting the rights of citizens.	☐	☐	☐	☐	☐
Understand the problems and accomplishments of the young American republic.	☐	☐	☐	☐	☐

Evaluation Check List for

Eighth Grade

Social Science

	Child's Name	Child's Name	Child's Name	Child's Name	Child's Name
Understand the expansion and development of the United States during the different presidential terms.	☐	☐	☐	☐	☐
Know the sectional differences that evolved as the America frontier expanded and the country developed culturally and economically.	☐	☐	☐	☐	☐
Know the causes, course, and consequences of the Civil War.	☐	☐	☐	☐	☐
Understand the causes and accomplishments of the Progressive Era.	☐	☐	☐	☐	☐
Know the events that led to American entry into World War I and the subsequent role played by American military forces.	☐	☐	☐	☐	☐
Understand America's return to isolationism and the disillusionment of the Roaring Twenties.	☐	☐	☐	☐	☐
Know causes of the Great Depression and the major efforts of the New Deal.	☐	☐	☐	☐	☐
Understand the causes and worldwide scope of American involvement in World War II.	☐	☐	☐	☐	☐
Understand the causes and events of the Cold War and its impact on American policies at home and abroad.	☐	☐	☐	☐	☐
Recognize a time period by a given mode of transportation.	☐	☐	☐	☐	☐
POLITICAL SCIENCE					
Understand the changes in American society brought about by the Industrial Revolution.	☐	☐	☐	☐	☐

EVALUATION CHECK LIST FOR

EIGHTH GRADE

SOCIAL SCIENCE

	CHILD'S NAME	CHILD'S NAME	CHILD'S NAME	CHILD'S NAME	CHILD'S NAME
Understand the concept of imperialism and the establishment of the United States as a world power.	☐	☐	☐	☐	☐
Understand the changes in American society brought about by the Civil Rights movement, technological advances, and economic and political challenges from other nations.	☐	☐	☐	☐	☐
Identify political parties in the United States.	☐	☐	☐	☐	☐
Understand the powers of the President.	☐	☐	☐	☐	☐
Understand the voting process.	☐	☐	☐	☐	☐
Identify political leaders in different levels of government.	☐	☐	☐	☐	☐
Understand the difference between rights and responsibilities of a United States citizen.	☐	☐	☐	☐	☐

ECONOMICS

Apply an understanding of the association of supply and demand.	☐	☐	☐	☐	☐
Understand what affects job satisfaction.	☐	☐	☐	☐	☐
Predict the results on a country if its exports were no longer available.	☐	☐	☐	☐	☐
Understand inflation.	☐	☐	☐	☐	☐
Understand the depression.	☐	☐	☐	☐	☐

PSYCHOLOGY/SOCIOLOGY

Define psychology.	☐	☐	☐	☐	☐
Determine what consequences different acts will have for an individual.	☐	☐	☐	☐	☐
Realize the changing role of women in society.	☐	☐	☐	☐	☐
Understand what subjects need to be studied for different professions.	☐	☐	☐	☐	☐

STATE HISTORY

Seat of State Government • Developments: Historic/Cultural/Economic

State governments require, usually by the end of seventh grade, that a child will have learned certain basic knowledge about the state. Check with the educational offices in your state about its requirement.

The following *Evaluation Check List* is the requirement for a child in the State of Tennessee. It reflects the acceptable level by the end of the seventh year of schooling.

Evaluation Check List for

Seventh & Eighth Grades

State History

	Child's Name	Child's Name	Child's Name	Child's Name	Child's Name
Know your state capitol	☐	☐	☐	☐	☐
Understand the diversity of your state's physical geography and its impact on the state's historic, economic, and cultural development.	☐	☐	☐	☐	☐
Know the major developments in the area that became your state prior to and during European exploration.	☐	☐	☐	☐	☐
Know the events that led to statehood for your state.	☐	☐	☐	☐	☐
Understand your state Constitution and its relationship to the United States constitution and national government.	☐	☐	☐	☐	☐
Recognize your state's leadership role in the expansion of the young republic.	☐	☐	☐	☐	☐
Understand political, economic, and social developments in the antebellum period on your state.	☐	☐	☐	☐	☐
Know the causes of the Civil War as reflected by your state's sectional differences, if applicable.	☐	☐	☐	☐	☐
Understand the role of your state during the Civil War, if applicable.	☐	☐	☐	☐	☐
Understand the political, social, and economic changes brought to your state through the Reconstruction.	☐	☐	☐	☐	☐
Understand the problems and progress that characterized your state at the turn-of-the-century.	☐	☐	☐	☐	☐
Recognize the impact of the Great Depression and World War II on your state and					

	CHILD'S NAME	CHILD'S NAME	CHILD'S NAME	CHILD'S NAME	CHILD'S NAME
the nation.	☐	☐	☐	☐	☐
Understand the political and social changes that came to your state in the post-World War II years.	☐	☐	☐	☐	☐
Recognize the growing diversity of your state's economy and its impact on national and world markets.	☐	☐	☐	☐	☐
Understand the organization and structure of state and local government.	☐	☐	☐	☐	☐

SECTION V
APPENDICES

GLOSSARY I
BIBLICAL EDUCATIONAL TERMS

From *International Standard Bible Encyclopaedia, Electronic Database* by Biblesoft.

A rich variety of words is employed in the Bible to describe the teaching process. The terms do not so much indicate an office and an official as a function and a service, although both ideas are often expressed or implied.

OLD TESTAMENT TERMS

discernment: *bin,* to separate: The word meaning "to separate," "to distinguish," is often used in a causative sense to signify "to teach." The idea of teaching was not an aggregation of facts bodily transferred, like merchandise. Real learning followed genuine teaching. This word suggests a sound psychological basis for a good pedagogy. The function of teaching might be exercised with reference to the solution of difficult problems, the interpretation of God's will, or the manner of a godly life (Dan. 8:16,26; Neh. 8:7-9; Ps. 119:34).

discipline: *lamadh,* to beat: A very common word for "to teach"; it may have meant "to beat with a rod," "to chastise," and may have originally referred to the striking and goading of beasts, by which they were curbed and trained. By a noble evolution, the term came to describe the process of disciplining and training men in war, religion and life (Isa. 2:3; Hos. 10:11; Micah 4:2). As teaching is both a condition and an accompaniment of disciplining, the word often means simply "to teach," "to inform" (2 Chr. 17:7; Ps. 71:17; Prov. 5:13). The glory of teaching was its harmony with the will of God, its source in God's authority, and its purpose to secure spiritual obedience (Deut. 4:5,14; 31:12-13).

illumination: *zahar,* to shine: This verbal root signifies "to shine," and when applied to the intellectual sphere indicates the function of teaching to be one of illumination. Ignorance is darkness, knowledge is light. Moses was to teach the people statutes and laws, or to enlighten them on the principles and precepts of God's revelation (Exo. 18:20). The service rendered by the teachers-- priests, Levites and fathers-- sent forth by Jehoshaphat, was one of illumination in the twofold sense of instruction and admonition (2 Chr. 19:8-10).

inspiration: *nabha´,* to boil up: The most significant word for "prophet" is derived from the verb which means "to boil up or forth like a fountain," and consequently to pour forth words under the impelling power of the Spirit of God. The Hebrews used the passive forms of the verb because they considered the thoughts and words of the prophets due not to personal ability but to divine influence. The utterances of the prophets were characterized by instruction, admonition, persuasion and prediction (Deut. 18:15-22; Ezek. 33:1-20).

knowledge: *yadha´,* to see (compare *oida*): This verb literally means "to see" and consequently "to perceive," "to know," "to come to know," and "cause to know or teach." It describes the act of knowing as both progressive and completed. The causative conception signifies achievement in the sphere of instruction. It is used of the interpretation and application by Moses of the principles of the law of God (Exo. 18:16,20), of the elucidation of life's problems by the sages (Prov. 9:9; 22:19), and of constant Providential guidance in the way of life (Ps. 16:11).

law: *yarah,* to cast, teach, instruct, inform: The teaching idea from which the law was derived is expressed by a verb which means "to throw," "to cast as an arrow or lot." It is also used of thrusting the hand forth to point out or show clearly (Gen. 46:28; Exo. 15:25). The original idea is easily changed into an educational conception, since the teacher puts forth new ideas and facts as a sower casts seed into the ground. But the process of teaching was not considered external and mechanical but internal and vital (Exo. 35:34-35; 2 Chr. 6:27). The nominal form is the usual word for law, human and divine, general and specific (Deut. 4:8; Ps. 19:8; Prov. 1:8). The following are suggestive phrases: "the book of the law" (Deut. 28:61; 2 Kings 22:8); "the book of the law of Moses" (Josh 8:31; 2 Kin 14:6); "the book of the law of God" (Josh. 24:26); "the book of the law of Yahweh" (2 Chr. 17:9). Thus even in the days of Joshua there was in the possession of the religious teachers a book of the Law of the Lord as given by Moses. This recorded revelation and legislation continued to be the divine norm and ultimate authority for priest, king and people (2 Chr. 23:11; Neh. 8:1-3).

nourishment: *ra`ah,* to feed a flock: The name "shepherd," so precious in both the Old Testament and the New Testament, comes from a verb meaning "to feed," hence, to protect and care for out of a sense of devotion, ownership and responsibility. It is employed with reference to civil rulers in their positions of trust (2 Sam. 5:2; Jer. 23:2); with reference to teachers of virtue and wisdom (Prov. 10:21; Eccl. 12:11); and pre-eminently with reference to God as the great Shepherd of His chosen people (Ps. 23:1; Hos. 4:16). (Ezek. 34) presents an arraignment of the unfaithful shepherds or civil rulers; (Ps. 23) reveals Yahweh as the Shepherd of true believers, and (Jn. 10) shows how religious teachers are shepherds under Jesus the Good Shepherd.

vision: *ra´-ah,* to see: The literal meaning of this verb is "to see," and the nominal form is the ancient name for prophet or authoritative teacher who was expected to have a clear vision of spiritual realities, the will of God, the need of man and the way of life (1 Sam. 9:9; 1 Chr. 9:22; 2 Chr. 16:7) f; (Isa. 30:10).

wisdom: *sakhal,* to be wise: The verb from which the various nominal forms for "wisdom" are derived means "to look at," "to behold," "to view," and in the causative stem describes the process by which one is enabled to see for himself what had never before entered his physical or intellectual field of consciousness. The noun indicates a wise person or sage whose mission is to instruct others in the ways of the Lord (Prov. 16:23; 21:11); and often in the Wisdom literature). In Dan. 12:3 we read: "They that are wise (margin, "the teachers") shall shine as the brightness of the firmament."

New Testament Terms

Further light is thrown upon religious teaching in Bible times by a brief view of the leading educational terms found in the New Testament.

acquisition: *manthano,* to learn: The central thought of teaching is causing one to learn. Teaching and learning are not scholastic but dynamic, and imply personal relationship and activity in the acquisition of knowledge (Mt. 11:29; 28:19; Acts 14:21). There were three concentric circles of disciples in the time of our Lord: learners, pupils, superficial followers, the multitude (Jn. 6:66); the body of believers who accepted Jesus as their Master (Mt. 10:42); and the Twelve Disciples whom Jesus also called apostles (Mt. 10:2).

authority: *prophetes,* one who speaks for: A prophet was a man who spoke forth a message from God to the people. He might deal with past failures and achievements, present privileges and responsibilites, or future doom and glory. He received his message and authority from God (Deut. 18:15-22; Isa. 6). The word refers to Old Testament teachers (Mt. 5:12), to John the Baptist (Mt. 21:26), to Jesus the Messiah (Acts 3:25), and to special speakers in the Apostolic age (Mt. 10:41; Acts 13:1; 1 Cor. 14:29,37).

care: *poimen,* a shepherd: The word for shepherd signifies one who tends a flock, and by analogy a person who gives mental and spiritual nourishment, and guards and supports those under his care (Mt. 9:36; Jn. 10:2,16; 1 Pet. 2:25; Eph. 4:11). Love is a fundamental prerequisite to the exercise of the shepherding function (Jn. 21:15-18). The duties are to be discharged with great diligence and in humble recognition of the gifts and appointment of the Holy Spirit (Acts 20:28).

elucidation: *diermeneuo,* to interpret: In the walk to Emmaus, Christ explained to the perplexed disciples the Old Testament Scriptures in reference to Himself. The work of interpreter is to make truth clear and to effect the edification of the hearer (Lk. 24:27; 1 Cor. 12:30; 14:5,13,27).

exposition: *ektithemi,* to place out: The verb literally means "to set or place out," and signifies to bring out the latent and secret ideas of a literary passage or a system of thought and life. Thus Peter interpreted his vision, Aquila and Priscilla unfolded truth to Apollos, and Paul expounded the gospel in Rome (Acts 11:4; 18:26; 28:23). True teaching is an educational exposition.

instruction: *didasko,* to teach: The usual word for "teach" in the New Testament signifies either to hold a discourse with others in order to instruct them, or to deliver a didactic discourse where there may not be direct personal and verbal participation. In the former sense it describes the interlocutory method, the interplay of the ideas and words between pupils and teachers, and in the latter use it refers to the more formal monologues designed especially to give information (Mt. 4:23); chapters 5-7; (13:36) f; (Jn. 6:59; 1 Cor. 4:17; 1 Tim. 2:12). A teacher is one who performs the function or fills the office of instruction. Ability and fitness for the work are required (Rom. 2:20; Heb. 5:12). The title refers to Jewish teachers (Jn. 1:38), to John the Baptist (Lk. 3:12), to Jesus (Jn. 3:2; 8:4), and often, to Paul (1 Tim. 2:7; 2 Tim. 1:11), and to instructors in the early church (Acts 13:1; Rom. 12:7; 1 Cor. 12:28). Teaching, like preaching, was an integral part of the work of an apostle (Mt. 28:19; Mk. 16:15; Eph. 4:1).

presentation: *paratithemi,* to place beside: The presentative idea involved in the teaching process is intimately associated with the principle of adaptation. When it is stated that Christ put forth parables unto the people, the sacred writer employs the figure of placing alongside of, or near one, hence, before him in an accessible position. The food or teaching should be sound, or hygienic, and adapted to the capacity and development of the recipient (Mt. 13:24; Mk. 8:6; Acts 16:34; 1 Cor. 10:27; 2 Tim. 4:3; Heb. 5:12-14).

supervision: *episkopos,* an overseer: The bishop or overseer was to feed and protect the blood-bought church of God (Acts 20:28). Among the various qualifications of the religious overseers was an aptitude for teaching (1 Tim. 3:2; Tit. 1:9). The Lord is pre-eminently shepherd and bishop (1 Pet. 2:25).

GLOSSARY II

MODERN EDUCATIONAL TERMS

achievement test. an objective examination that measures educationally relevant skills or knowledge about such subjects as reading, spelling, or mathematics.

addend. A number added to another number. In the problem "40 + 73 = ?" the addend is 73.

age norms. values representing typical or average performance of people of age groups.

antebellum. A period before the United States Civil War.

antonym. A word that means the opposite of another word.

average. a statistic that indicates the central tendency or most typical score of a group of scores. Most often, average refers to the sum of a set of scores divided by the number of scores in the set.

battery. a group of carefully selected tests that are administered to a given population, the results of which are of value individually, in combination, and totally.

ceiling. the upper limit of ability that can be measured by a particular test.

clause. A group of words that contain a subject and a verb or verb phrase and forms part of a compound or complex sentence.

congruent. *Geometry,* exactly coinciding: Congruent triangles have the same size and shape. *Algebra,* producing the same remainder when divided by a given number.

contraction. One word made up of two words that have been shortened. It's—it is, hasn't—has not.

Criterion-Referenced Test. A measurement of achievement of specific criteria or skills in terms of absolute levels of mastery. The focus is on performance of an individual as measured against a standard

diacritical. A mark placed over, under, or attached to a letter to indicate pronunciation, stress accent or other value.

diagnostic test. An intensive, in-depth evaluation process with a relatively detailed and narrow coverage of a specific area. The purpose of this test is to determine the specific learning needs of individual students (rather than comparing students to other students, as the standardized tests) and to be able to meet those needs through regular or remedial classroom instruction.

digraph. Two letters used together to spell a single sound. Example: *ea* in each, *th* in with, *sh* in shop.

diphthong. A vowel made up of two vowel sounds pronounced as one syllable. Such as *ou* in house.

Dolch Sight Words. See page 288.

domain-referenced test. A test in which performance is measured against a well-defined set of tasks or body of knowledge (domain). Domain-referenced tests are a specific set of criterion-referenced tests and have a similar purpose.

ecosystem. A system made up of living organisms and its physical environment. A pond, a lake, a forest or an ocean may be an ecosystem. An ecosystem includes such factors as food supply, weather and natural enemies.

factor. Any one of the numbers or expressions which produce a given number of quantity when multiplied together. Example: 2 and 5 are factors of 10.

food chain. A group of organisms so interrelated that each member of the group feeds upon the one below it and, in turn, is eaten by the one above.

food web. 1. A group of interrelated food chains in a certain community. **2.** food cycle.

grade equivalent. The estimated grade level that corresponds to a given score.

heteronym. A word spelled the same as another, but having a different sound and meaning. Example: lead, to conduct and lead, a metal.

homograph. See homonym.

homonym. 1. A word having the same pronunciation and spelling of another word, but different in meaning and origin. Example: bass meaning a fish and bass meaning a male singing voice. **2.** homograph. **3.** homophone.

hyperbole. An exaggerated statement used for effect and not meant to be taken literally. Example: Waves as high as mountains broke over the reef.

inflection. A variation in a word to show case, number, gender, person, tense, mood, voice or comparison. A suffix or other ending used in inflecting: *-est* and *-ed* are common inflections.

informal test. A nonstandardized test that is designed to give an approximate index of an individual's level of ability or learning style; often teacher-constructed.

integer. A whole number (as distinct from fractions). Any positive or negative number including 0.

interrogative. Having the form of asking a question.

inventory. A catalog or list for assessing the absence or presence of certain attitudes, interests, behaviors, or other items regarded as relevant to a given purpose.

item. An individual question or exercise in a test or evaluative instrument.

normal curve equivalent. standard scores with a mean of 50 and a standard deviation of approximately 21.

norm. performance standards that is established by a reference group and that describes average or typical performance. Usually norms are determined by testing a representative group and then calculating the group's test performance.

norm-referenced test. An objective test that is standardized on a group of individuals whose performance is evaluated in relation to the performance of others; contrasted with criterion-referenced test.

objective percent correct. The percent of the items measuring a single objective that a student answers correctly.

ordinal. A number that shows position in a series. First, second, etc.

percent score. The percent of items that are answered correctly.

percentile. The percent of people in the norming sample whose scores were below a given score.

performance Test. Designed to evaluate general intelligence or aptitudes. Consists primarily of motor items or perceptual items because verbal abilities play a minimal role.

polysyllabic. A word with more than three syllables.

predicate. The word or words in a sentence that tell what is said about the subject. In *men work, The men dug wells,* and *The men are soldiers, work, dug wells,* and *are soldiers* are all predicates.

published test. A test that is publicly available because it has been copyrighted and published commercially.

Pythagorean theorem. The theorem that the square of the hypotenuse of a right triangle equals the sum of the squares of the other two sides.

rating scales . Subjective assessments made on predetermined criteria in the form of a scale. Rating scales include numerical scales or descriptive scales. Forced choice rating scales require that the rater determine whether an individual demonstrates more of one trait than another.

raw score. The number of items that are answered correctly.

reliability. The extent of which a test is dependable, stable, and consistent when administered to the same individuals on different occasions. Technically, this is a statistical term that defines the extent to which errors of measurement are absent from a measurement instrument.

schwa. An unstressed vowel sound such as *u* in *circus.* Represented by the symbol of an upside-down *e*.

screening. A fast, efficient measurement for a large population to identify individuals who may deviate in a specified area, such as the incidence of maladjustment or readiness for academic work.

specimen set. A sample set of testing materials that are available from a commercial test publisher.

standard scores--A score that is expressed as a deviation from a population mean.

standardization--Is obtained by administering the test to a given population and then calculating means, standard deviations, standardized scores, and percentiles. Equivalent scores are then produced for comparisons of an individual score to the norm group's performance.

standardized test. A form of measurement that has been normed against a specific population.

stanine. One of the steps in a nine-point scale of standard scores.

synonym. Words of similar meanings. *Small* is the synonym of *little*.

validity. The extent to which a test measures what it was intended to measure. Validity indicates the degree of accuracy of either predictions or inferences based upon a test score.

Dolch Sight Words

a	clean	got	made	red	too
about	cold	green	make	ride	try
after	cam	grow	many	right	two
again	could	had	may	round	under
all	cute	has	me	run	up
always	did	have	much	said	upon
am	do	he	must	saw	us
an	does	help	my	say	use
and	done	her	myself	see	very
any	don’t	here	never	seven	walk
are	down	him	new	shall	want
around	draw	his	no	she	warm
as	eat	hold	not	show	was
ask	eight	hot	now	sing	wash
at	every	how	of	sit	we
age	fall	hurt	off	six	well
be	far	I	old	sleep	went
because	fast	if	on	so	were
between	find	in	once	some	what
before	first	into	one	soon	when
best	five	is	only	start	where
better	fly	it	open	thank	which
big	for	it’s	or	that	white
black	found	jump	our	there	who
blue	four	just	out	them	why
birth	from	keep	over	then	will
bring	full	kind	own	these	wish
brown	funny	know	pick	they	with
but	gay	laugh	play	think	work
buy	get	let	please	this	would
by	give	like	pretty	those	write
call	go	little	pull	three	yellow
came	goes	live	put	to	yes
can	going	long	ran	today	you
carry	good	look	read	together	your

Bibliography

Books marked with a ***V*** are available through Family Christian Academy (1-800-788-0840) and many other home school supply stores.

Adams, Dan. *The Child Influencers: Restoring the Lost Art of Parenting*. Cuyohoga Falls, OH: Home Team Press, 1990. ***V***

Auch, Ron. *The Heart of the King: A Devotional Commentary on Psalm 119*. Green Forest, AZ: New Leaf Press, 1995. ***V***

Bacon, Earnest. *Spurgeon, Heir of the Puritans*. Arlington Heights, IL: Christian Liberty Press, 1996.

Bean, E. William. *New Treasures: A Perspective of New Testament Teachings Through Hebraic Eyes*. Oak Creek, WI: Cornerstone Publishing, 1995. ***V***

Beechick, Ruth. *The Language Wars: and Other Writings for Homeschoolers*. Pollock Pines, CA: Arrow Press, 1995. ***V***

———. *You Can Teach Your Child Successfully*. Pollock Pines, CA: Arrow Press, 1993. ***V***

———. Teaching Primaries: Understanding How They Think and How They Learn. Denver, CO: Accent Books, 1985. ***V***

Bloch, Abraham P. *The Biblical and Historical Background of Jewish Customs and Ceremonies* New York, NY: . KTAV Publishing House, Inc., 1980. ***V***

Blumefield, Samuel. *Is Public Education Necessary?* Old Greenwhich, CT: The Devin-Adair Company, 1981.

Brummelen, Harro Van. *Steppingstones to Curriculum: A Biblical Path*. Seattle, WA: Alta Vista College Press, 1994.

———. *Walking with God in the Classroom: Christian Approaches to Learning & Teaching*. Seattle, WA: Alta Vista College Press, 1988.

Burtness, Bill. *Judah Bible Curriculum: Education for Liberty*. Urbana, IL: Judah Bible Curriculum, 1988.

Cannon, Inge P. *Education Plus: Patterning Learning Upon Scripture*. Education Plus, 1995.

Cavett, Rick. "Goals, Standards, and All That." *The Mississippi Conservative*. May, 1995.

Clarkson, Clay and Sally. *Educating the Whole Hearted Child: A Handbook for Christian Home Educators*. Walnut Springs, TX: Whole Heart Ministries, 1996. ***V***

Coder, S. Maxwell. *First Steps To Knowing God's Will: Everything You Need to Live A Christian Life*. Meridian Publication, 1996.

Coke, Karl D., Ph.D. "Restoring The Home As The Center For Spiritual Growth." Charlotte, NC: Family Restoration Fellowship.

David de Sola Pool. *Why I Am a Jew*. Boston: Beacon Press, 1957.

Deparrie, Paul and Mary Pride. *Ancient Empires of the New Age*. Westchester, IL: Crossway Books, 1989.

Deporter, Bobbi and Mike Hernacki. *Quantum Learning: Unleashing the Genius in You*. New York, NY: Dell Publishing, 1992.

Duffy, Cathy. *Government Nannies: The Cradle - To - Grave Agenda of Goals 2000 & Outcome Based Education*. Gresham, OR: Noble Publishing Associates, 1995. ***V***

Eakman, B. K. *Educating for the New World Order* Portland, OR: Halcyon House, 1991. ***V***

Edersheim, Alfred. *Sketches of Jewish Social Life*. Peabody, MA: Hendrickson Publishers, 1994. ***V***

———. *The Temple: Its Ministry and Services*. Peabody, MA: Hendrickson Publishers, Inc.,1994. ***V***

Education Liberator, the monthly publication of the Separation of School & State Alliance. 4578 N. First St., #310, Fresno, CA, 93726; email (separate@sepschool.org) or WWW (http://www.sepschool.org), voice (209-292-1776).

Feder, Don. *A Jewish Conservative Looks at Pagan America*. Lafayette, LA: Huntington House Publishers, 1993. ***V***

Feldman, Abraham J. "Contributions of Judaism to Modern Society." New York: The Union of American Hebrew Congregations, n.d., p. 5.

Finn, Chester E. Jr. "What To Do about The Schools." *Commentary Magazine*, October, 1994.

Follette, John Wright. *Broken Bread: A Devotional Classic for Developing Christian Character* Springfield, MO: Gospel Publishing House, 1957.

Frangipane, Francis. *Holiness, Truth and the Presence of God: A Powerful , Penetrating Study of the Human Heart and How God Prepares it For His Glory*. Marion, IN: Francis Frangipane, 1986.

Freeman, James M. *Manners And Customs of the Bible: A Complete Guide to the Origin and Significance of Our Time - Honored Biblical Tradition.*

Fugate, J. Richard. *What the Bible says about Child Training*. Tempe, AZ: Aletheia Publishers, Inc., 1980. ***V***

Gatto, John Taylor. *Dumbing Us Down: The Hidden Curriculum of Compulsory Schooling*. Philadelphia, PA: New Society Publishers, 1992. ***V***

Goodrich, Donna, Mary Lou Klingler and Jan Potter. *100 Plus Motivational Moments for Writers and Speakers*. San Juan Capistrano, CA: Joy Publishing, 1991.

Green, Albert. *Thinking Christianly*. Seattle, WA: Alta Vista College Press, 1990.

Gruber, Dr. Gary. *Dr. Gary Gruber's Essential Guide to Test Taking for Kids Grades 3-4-5*. New York, NY: Quill William Morrow, 1986.

Hawkins, O. S. *In Sheep's Clothing: Jude's Urgent Warning about Apostasy in the Church*. Neptune, NJ: Loizeaux, 1994.

Haycock, Dr. Ruth C. *Encylopedia of Bible Truths for School Subjects*, Association of Christian Schools International.

Henry, Matthew. *Commentary of the Whole Bible by Matthew Henry*. Grand Rapids, MI: Zondervan Publishing House, 1960.

Howse, Brannon. *An Educational Abduction: Do You Know What Your Child Is Being Taught?* Green Forest, AR: New Leaf Press, 1993.

Hubbard, David A. *The Wisdom of the Old Testament*, Messiah College Occasional Papers, no.3 (Grantham, PA: Messiah College, August, 1982) p. 23.

Independence Institute is a nonprofit, nonpartisan Colorado think tank. It is governed by a statewide board of trustees and holds a 501(c)(3) tax exemption from the IRS. Its public policy focuses on economic growth, education reform, local government effectiveness, equal opportunity, and the environment.

International Institute for Christian Studies. WWW. 73754.1132@compuserve.com

International Standard Bible Encyclopedia. Electronic Database by Biblesoft, 1996.

Jacoby, Russell. *Dogmatic Wisdom: How the Culture Wars Divert Education and Distract America*. New York, NY: Doubleday, 1994.

Johnston, Henry P., ed., *The Correspondence and Public Papers of John Jay,* reprint. New York, NY: Burt Franklin, 1970.

Juster, Dan. *Jewish Roots: A Foundation of Biblical Theology*. Shippensburg, PA: Destiny Image, 1995.

Kahn, Gary H. *The Demonic Roots of Globalism: En Route to Spiritual Deception*.

———. *En Route to Global Occupation: A High Ranking Governmental Liaison Exposes the Secret Agenda for World Unification*. Lafayette, LA: Huntington House Publishers, 1991.

Kandel, I. L. *Colliers Encyclopedia CD-ROM*. Education, History of, Vol. 8, 02-28-1996. P.F. Collier, A Division of Newfield Publications, Copyright © 1996.

Kimeldorf, Martin. *Creating Portfolios: For Success in School, Work, and Life*. Minneapolis, MN: Free Spirit Publishing, 1994.

Lahaye, Tim. *The Race for the 21st Century: What Christians must do to Survive*. Nashville, TN: Thomas Nelson, Inc., 1986.

Lapide, Pinchas E. *Hebrew in the Church*, trans. Erroll F. Rhodes. Grand Rapids: William B. Eerdmans Publishing Co., 1984, p. x.

Leitch, Cliff. Wisdom of the Bible Shareware, 1996.

Limburg, James, ed. *Judaism: An Introduction for*

Christians Minneapolis, MN: Augsburg Publishing House, 1987.

Luksik, Peg and Pamela Hobbs. *Outcome Based Education: The State's Assault on Our Childrens Values*. Lafayette, LA: Huntington House, 1995.

MacDonald, William ed. *Believers Bible Commentary*: A Thorough, Yet Easy To Read Bible Commentary That Turns Complicated Theology Into Practical Understanding, Nashville, TN: Thomas Nelson Publishers, 1995.

Marx, Karl and Friedrich. Engels. *Basic Writings on Politics and Philosophy*, ed. Lewis S. Feuer. New York: 1959.

Mason, Charlotte, *Home Education*. London: England, 1925. Wheaton, IL: Reprint by Tyndale House Publishers, Inc., 1954.

———. *Formation of Character.*

———. *Ourselves.*

———. *Parents and Children.*

———. *School Education.*

———. *A Philosophy of Education.*

Mathis, James and Susan. *Foundations of A Christian World View*. Gainesville, FL: Christian World View Publishing, 1993.

McCarthy, Bernice. *The 4Mat System.* Barrington, IL: Excel, Inc., 1987.

McGill-Franzen, A. and R. L. Allington. "Flunk 'em or Get Them Classified: The Contamination of Primary Grade Accountability Data." *Educational Researcher* 22 (1, Jan-Feb): 19-22. (1993). EJ 464 906.

Meisels, S. J. "Doing Harm by Doing Good: Iatrogenic Effects of Early Childhood Enrollment and Promotion Policies." *Early Childhood Research Quarterly.* 2 June 1992, 155-174. EJ 450 523.

———, A. Dorfman, and D. Steele. "Equity and Excellence in Group-Administered and Performance-Based Assessments" in M. T. Nettles, and A. L. Nettles (Eds.) *Equity And Excellence In Educational Testing And Assessment* (Boston: Kluwer Academic Publishers, 1995). 243-261.

———, J. R. Jablon, D. B. Marsden, M. L. Dichtelmiller, A. B. Dorfman, and D. M. Steele. *The Work Sampling System: An Overview*. Ann Arbor: Rebus Planning Associates, Inc., 1995.

———, Fr. Liaw, A. B. Dorfman, and R. Fails. "The Work Sampling System: Reliability and Validity of a Performance Assessment for Young Children." *Early Childhood Research Quarterly* 10 (Sept. 3, 1995).

———. "Remaking Classroom Assessment with The Work Sampling System." *Young Children,* 5 July 1993, 34-40. EJ 465 921.

Microsoft® Encarta® 97 Encyclopedia. Microsoft Corporation, 1993-1996.

Millar, Keith ed., student at Northwest Nazarene College (Nampa, ID), with corrections by George Lyons for the Wesley Center for Applied Theology, September 30, 1995 from the Christian Classics Ethereal Library Server at Wheaton College.

Moody, Joshua, "Teaching of the Puritan Thinker." See Henry L. Feingold, *The Jewish Role Shaping America Society*, ed. A James Rudin and Marvin Wilson (Grand Rapids: William B. Eerdmans Publishing Co., 1987), p. 46

Moseley, Dr. Ron. *Yeshua: A Guide to The Real Jesus and The Original Church*, Hagerstown, MD: EBED Publications, 1996.

Mulligan, David. *Far Above Rubies: Wisdom in the Christian Community*. Marshfield, VT: Messenger Publishing, 1994.

Nash, Ronald H. *The Closing of the American Heart: What's Really Wrong With America's Schools.* Probe Books.

National Home Education Research Institute (NHERI) is actively engaged in collecting and analyzing original research data. This type of information could be invaluable in helping you educate legislators, friends, media, grandparents, and others. A subscription to the *Home School Researcher* will keep you abreast of the ever-growing body of research in the area of home education ($25/year individual, $40/year organization or library). An extensive bibliography and various research papers are also available. Tax-deductible donations greatly assist the essential work of the non-profit, 501(c)(3), *NHERI*. National Home Education Research Institute, Brian D. Ray, Ph.D., Western Baptist College, 5000 Deer Park Dr. SE, Salem, Oregon 79301-9392, ph. (503) 375-7019.

Nourse, Ruth. *The Hijacking of American Education*: "Part 2 - War of the Poets: Longfellow vs. Poe."

Packer, J. I. *A Quest For Godliness: The Puritan Vision of the Christian Life*. Wheaton, IL: Crossway Books, 1994.

Phillips, John. *Exploring the World of the Jew.* Neptune, NJ: Loizeaux, 1993.

Pride, Mary. *School Proof: How to Help Your Family Beat the System and Learn to Love Learning - The Easy, Natural Way.* Wheaton, IL: Crossway Books, 1988.

Richards, Lawrence O. *The Teacher's Commentary: Explains and Applies the Scriptures in a Way That Will Help You Teach Any Lesson From Genesis to Revelation.* Wheaton, IL: Victor Books, 1987.

Riese, Alan W. and Herbert J. La Salle. *The Story of Western Civilization: Greece and Rome Build Great Civilizations.* Cambridge, MA: Educators Publishing Service, 1990.

Rosovsky, Nitza. *The Jewish Experience at Harvard and Radcliff.* (Cambrage: Harvard University Press, 1986,

Scarlata, Robin, *A Family Guide to the Biblical Holidays.* Madison, TN: Family Christian Press, 1997. *V*

———. *Far Above Rubies Companion.* Madison, TN:, Family Christian Press, 1995. *V*

———. *Far Above Rubies Lesson Plans Volume 1.* Madison, TN: Family Christian Press, 1996. *V*

Schaeffer, Francis A. *A Christian View of the Bible as Truth*, vol. 2 of *The Complete Works of Francis A Schaeffer, A Christian World View.*

———. *A Christian View of Spirituality*, vol. 3 of *The Complete Works of Francis A Schaeffer, A Christian WorldView.*

———. *A Christian View of the Church*, vol. 4 of *The Complete Works of Francis A Schaeffer, A Christian WorldView.*

———. *A Christian View of the West*, vol. 5 of *The Complete Works of Francis A Schaeffer, A Christian WorldView.*

———. *A Christian View of Philosophy and Culture*, vol. 1 of *The Complete Works of Francis A Schaeffer, A Christian WorldView.* Westchester, IL: Crossway Books, 1982.

Schoeder, John F. ed., *Maxims of Washington.* Mt. Vernon: Mt.Vernon Ladies Association, 1942.

Skillen, James W., ed. *The School Choice Controversy: What is Constitutional?* Grand Rapids, MI: Baker Books, 1993.

Slater, Rosalie J. *Teaching and Learning America's Christian History: The Principle Approach.* San Francisco, CA: Foundation for American Christian Education, 1965.

———. *A Family Program For Reading Aloud.* San Francisco, CA: Foundation For American Christian Education, 1991.

Smith (Eds.), *Assessment For Instruction In Early Literacy.* Englewood Cliffs, NJ: Prentice Hall, 7-44. (See ED 324 647 for original version of this report.)

Stallman, A. C. and P. D. Pearson. (1990). "Formal measures of early literacy" in L. M. Morrow and J.K.

Stamps, Don. Study notes and articles from *The Full Life Study Bible KJV.* Life Publishers International, 1992.

Thayer, William M. *Gaining Favor With God & Man.* Madison, TN: Family Christian Press, 1997. *V*

Tozer, A. W. *The Quotable Tozer: Wise Words With a Prophetic Edge.* Camp Hill, PA: Christian Publications, 1994.

Ward, Kaari, ed. *Jesus and His Times.* Pleasantville, NY: Readers Digest Association, Inc., 1987.

Waring, Diana. *Beyond Survival: A Guide to Abundant-Life Homeschooling.* Lynnwood, WA: Emerald Books, 1996. *V*

Wilkins, Steven. *America: The First 350 Years.* Monroe, LA: Covenant Publications, 1988. *V*

Wilson, Douglas. *Recovering The Lost Tools of Learning: An Approach to Distinctively Christian Education.* Wheaton, IL: Crossway Books, 1991.

Wilson, Marvin R. *Our Father Abraham: Jewish Roots of the Christian Faith.* Grand Rapids, MI: William B. Eerdmans Publishing Company, and Dayton, OH: Center For Judaic-Christian Studies, 1989.

REPRODUCIBLE FORMS

Spiritual Fruits Evaluation Form												
	August	September	October	November	December	January	February	March	April	May	June	July
Love (seeking the highest good for others)												
Joy (gladness based on the nearness of God)												
Peace (quietness of heart)												
Kindness (desire not to cause anyone pain)												
Gentleness (restraint, strength, and courage, angry when needed and submissive when needed)												
Self-control (mastering one's own desires and passions)												
Goodness (zeal for the truth and righteousness)												
Faithfulness (firm loyalty)												
Patience (endurance, longsuffering)												

1=Weak in this area
2=Needs Improvement in this area
3=I am proud of my child's efforts in this area

Comments: ____

____

____

____

____

Work and Study Habits Evaluation Form

	August	September	October	November	December	January	February	March	April	May	June	July
Listening Ability												
Sits Attentively												
Follows Directions												
Completes Work in Given Time												
Organized												
Uses Time Wisely												
Neat Work												
Works to Potential												
Attempts Difficult Work												
Does Not Complain												

1=Weak in this area
2=Needs Improvement in this area
3=I am proud of my child's efforts in this area

Comments: ______________________________

____

____

____

____

Attitude Evaluation Form

Shows:	August	September	October	November	December	January	February	March	April	May	June	July
Courtesy for Others												
Willingness to Help												
Attitude Towards Correction												
Self-control												
Respect for Other Children												
Respect for Adults												
Handling of Problems												
Cooperation in a Group												

1=Weak in this area
2=Needs Improvement in this area
3=I am proud of my child's efforts in this area

Comments: ______________________________

____

____

____

____

Responsibilty Evaluation Form	August	September	October	November	December	January	February	March	April	May	June	July
Does Not Complain or Grumble												
Stays within Chain of Authority												
Receives Disipline with Proper Attitude												
Completes Chores on Time												
Completes School Work on Time												
Respects Others' Property												
Works Well with Siblings												
Accepts Responsibility for Belongings												
Resolves Conflicts with Siblings												
Gives and Receives Empathy												

1=Weak in this area
2=Needs Improvement in this area
3=I am proud of my child's efforts in this area

Comments: ____________________

Character Traits Evaluation Form

	August	September	October	November	December	January	February	March	April	May	June	July
Faith												
Loyalty												
Responsibility												
Punctuality												
Patience												
Self-control												
Modesty												
Self-respect												
Honesty												
Tact												
Giving												
Perseverance												
Hard Work												
Patriotism												
Using Time Wisely												

1=Weak in this area
2=Needs Improvement in this area
3=I am proud of my child's efforts in this area

These are traits we need every hour. Children will not need algebra or spelling rules at all times, and in all places, but they need these traits.

Comments: ____________________